CW01631633

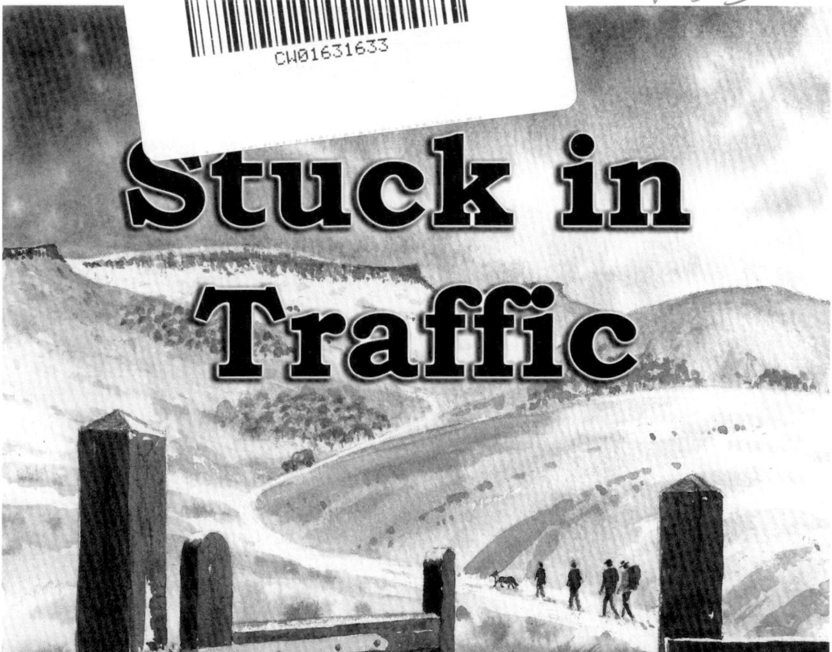

Author's note

We'd like to acknowledge the magnificently denominated Lefty Frizzell as the writer of *If You've got the Money,* released in 1950 on Columbia records. As far as we can tell, copyright of the song was at first part purchased by Jim Bulleit of Bullet Records in 1950, and then sold on to (Ralph) Peer Southern Publishing. Peermusic, the successor to Peer Southern Publishing were contacted in April and October 2020 for either clarification as to who now owns the copyright or for permission to cite the lyrics but no response was forthcoming. *If you've got the money* has been covered by a 'Who's who' of country music legends, including Texas Jim Robertson and the Pan Handle Punchers, Hank Dalton and the Buckeye Boys, Agnes and Orville and, in a Swedish version entitled *Om Du Har Kovan, Johan,* Elof Ahrl. However, on P13, Dave Strives was singing along to Willie Nelson's 1976 version of the song, from the platinum award winning album *The Sound in Your Mind,* released by Columbia Records. Lefty himself was inaugurated into the Country Music Hall of Fame in 1982 and his J-200 customised Gibson guitar was later sold at auction with a reserve of $350 000. He played a highly influential role in popular music in the 1950s and was described by Merle Haggard as "the most unique thing that ever happened to country music." Lefty led the archetypal country singer's life, full of ups and downs but he left a musical legacy that, although now largely forgotten, continues to influence country music to this day.

References

https://countrymusichalloffame.org/artist/lefty-frizzell/
https://lyricsplayground.com/alpha/songs/i/ifyouvegotthemoneyivegotthetime.html

Whatever is true, whatever is noble, whatever is right, whatever is pure, whatever is lovely, whatever is admirable, if anything is excellent or praiseworthy, think on these things.

St Paul

A word from Dave

No, what it is see …

I didn't want *tha lot* thinkin' I were one o' them *influenzas*. 't i'n't fo' me, that carry on – 'ave already enough on me 'ands what wi 'yard 'n' that. So before tha gets crackin', I wanted t' 'ave a word. See, what 'appened is, Kensson took so long t' finish 'job that by 'time e' were done, all gear were out o' date. Any roads, I said I'd 'elp t'old lad out 'n' 'ave a quick butcher's on 'web. Upshot is, all 'gear's proper job 'n' as up t' date as I can make it. Problem is, it's one o' them; soon as they put stuff on, they sell out 'n' tha can't get 'old on it.

Any roads, like I say, that's between thee 'n' them; 'am not makin' owt, 'n' I doubt if Kensson'll get 'is 'and in 'is pocket. Tha can suit theesen whether or not tha gi's it a coat o' lookin' at, but it's all proper job - no cheap tack 'ere tha knows, n' tha might pick up a reet deal.

Oh aye, 'n' 'fore I forget; gi' lad a chance, 'e's a bit green but 'e's doin' 'is best.

'n' last thing; if tha's in 'n' around 'God's own' 'n' lookin' for a new set o' wheels, don't be forgettin',

Tha saves at Dave's.

Si' thee ….

'Front cover: Winter walk below Stannage Edge, Derbyshire. Original watercolour by Christopher Atkins'

First published in the United Kingdom by Arc Publishing and Print 2022

Copyright © Mark Kensson 2022

All rights reserved. No portion of this book may be reproduced, stored in a retrieval system or transmitted at any time or by any means mechanical, electronic, photocopying, recording or otherwise, without the prior written permission of the author.

The right of Mark Kensson to be identified as the author of this work has been asserted by him in accordance with the Copyright, Designs and Patents Act 1988.

The information in this book is given in good faith and is believed to be correct at the time of publication. Neither the author or the publisher accepts any responsibility for errors or omissions.

All views and comments in this book are those of the author and should not be attributed to the publisher.

1

Dave loved traffic jams. They gave him an excuse to drive slowly, time to gaze into the Friday night reflections of the city lights in the oil-tinted waters gathered in the creases and crevasses of roads scarred by a thousand repairs; gave him permission to back off, to stop chasing. So, revelling in the *nowt else t' do*, he eased himself back into the warmth of the customised hand-stitched leather of the Recaro Cross Sportster CRS driver's seat, let out a deeply self-satisfied sigh and took in the twilighting views of the only city he'd ever known and could ever love. There was nothing much left to prove these days, not when he was stuck in traffic.

It was true, he loved his city; it reminded him of where he'd come from and, more importantly, who he was now. This was where he'd made it; here he'd been able to show the world what he could do. The city had given him his chance, but he'd still had to take it and although he would never forget where he'd come from, once he'd done what he had to do, the city had allowed him to escape and he'd grabbed the opportunity with both hands. For this, he would always be grateful and, as much as he loved being away, he would always love coming back

But more even than all of this, Dave loved the way that the men looked at him when he was stuck in traffic; loved to inhale their recognition of his success as he sat high above them, looking down from the glistening silver and cream cab of his flat-bed truck. He would 'tut' and raise his eyebrows in mock consternation at their double take towards the empty driver's seat and sigh and shake his head forlornly at the embarrassment of being unable to recognise that such a huge truck could only ever be an American import - *nobody knows nowt these days; 'least abaht owt that matters, any roads*. But he would still follow the men's gaze as it caressed the oh so slow-moving vehicle, taking in every detail: the water spinning off the eighteen enormous beadlock bolts on each of the four Hutchinson 17in Rock Monster wheels (with internal CTIS valves), or the way in which the personalised Westin Fey Diamond Step import chrome fenders gleamed gold in the streetlights, before becoming mesmerised by the beads of rain skiddling down the cab's glossy wax coating that the lads had applied afresh this afternoon whilst he was trying to clear his desk. It had been a mad rush to finish early but he'd finally made it and so, at last, was able to wind his neck in and enjoy the wistful glances of the rush hour workers, leaning into the wind and rain as they walked along the greasy pavements towards the car parks if they were doing all right or the bus station if they weren't.

Dave knew these men, who gazed so longingly at the enormous flat-bed truck and its obviously well-to-do owner, and exactly what each one of them wanted; they wanted what he had, to sit where he sat, to swap places with him. That's why they came to the car lot sporting their big coats and their heavy watches and why their eyes never left him as he toured the yard. And he knew that they knew that a nod from him could make or break any one of them in that tight-knit community, where anybody who was anybody knew Dave Strives and anybody with any sense stayed on the right side of him. He also knew that, given half a chance, they would take him for everything he had and this too made him smile, because try as they might, no one ever would.

In his city there would only ever be one silver and cream American import flat-bed truck. Only one with Hutchinson 17in Rock Monster wheels (with internal CTIS valves) and personalised Westin Fey Diamond Step chrome fenders. Only one with custom made Recaro Cross Sportster CRS seats. Only one …. Only one Dave Strives. That's why he loved traffic jams, on Friday nights, when he could drive slowly along Sheaf Street in the rain, looking down from the silver and cream cab of his American import flat-bed truck.

All of the above meant that he could afford to pull up nonchalantly as the lights of the pedestrian crossing changed to amber. He could have accelerated through but chose not to; he'd already said, *there were nowt to prove*. His smile broadened again, unseen behind the black-tinted windscreen, as the youth with the dark, rain sodden patch across his shoulders glanced up at the truck. He'd probably seen the number plate and, like so many others before, was so intrigued that he'd not noticed the woman hurrying across in the other direction. Their shoulders glanced off one another, and as the youth turned to mumble his apology from beneath the hood of his cold, damp sweatshirt, Dave asked out loud, "Nah den, young 'un, what is it this time? 'What's it stand fo'?' or ''ow much did it cost?'" Either way, the youth had something to tell his mates later that night in the pub.

As the crossing emptied, the red lights were joined by amber and then replaced by green and the last of the rain-swept pedestrians scurried across the road. Dave noticed that his headlights were on full beam and so flicked the lever towards him and pulled slowly away. The change in the pedestrian lights had opened up the road in front of him. He pressed his foot against the customised chrome-covered plate of the accelerator pedal and the truck suddenly shot away from the Fiesta behind him. He thought he recognised it from the yard but couldn't be sure. How many red Fiestas had he sold in the last twenty years? Must have been hundreds. He smiled again as he remembered the nails he used to pick up from the auctions, when everyone had left except for the few desperate private sellers who hadn't made their reserves. He remembered how he'd driven them home in the middle of the night, haggling all the way, following the back streets, where he was safe from the police. He thought about the days he and Danny had wagged school and college to do up their latest acquisitions and flip them over in the Star. But when he remembered Danny, he stopped smiling and concentrated once more on the road

He didn't allow the acceleration to last for long. He pivoted his right foot up against the monogrammed silver heel of his handcrafted, Corral natural rattlesnake-skin boot and allowed the enormously powerful engine to coast in second, just below the thirty M.P.H. limit. "Just enough....," he whispered, ".... just enough t' let 'em know." His smile widened again as he thought of all the scrapes his father's advice had saved him from over the years and how well he'd done for himself on the back of it. He had done well; he'd done *very* well and, as if to reassure himself, he eased back once more into the hand-stitched black leather seat to feel its warmth through his brown suede jacket. He checked his position on the integral GPS and flicked the radio button on the steering wheel. As the newscaster announced slow moving traffic around the station, he leant his head back against the headrest, half-closed his eyes and allowed his smile to relax.

He braked just in time. "Chuffin' road works!" he exclaimed. "It's a reet tangle, this; they've been doin' 'em fo' 'last five years. *New roads fo' 'new millennium* – 'ow's that workin' out, then lads?... Council – couldn't organise a riot, 'n' what's this joker think 'e's playin' at?" His right hand reached down for the window button as the workman, who had been hurriedly removing cones from the centre of the road, scuttled past, then he remembered that he'd stopped swearing and flagging him off would be pointless behind the darkened windows. So, he sighed ruefully and shook his head instead and, as the traffic moved off once more, he drew the enormous truck slowly down the slip road, and with studied concentration to ensure that he manoeuvred its huge chassis evenly between the yellow criss-crossed lines of the disabled parking space, he announced his arrival at the station.

Jenny and David were cold. They'd been waiting for nearly two hours.

"Try him again," Jenny moaned to her brother.

"What's the point? He's not answering and Mum said we had to wait."

"Well try Mum again then; she'll be at the airport by now."

But David didn't want to speak to his mother. He somehow knew the reaction that their news would provoke, and although he was only vaguely aware of the change of mood whenever his uncle came up in conversation, he felt sure that his failure to meet them would only make things worse. He barely knew his uncle, but what little he had seen of him had left him totally in awe, and true to his simple, honest nature, David had already pledged him his undying loyalty. In complete contrast to his sister, he'd leapt at the chance at staying with him for the weekend and he had no intention now of doing anything that might undermine him.

"Stop telling me what to do," he snapped, "he'll be here. He's probably just stuck in traffic."

"Well I've had enough; I'm going to find a taxi." Jenny had just placed her foot on the bottom step of the flight of stairs that led to the overhead walkway when she suddenly froze.

"Nah den, cocker!" came the over-loud, gruff voice from under the Stetson El Alamo premium fur felt – *'when only the best will do'* - cowboy hat, $1 605, "Where's 'fire?" Jenny felt her face redden and looked round as if trying to identify the person being addressed. Dave leaned further over the balcony, shouting even louder, "Up 'ere me old fruit. Is tha deaf as well as daft?"

"You're late!" responded Jenny, as Dave bounded down the stairs. She was trying to sound cross, but not so cross as to risk her uncle's infamous temper.

"Late? Gi' o'er. Quarter past five on 'dot. I even asked Christine t' double check 'fore I left; 'Fifteen- fifteen,' she said 'n' 'ere I am, bang on 'money…. Eh, what's tha think o' new 'at? Belter i'n't it?"

"Fifteen-fifteen is quarter past *three*!" snarled Jenny, the start of a headache, the two hour wait on the cold, intimidating platform and the embarrassment of her uncle's arrival suddenly converging to push her way past caring about his temper, "Are you *totally* stupid?"

Dave visibly flinched at the insult. "'tha sure abaht that? … Don't sound reet t' me." He quickly turned to David, "… Davey boy! Still supportin' that load o' old rubbish?"

"Better than thou's lot," replied David, missing the target by some distance with his Sheffield accent.

"Eh, a true blue allus beats a glory fan; I'll tell thee now fo' nowt, young 'un, tha'll be burnin' that piggy shirt 'fore 'season's out." "Thou knows nothing about it," laughed David, punching his uncle on the arm as hard as he could.

"Is that all tha's got? I'm not ticklish tha knows," said Dave, trying his hardest not to wince. He picked up the children's two smallest bags and swung them up and round his shoulder, almost knocking a woman's coffee cup out of her hand as he turned back to grin at Jenny. "Come on then, get a wiggle on – we've things t' do. I'm not lakin' round 'ere all night waitin' fo' *tha pair*; some reet dodgy characters round 'ere, tha knows." And with a wink he removed any last trace of resentment at the confusion and bounded back up the steps two at a time. David jumped up after him singing *I never felt more like swinging a pig* to the tune of Never Felt More like Singing the Blues· with as much gusto as his unbroken voice would allow.

· A song of endearment popular with Sheffield Wednesday fans but subsequently hijacked and reworded by their Sheffield United counterparts. Each side affectionately refers to the other as 'piggies', hence the reference in David's version, intended to antagonise his uncle.

Jenny, however, stood stock still on the platform, unable to move. As her mind caught up with the true awfulness of her situation, she let out a deep sigh, rolled her eyes and slowly shook her head: here she was, a highly intelligent, independent, soon to be fifteen-year-old young woman, forced to spend the weekend babysitting her hopelessly immature, twelve-year-old brother and their equally infantile uncle, who had left them waiting for two hours on a freezing cold railway platform, in a city they hardly knew, before arriving to pick them up wearing snakeskin cowboy boots and a truly ridiculous hat. … It was definitely worth a second sigh. … It didn't help. So, resigning herself to her fate, she watched the sigh drift away into the cold night air, picked up her and David's holdalls and trudged slowly towards the stairs. It was going to be a long weekend.

Jane was tired. Despite having reclined her seat back as far as it would go and asking for a better pillow, the tension in her neck and shoulders made it impossible to find a comfortable position. She stared out through the window, unable to see anything but her own reflection. She looked old. Eight hours earlier, the beautician in the executive lounge had carried out her work with her usual proficiency, and in the skilfully lighted salon Jane had been quietly delighted to see her rejuvenated face in the mirror. Ignoring the one hundred and one messages demanding her attention, she'd willingly allowed herself to be taken through the range of skin care products and hardly taken note of the £270 on the bottom of the credit slip, but in the half-light of the 'plane's interior she could see all of her forty-three years.

She felt old. The last few days had been a non-stop whirl of activity as she fought to bring the London office up to speed before she left. She knew it was hopeless and that by the time she landed in New York there would be a flood of messages waiting for her – dilemmas to which she alone would know the answer and decisions which only she could make. But none of this had stopped her trying – nothing ever stopped her trying – that's why she was on a 'plane, soon to be heading back out across the Atlantic Ocean when she should really be at home spending Friday evening with her children. … The Children! She was supposed to 'phone them! Against all her better judgement, in her dash to get to the airport she'd left it to Jenny to find their way to St Pancras and then on to Sheffield, where hopefully Dave would pick them up. What on earth was she thinking? The enormity of her irresponsibility hit her like a train: she actually had no idea where they were. How could she? In her panic, she slammed her fist down onto the seat return button. The force with which she shot forward sent the contents of her newly arrived drink flying towards her, drenching her blouse and flooding the carrier bag by her feet with a mixture of gin, ice, lemon and slimline tonic water. Still panicking, she reached down into one of the bags and fished around until she found the lemon and most of the ice, but the bag was soddened and she was sure that the make-up would be ruined. She pressed the buzzer for attendance. "Get something to wipe up this mess!" she snapped at the flight attendant, who immediately turned back towards the galley, biting her lip. She returned promptly and began cautiously wiping up the remains of the drink from the arms of the leather seat. "Would you like me to bring you another drink?" she asked in the politest, most caring tone she could muster.

"No. You're just making things worse. Give that to me!" The attendant compliantly handed over the cloth with which she had been mopping up the drink, and when Jane had finished rubbing her blouse she carefully took it back. "Would you like me to store your hand luggage in the overhead compartment *now*?"

"I've already told you that won't be necessary," Jane could

hardly control her anger as she sucked in the words. … The Children! How could she be so forgetful? They were the reason why she was doing this. She checked her watch: 4.30 p.m. GMT. Where was her 'phone? She reached down into her handbag for it, but as she 9liped open the cover, the remains of her drink poured out in a small, thin line, staining her skirt to match her blouse.

"Aargh!" *Why* had she thought this was a good idea? She should have admitted that it was the wrong decision when first Karen had gone home to her mother's with the so-called *'flu* and then her own mother had refused to undo her plans for the weekend. Why was everyone so selfish? Couldn't anyone see how important this was? – they could lose everything here just because people weren't prepared to go out of their way for once. It wasn't like they ever asked for much, but on this one occasion, when she'd really needed people to step up, they were nowhere to be seen. And what in the world had made her 'phone Dave? She hadn't spoken to him for three years, hadn't seen him for five. As soon as he'd said 'yes' she regretted it, but by then she was being swept along on a current she could no longer control. And now she was about to leave her children three thousand miles away in the care of man she wouldn't buy a second-hand car from. She bit her lip in frustration, mostly at herself. Then, as her anger suddenly pushed her way past the point of caring, she pounded her fists into the back of the seat in front of her and stamped her foot on the floor. She felt a crunch under her foot as a glass bottle succumbed to the point of her stiletto heel and the sweet smell of perfume began to overpower the lingering aroma of gin. At the same time, a small, elderly face framed in a black cowl appeared over the back of the chair in front of her. "Can I help you at all, my dear?" asked the nun.

"No … er … no, thank-you," mumbled Jane, now overwhelmed with embarrassment, "I'm fine, thank you," and as her mind caught up with the true awfulness of her situation, she too let out a deep sigh. … It didn’t help, so, resigning herself to her fate, she hailed the flight attendant once more, ordered a replacement drink, asked politely if she would mind finding her another seat, and responded with no more than a submissive smile when the stewardess reminded her that the use of mobile ‘phones was prohibited whilst the aircraft was in flight. Finally, she and her daughter had found something about which they agreed: it was going to be long weekend.

2

Dave loved the dark. As a boy he had never been able to overcome the sense of intrusion he felt at the orange glow from the streetlight outside their bedroom window. Danny never bothered, he was asleep in no time, but Dave would lie awake for hours, unable to relax, scouring the classifieds or reading car magazines by torchlight. Whenever he spotted their next project, he would whisper Danny's name, hoping to share the excitement, but he never received more than a groan or half-formed mumble in return. Sometimes, if he'd had a particularly brilliant idea, he would shake him or lean over and hiss some term of abuse in his ear, but Danny never stirred, so, like a miser guarding his riches, Dave would leap out of bed, dash over to the curtains and pull them as tight as he could, dreading that the streetlight would give away his secret before he'd had time to close the deal. He would dive back into bed, pull the blankets tight around his head and squeeze his eyes tight shut, but he could never quite block out the prying glow from the never-sleeping streetlight fingering its way through the chinks in the curtains. He would grip his magazines so tightly that the print would rub off onto his hands, and in the morning he would have to swap pillows before Danny woke in order to save himself a tongue-lashing from their mother. He'd promised himself back then that one day he would live far away from the streetlights, where his plans and his secrets would be safe from the orange glow.

Sat in the driver's seat in the cabin of his silver and cream flat-bed truck – that was when the dark was truly exciting: enveloping everything outside, isolating him from the world, and keeping his secrets safe from prying eyes. The dark made the lights on the dashboard burn brighter in their shades of red and green and blue and seemed to accentuate the smell of the hand-stitched leather of the Recaro Cross Sportster seats. In the dark it was clearer than ever that the cabin emanated wealth, luxury and success, reminding him once more of who he was and how well he'd done. So, he sank back into the warm, welcoming black leather driver's seat, turned up the volume via the two Rockford Fosgate TM1000X5 marine amplifiers and grinned in response to the pulsing beat coming from the four Bowers and Wilkins Marine 8 speakers – *what's point 'avin' quality amp 'n' then cheap-skatin' on 'speakers?* Very deliberately, he began to tap his snakeskin boot and nod his head in time to Willie Nelson.

"Do we have to listen to this? I can't stand country music," hissed Jenny from the back seat. She was still fuming at her uncle for his behaviour at the railway station:

"I can't see any disabled passengers," the woman in the wheelchair had chided Dave.

"Aah, but can tha see this disabled sticker wi' my fancy number plate on it?"

"Yes I can, and I can also 'phone the council and the police."

"Gi' o'er, we was only ten minutes. Let me gi' thee ''and up 'curb."

The woman had tried to protest, but Dave either didn't hear or didn't care. "I'll tell thee what; is tha on that Motability? 'ere's me card, when tha's ready, gi' us a ring 'n' I'll sort thee out wi' summat a bit special. Off tha trots then, love, I've me niece 'n' nephew t' sort out 'ere. They're southerners, from 'Smoke, come t' stay fo' weekend. Mam 'n' dad's big shot lawyers; I'd best not leave *them* out in 'cold."

Dave ran round to the driver's side of the truck, firing the key at the lock. "Come on, *tha pair*, last one in's a southern softy. It's frosty enough wi'out standin' 'round chattin' t' 'ice queen. Eh, 'n' no dibbin' shotgun neither. In 'back wi' both o' thee; we need t' crack on 'ere."

David climbed in but Jenny had waited until her uncle had closed his door. "Sorry," she mouthed to the woman with an apologetic smile and a weary shake of her head. She opened the rear door and hurled in the luggage. And as she climbed in, she made an extra effort to slam it with all her strength.

"Does tha 'ave t' do that on tha Dad's poncy Mercedes?"

"No!"

"Well don't do it on mine then! I've worked 'ard fo' this motor 'n' it's gonna 'ave t' do me a while yet." Jenny didn't respond, but inside she was seething at her uncle's insensitivity and his willingness to embarrass them in public. It was just the latest example of his ridiculous need to impress. She slammed the blade into the seat belt block with as much force as possible. Dave jumped on the brakes. "It's a long walk t' my 'ouse 'n' an even longer 'un t' thine. Make thee mind up, lass!" Dave had raised himself up in the driver's seat, making quite sure that Jenny could see his face in the rear-view mirror.

"Sorry," she said quietly.

"Aye, well maybe tha's sinkin' a bit after 'journey; 'stomach'll reckon 'throat's been cut," Dave continued in a more conciliatory tone. "What it is see, is 'tha's just not used t' Northern ways; we tell it like it is up 'ere, lass. Tha'll learn soon enough. … Let's get 'ome, eh Davey lad, 'n' see what's fo' tea."

So, they had travelled on in silence, Dave enjoying the easy atmosphere, Jenny staring out of the window, until they reached the outskirts of the city, when Dave had turned up the music system to greet the arrival of the countryside.

> *"If tha's got 'money, 'oney,"* he sang over Willie,
> *"I've got 'ride,*
> *We'll g' 'onky tonkin' 'n' we'll 'ave a time*
> *Tha take me Cadillac 'n' leave tha old wreck behind*
> *If tha's got 'money 'oney, I've got 'ride."*

And in spite of everything, Jenny couldn't stop the smirk spreading across her face as she considered her uncle's ridiculous attempt at country singing. But, true to form, Dave didn't let the relief last long. "What's tha into then?" he taunted in response to Jenny's outburst, "not that daft dance music?"

"It doesn't matter," sighed Jenny.

"What abaht thee, Davey lad, what's tha into then?"

"I dun't really like listenin' t' music, me old mate."

Jenny scowled at her brother.

"Just me 'n' Willie then; *If tha's got 'money, 'oney, I've got 'ride* ...don't know what tha's missin', *tha pair*; can't beat a bit o' Shotgun .... *We'll g' 'onky tonkin' 'n' we'll 'ave a time* ... Reet then, let's 'get 'ome; 'stomach reckons 'throat's been cut."

Dave gently pressed the accelerator towards the floor and, even at this, the truck surged forward through the night. He allowed himself a sly grin as he anticipated what was to come. In five minutes, they had left the streetlights far behind and as the darkness closed out the last embers of the city's glow, Dave swung the truck left and they sped along the top of one of Sheffield's famous dams.

"If tha looks out o' Davey's window, tha can see floodlights o' ''Promised Land' when there's a game on."

"Great," muttered Jenny, not really understanding but sure she wouldn't be interested even if she did.

"'n' this 'ere's where I take me boat out when no one's abaht."

Despite herself, Jenny turned to the right and glimpsed the early moonlight laying full length across the slate black water of the reservoir. Even her annoyance with her ridiculous uncle couldn't prevent her from being instantly drawn to the remote beauty of the place. It was so far away from the lights and noise of London and the anxieties she'd left behind. She almost felt as though she could begin to relax.

“’n’ this ’ill ‘ere, that’s where we’re walkin’ from tomorra.”

“What?!”

“Aye, ‘thought tha’d like t’ see a bit o’ ‘countryside while tha’s ‘ere – get a bit o’ fresh air in them city lungs.”

“Huh, yeah, gonna happen.”

“Aye, it is gonna ‘appen, lass *and* tha’s gonna enjoy it; twenty-two miles o’ finest Yorkshire air. Can’t beat it.”

“What’s the plan Uncle Dave?” asked David, forgetting his accent in his enthusiasm.

“Wouldn’t tha like t’ know?”

“Please!”

Dave couldn’t help himself; “Reet then; John’ll be round after ‘e’s done a few bits, then as soon as we’ve tha’ pair kitted out, we’re off.”

“Kitted out?” gasped Jenny, unable to contain her exasperation.

“Aye lass, tha need’s proper gear out ‘ere tha knows; this i’n’t poncin’ round Convent Garden – far too many city-folk come out ‘ere not knowin’ what they’re up against; I’ ‘emselves in a tangle – draggin’ out Mountain Rescue, causin’ no end o’ bother fo’ locals.” David looked out nervously at the looming shadows of the hills surrounding the reservoir.

“If you think I’m dressing up like some stupid Girl Guide,” Jenny fumed, “you’ve got another think coming. … And it’s *Covent* Garden.”

“Is it? Same difference.”

“No it isn’t! A convent’s where nuns live. Seriously, don’t you know anything?”

“Alreet, lass, none’s the worse; no need t’ wet theesen. Eh …. – NONE’S THE WORSE! *NUN’S* THE WORSE!! – What abaht that ‘un, Davey lad? *NUN’S* THE WORSE!” and Dave and his nephew roared with laughter.

Jane had calmed down. Her new seat, well away from the nun, seemed to relax her and somehow she had been able to make herself more comfortable. There were fewer passengers in this section and this, too, had a calming effect; by the time the plane had come to a halt, she was fighting to keep her eyes open. Her brief respite was broken by a new cabin assistant, dark and French to the other's British and blond, telling her that as the 'plane was now stationery, she could use her 'phone.

"Thank you, I need to contact my children," she explained modestly, hoping to communicate her anxiety and so excuse her earlier behaviour. She dialled Jenny's number but there was no connection. She tried again without success. She tried David's; again, no connection. She tried Jenny's *again*; still no success. Exasperated, she placed the 'phone on the tray in front of her, closed her eyes and bit hard on her lip as the stinging sensation behind her eye lids threatened to overwhelm her. In acknowledgement of her defeat, she let her forehead fall forward against the tip of her left thumb and index finger as her elbow rested on the arm of the seat. She closed the thumb and finger together and began to tap rhythmically on her forehead as if trying to force a decision into her mind. She could feel her fingernails cutting into her skin; she welcomed the pain. She stopped tapping and began to move her head up and down against her nails. How could she phone *him* already? She swapped hands and began to chew the skin on her right index finger and then suddenly, as if the tapping and the rubbing and the chewing had worn away the uncertainty and confusion, she knew what to do. She lifted the 'phone again, dialled the number from memory and squeezed her fist tight as the connection was made. The 'phone rang and the familiar voice on the other end of the line announced, "Sheffield 2457632, Audrey Strives speaking."

"Audrey, it's me, Jane."

"Jane, where are you?"

"I'm on my way to New York, to meet Daniel."

"Have you stopped off somewhere?"

Jane smiled. "Oh Audrey, it's so good to hear your voice. I'm in Montreal; we're picking up more passengers."

"Ooh, you're not going anywhere near Marks and Spencer's are you?"

Jane furrowed her brow and creased up her eyes, then slowly, for the first time in days, an unthought of smile spread itself irresistibly across her face. "No, Audrey, Montreal, not Meadowhall; it's in Canada."

"Don't they have egg-custards then?"

Jane fought with all her might to hold back the laughter threatening to explode inside her and could only offer a cough and a splutter in response. Then, as she finally felt the tension release, she let out an almighty sigh.

"Are you alright dear?"

"Yes, yes, I'm fine," said Jane, desperately trying to recover her poise, "I'm on my way to meet Daniel and was just trying to 'phone Jenny and David, to see how they were getting on …." Her voice trailed away. She knew Audrey was aware of the ill-feeling between her and Dave and she was far from confident in her ability to disguise her true feelings.

"Oh yes, it's this week-end isn't it?"

Jane sighed at the excitement in Audrey's voice. "Have you heard from them?"

"No, why should I have?"

"No, no, it's just that I can't get through to them and I wasn't sure about 'phoning your David …." Jane's voice trailed off again. She was embarrassed at her willingness to manipulate her mother-in-law but still hoped that Audrey would understand without her having to ask directly. She needn't have worried.

"Now listen to me, Jane Strives (it just would not register with her that Jane had kept her own name), I'm not *completely* behind the door just yet." Audrey's voice had taken on the steely defiance of those who had looked after their own all their lives and now bridled at even the slightest inference that they were no longer up to the job. “Would you like me to ring my David and then ‘phone you back?”

“That would be *so* good, Audrey. But look, let me give you ten minutes and then I’ll ‘phone you.”

“Alright, if that’s how you want to do it.”

“Thanks Audrey, thank-you so much.”

“Don’t you worry yourself about anything; I’ll give my David a ring and then you ring me when we’ve done. Oh, but what about if you’ve left the services?”

Jane smiled again. “Don’t worry, Audrey, I’m sure we’ll still be here. I’ll talk to you in a few minutes. Bye now.” As she carefully placed the ‘phone back on the tray, a single tear broke through her defences and rolled slowly down her cheek. She brushed it away, not caring that she could feel the mascara smudging across her face. Audrey was going to talk to the children; it was going to be alright.

The road turned away from the reservoir and up a slight gradient into a deep, evergreen wood. Dave knew this was the long way round, but he nearly always took it and tonight it would give the young ‘uns chance to see what the truck could really do. As the trees cleared and the road stretched out into the cold, clear night, Dave finally put the pedal to the metal. The acceleration forced David back into his seat and a huge grin spread across his face as the Littlefield LB-22 Series custom-made supercharger screamed into life. “How fast are we going, Uncle Dave?” he shouted over the engine’s roar.

Dave coolly reached down and turned off the headlights. The lights on the dashboard dimmed just in time to stop his nephew leaning over between the two front seats to read the speedometer. "Never tha mind, young 'un," teased Dave as he lifted his foot from the accelerator.

"Dave, what do you think you're doing?" shouted Jenny, suddenly aware that the road in front of them was barely visible. "Turn on the lights! This is dangerous!!"

Dave chuckled at the panic in her voice. "Alreet, don't wet theesen, lass, it's just a bit o' messin'. Eh, 'n' it's *Uncle* Dave t' *tha pair.*" He turned on the headlights and pressed his foot gently on the accelerator once more, "Any roads, I know this drag like 'back o' me 'and. ... Urgh what's that?" He took one hand off the wheel and waved it around in front of the windscreen. David was roaring with laughter.

"Pathetic," Jenny groaned from the back seat, rolling her eyes and slowly shaking her head once more.

Dave let it go, he was having far too much fun to let his niece's mardiness spoil things. "'Any roads'; heh, heh! ANY ROADS!! – What abaht that 'un, Davey lad? ANY ROADS!" Dave's voice could rise to an unbelievably annoying pitch when he was excited and by now he was nearing the top of his range. "Quick, Davey, phone fo' ambulance!"

David turned to Jenny in blind panic.

"Just ignore him."

"Tha can't do that wi' broken ribs."

"I don't understand."

"Keep up, Davey lad - tha sister's broke 'er ribs wi' laughin' at me 'jokes. It'll be *tha pair* calling Mountain Rescue out if I carry on like this." Dave's crescendo was finally tailing away, but he was so pleased with himself that he couldn't resist telling them a joke he'd heard from one of the lads that morning about a bloke buying a racing car for his dog. He'd been saving it up for the right moment, but just as he was starting he and Willie were interrupted:

"NOBODY MOVE! THIS IS A BUST," ordered a gruff New

York voice from behind the dashboard.

"Cool!" said David.

"What a surprise," muttered Jenny.

Dave glanced down at the screen on the dashboard and instantly recognised his mother's 'phone number. He nonchalantly flicked a button on the steering wheel. "Thou saves hat Dave's, 'ow can hi 'elp you, madam?"

"Stop it, you know full well it's me," scolded Audrey.

"Hi've told you before, Madam, hit just hisn't possible to fit a Zimmer frame into the boot of a Porsche Boxster." David clasped his arms across his stomach and squeezed his ribs in a desperate effort to control his laughter.

"David, stop messing about! This is important."

"What's up Ma?"

"Jane 'phoned."

Jenny froze.

"She wants to know if you collected the children alright."

"Children, what children? I've only just finished work. Busy man me; no time fo' mitherin' abaht children."

"Hi Gran, it's me," interrupted Jenny, tired of her uncle's showing off.

Dave frowned but said nothing. There was a pause on the other end of the line.

"Are there two 'phones in that car?"

"No Mam, we're on speaker 'phone. Course I picked 'em up; wouldn't want t' upset Jane. 'n' ow many more times? – it's a *truck*."

"Oh I don't know. Anyway, Jenny, your Mum's fine and she just wanted me to check up on you. She's on her way to New York and has stopped off at Meadowhall."

A bemused silence filled the cabin. Then a smile more accurately reflecting her mother's than any she'd seen in the 'plane's window crept across Jenny's face. "I think you mean *Montreal*, Gran."

"Oh yes, that's right. Did you know they don't have egg custards there?"

Knowing better than to ask, Jenny only smiled.

"She did try to ring you, but the 'phone wouldn't work."

"Course it not," butted in Dave, "them poncy little mobiles not work out 'ere. Tell t'old lass she needs one o' these proper satellite 'phones. Eh, I can do 'er a reet deal this week-end."

"I'll tell her no such thing and you stop showing off in front of the children. Keep your beaky nose out of it! I'm talking to Jenny and David - the sensible ones." She paused and then added, "I should come over - he's banned me you know."

"Be told, Mother," chided Dave, only half-playing, "this is nowt t' do wi' thee. Jane put me in charge 'n' if I need owt, I'll tell thee."

There was another pause.

"Can you put David on a minute?"

"Hi Gran," called David from the back, "how are you?"

"I'm fine thank-you. I hope that son of mine is behaving himself. You tell your Gran if he isn't and I'll be over in a flash."

"Any roads," Dave butted in again, "why didn't she wait 'n' 'phone me 'er sen if she were mitherin' 'bout summat?"

"She didn't have your number with her."

"Tha's a rubbish liar, old lass. Tha'll not be workin' fo' me just yet."

"Oh get off with you. I've got to go now, Jane's ringing back soon. Am I to tell her everything's fine?"

"Yes Gran," replied Jenny, trying to sound optimistic, "everything's fine."

"I'll leave it at that then. Talk to you soon. And David, just you remember. Bye."

"Bye Gran."

"Bye Gran."

"See thee Monday, Mam."

"Oh, and Jenny and David, I'll tell your Mum to 'phone you

at my David's about ten."

"Thanks, Gran. Bye."

"That's fine then," mused Dave, "although she could 'ave just waited 'n' phoned me at 'ome 'er sen if she were that mithered; we'll not be above five minutes. Never 'ad any patience that 'un. 'n' why'd she need t' bring Mam into it? Well, maybe she's got reason," he conceded after a few seconds reflection, "any roads, nowt's spoilin'." He peered into the mirror, hoping for a glimpse of the children's faces. "Alreet, *tha pair*?"

"Fine," replied David quietly.

Jenny didn't respond.

Dave turned back to the road, looking for reassurance. This was his favourite part of the journey. The road dipped slightly and there, framed in the truck's brilliant LED matrix headlights was the sign, *Highfield*. This was where Dave lived now, in this beautiful village, where his father had driven them out on Sundays when they were boys to watch the cricket and eat ice cream in the fresh air. This was his home: the white sign with the black border, the ancient dry-stone wall behind it and the dark green hills stretching out beyond all told the same story; Dave had made it. He'd escaped the city with its estates and noise and lights and crowds. He lived here now in the quiet and the dark and the solitude. He and his secrets were finally safe. The peace and tranquillity of the village and its surrounding countryside had gently but irresistibly melted away the loneliness that he'd felt so keenly after Danny had left. He was as close to contentment as he could be.

It was true, this *was* his home now; it reminded him of who he was and how well he'd done. Dave knew himself well enough to know why he'd driven the long way round - why he always drove the long way round; he wanted David and Jenny to see where he lived and be pleased with everything he'd done. He needed to share it with them and he needed them to love it too.

He slowed down at the T-junction by the Crown and rolled

down his window to shout, “Alreet, old pal?” to a dog-walker he’d never seen before. He indicated right and turned slowly down the steep hill past the old pumping station. For the last two years, Dave had been trying to buy it from the water company, knowing that his contacts in the town hall could see to the planning permission. The semi-derelict building had a double-pitched roof made of local stone, running about fifty metres from front to back. Dave loved stone roofs; under one half he would build his dream home and under the other a swimming pool. Everyone would come out from Sheffield on Sundays and they’d have barbeques in the garden with the doors to the pool swung open to the hills that encircled the village. Well, he would if the water company would sell, but up to now it was ‘no go’ - probably just waiting for a better offer once the market picked up. Dave shrugged his shoulders. He could wait, he was fine where he was for now.

At the bottom of the hill, Dave turned right again, over the beautifully arched stone bridge, where late on summer nights, after auctions, he would pull over and listen to the river welcome him home. Some nights the beauty of the place and all that it stood for almost moved him to tears. Tonight, however, he drove slowly over it without stopping and past an immaculately manicured bowling green to their left. The road followed a long, left-hand curve around a cricket pitch and then straightened towards what looked like a dead end. Suddenly Dave opened the truck’s throttle and swung sharply to the right.

They were climbing the steepest hill the children had ever seen. For a moment, Jenny thought they might tip over backwards, but the truck glided effortlessly to the top, before stopping momentarily at a Give Way sign. A left turn took them past the top pub with its welcoming lights and intoxicating aromas of woodsmoke, handcrafted beer and hot pies. Then up again and back out into the night; to Jenny it seemed as if they were on top of the world. A left and a right, still climbing, but now more gently and Dave finally slowed the truck for the last time. He pulled over to the edge of the deserted road, pushed a small black button on the dashboard and studiously manoeuvred the truck into a driveway laid with ancient setts. The five-bar gate in front of them swung open and Dave drew up ceremoniously in front of a beautiful stone-built farmhouse. He reached down and turned off the engine. They were home.

3

"Hello Audrey, were you able to speak to them?" Jane fought to keep her voice calm.

"They're fine. Are you on your way again?"

"Soon. … What did they say?"

"They were glad you rang and said to tell you not to worry and that they're having a lovely time. My David sends his love."

Jane swallowed hard. "That's thoughtful. Are you *sure* they're okay?"

"Yes, stop worrying and enjoy your trip. It will be nice for you and Daniel to spend some time together; it must be hard for him being on his own in New York like that."

Jane smiled. She was physically and emotionally drained and Audrey was as sharp as a pin when it came to her boys, but she wasn't falling for that. "Listen, I'll have to go, we're about to take off and I've had a bit of a problem with my 'phone."

"Alright, you get off, Love, and give my love to Daniel. I'm sure everything will be fine. Oh, and I've told the children that you'd give them a ring about ten tonight. Have I done right?"

"Of course you have, Audrey, and thanks for everything."

"Don't worry, Jane, everything will work out how it's meant to. See you soon, bye."

"Bye Audrey, and thanks."

As she closed her 'phone, Jane noticed the warning sign telling her that moisture had been detected in the charging port and she should not attempt to attach it to the mains - the gin and its accomplices were still hard at work. She smiled to herself - she could use Dan's 'phone. At least that was one problem she could solve.

To the stewardesses' relief, Jane closed her eyes and overcome by the intensity of the day, dozed off and on for the rest of the flight. She didn't wake until the change in air pressure announced their descent. She'd never come to terms with the feeling of someone squeezing her head between his hands and she shuddered with the cold and the start of a headache. She looked out of the window, and for the second time that day the care worn reflection that stared back reawakened the awful fear that she might be losing everything that mattered to her. Just as the despair threatened to overwhelm her once more, the plane banked hard to the left, presenting her with a spectacular view across the East River and over to Manhattan. She eagerly embraced the distraction and allowed herself to be drawn into the scene below as if she were slipping into a warm bath.

Jane loved New York. From her very first visit she had been captivated at every turn by the unremitting noise and unrelenting, breath-taking frenzy of the place, bringing every sense and nerve to life as though a bolt of electricity were coursing through her. She loved its restlessness and drive, its confidence and optimism; things could be done in New York and, when they were, they were recognised. There was no false modesty in New York; here it was okay to be a success.

She loved, too, the people's appreciation of that success, their surreptitious admiration of every tiny detail of her demeanour and appearance, revelling in the way they noted the style of her outfits and their furtive attempts to identify their brand. Without needing to speak, they betrayed their admiration of her elegant hands with her long fingers and pearl-like nails, faultlessly under-stated - the expression of success without ostentation. She loved the way that shop assistants waited for her response until she had removed her gloves finger by finger from those hands. Caressing the suppleness of their Ethiopian lambskin's leather, she would smooth out the gloves until they were perfectly straight, fold them one at a time carefully into her pocket and then lift her head and smile before deigning to reply. In the busiest city on earth, she loved to take her time.

She loved, too, the way the *Maitre d's* fluttered round her, how nobody ever ordered from the menu and the waiters always apologised when she sent back her food. Dining out here, like most things, was better than anywhere. She loved the shops and the bars, where you were never without conversation, she loved the bewildering array of smells from the street vendors' carts and being swept along in the irresistible hustle and bustle of the sidewalk and the subways, like a surfer catching a stupendous wave. She loved it all. New York was the best city in the world, reminding her, like nowhere else, of everything she dreamed of and how much she'd already achieved. She never ceased to be amazed at how easily she could let go of the guilt and fear and allow herself to be carried away by this wonderful city. New York had given her time to breathe, to feel fully alive and, no matter what came next, for that she would always be grateful.

Perhaps more than anything, Jane loved the way New Yorkers responded when she told them she was a lawyer; the raised eyebrows and approving, yet gratifyingly discomfited smiles at the corporate gatherings, the subtle increase in the speed of their response from the receptionists and p.a.s, or even the faint change of pitch in the voice of the hotel floor manager all betrayed their admiration and desire to please. At first she had thought that she needed to slip her career into every conversation but, as she grew in confidence, she realised that her bearing would get her most things and that, if she waited, people would soon ask.

When she'd first arrived, she'd practised saying it: "I'm a lawyer," first with a raised inflection and a slight lift of her head and arch of her eyebrows, then flat and emotionless, without any noticeable expression. Nothing proved quite satisfactory until she'd finally hit upon a slightly downward intonation, accompanied by the subtlest nod of her head that registered the significance of her profession, whilst suggesting that they shouldn't dwell on it just at this moment. Now she had said it so many times, she couldn't think how she said it, but however she said it, she *was* a lawyer, with a practice that had crossed the Atlantic to carry all before it in this wonderful city just as it had done before in London.

In New York she'd felt young and daring and her smile had returned; New York was where she had finally felt at home. It reminded her of who she was and what she'd done … *they'd* done; Dan had been there from the beginning. He'd been such a support in those early days, but now when she thought of him her smile faded.

The 'plane banked up and away from the city and the taught lines, which the beautician had worked so skilfully to hide, re-drew themselves in the oval window as the weariness and concern washed over her again. How had it come to this? She hadn't seen him for three months and in that time their exchanges had become increasingly business-like and less and less like those of a wife and her husband. He rarely spoke to the children anymore, asking them to 'fetch Mum' after the most cursory conversation. He had never been a great talker, over the 'phone he was worse and in New York it felt as though he drifted further away from her with every call. She'd realised months ago that they might be losing their business, but now she was terrified that they might be losing their marriage.

Five years earlier it had been the perfect solution - *Strive and Whynn*, a new and exciting venture for the new millennium. At first Dan had argued over the name: "Sounds like a couple o' con artists. 'n' anyway, why should I drop ''S'? 'n' 'as tha any idea o' 'stress o' married couples workin' together?"

But she'd made him see the advantages; no more worries over childcare, leave at a moment's notice, time together driving in and out of the city. And what about the way their talents complimented one another? Her drive and imagination, his organisation and attention to detail; it couldn't fail.

It didn't. The City loved them and as word spread, the list of companies wanting their services grew faster than even Jane had dared to imagine. Then one day, when Dan was at the doctor's with David, the call came from New York; would they be interested in helping with a trans-Atlantic merger?

Jane had 'phoned Dan in the car. He was so shocked that he was at a loss for words and could only stumble over his half-hearted congratulations, but that night they had celebrated in style with champagne in the kitchen before she and Dan had driven out to stay at their favourite hotel. Even Jenny was allowed her first glass, whilst Sally and David washed down his cough medicine with strawberry milkshake.

Over dinner, Jane had hardly eaten, hardly paused for breath as she'd explained how everything was finally falling into place. They'd worked so hard and now their efforts had been recognised in the biggest game of all. Of course it would mean changes, but the children were older now and if they had to choose one person in the whole world to take care of them, it would be *Sally*; she was already pretty much part of the family, was as honest and reliable as the day was long and had never once let them down. On top of all that, the children adored her and wouldn't ever dream of challenging her. Obviously, to begin with Jane and Dan would have to go out to New York together, but if for any reason Sally needed help, Audrey could come and stay, or even her own mother. They were always dropping hints about seeing more of the children and this could turn out to be the perfect opportunity. Once the groundwork had been laid, she and Dan could take turns in New York and in time they could train up their own NY team to shoulder most of the responsibility for the day-to-day details. This was their big chance – you'd have to be blind not to see it.

That night, after dinner, she couldn't sleep. This was what she was destined to do and she and Dan would do it together. A thousand thoughts ran through her mind as she plotted the course of the company's success. She called his name softly, wanting to share them with him, but he was asleep and wouldn't stir. Eventually she had given up and turned over. She pulled the sheets close about her and finally drifted off into the contented repose of a woman in touching distance of her dreams. Dan lay quietly beside her, almost weeping. It was happening again, and again he could do nothing to stop it. As the weight of his despair forced his head down into the pillow, he could only remember one thing; that afternoon, when she'd 'phoned him in the car, she hadn't asked about David.

Jenny hadn't been able to explain why she had felt so uneasy about New York. Mum had been so excited and Dad was obviously pleased for her, but even as they'd been drinking champagne in the kitchen it had felt as though little cracks had begun to appear all over the surface of their lives. She'd been unable to sleep and so crept downstairs to talk to Sally about ponies, which was what she always did whenever her parents went out for the evening. But this time, when she opened the lounge door, Sally reddened and looked at Jenny in the same way David did when their mother or Sally caught him rummaging through the kitchen cupboards.

"… they haven't the time to spend what they've already made … I just don't know what to think … look, I'll have to go; the children need me … I'll talk to you in the week. Bye." Sally quickly put down the 'phone and smiled uncomfortably.

"Who was that?" asked Jenny, suddenly feeling very frightened, as if the cracks were widening all around her.

"Oh just my sister - just catching up on each other's news."

"You're not in trouble are you?"

"Of course not, dear…. you do ask some funny questions. There was definitely no mix up at the hospital when you came along – you're your mother's daughter if ever I saw one! *Three* lawyers in the family cross-examining me; not sure how long I can cope with that!"

"Don't say that!" Jenny blurted out in blind panic.

"Oh sweetheart, I was only joking; you and David mean the world to me, I'd never do anything to harm you, you know that. Come on, let me warm you up some milk and you can tell me again about that white pony of yours; I'm sure there must be *something* left you haven't told me a hundred times before."

So she did, as she'd done for longer than she could remember and as Jenny pulled her dressing gown tight around her feet and gazed into Sally's broad, kindly face, the fear began to subside. They talked for longer than usual, Jenny needing the reassurance of the bond between them more than ever. She sensed that in Sally too, but there was something else: a strange sadness, as if something special were being lost or someone they loved was about to die and every remaining moment had to be treasured, and as the fire began to fade in the grate, so the apprehension slowly crept back over her. With her heart racing, she returned to the kitchen and began slowly washing her mug at the sink.

"Time for bed," announced Sally, returning from checking on David. Jenny stood stock still, unable to move. "If I move, I'll fall down a crack and never stop falling," she said to herself. Screwing up her courage, she picked up the tea towel in one hand and the mug in the other and turned to face Sally, who tilted her head to one side and smiled in the manner than Jenny and David loved so much, even when they teased her about it.

"Would you like me to come up?" Sally asked, and without waiting for a reply, she took the tea towel and the mug, placed them carefully on the work surface, grasped Jenny's hand and led her slowly up the stairs. Now she was older, Jenny would never normally invite her into her bedroom and Sally would never presume, but tonight nothing was said. Jenny took off her dressing gown and rolled over into bed. Sally tucked the sheets in around her, bent over and kissed her gently on the forehead.

"Thank you," whispered Jenny, "for everything."

"Good night," Sally responded quietly, trying not to let Jenny hear the tremor in her voice.

Two mornings later, Jenny came downstairs and was amazed to find her parents silent and ashen-faced at the kitchen table. "Where's Sally?" she asked in alarm.

"Is David awake?"

"I'll go and fetch him," said Jenny, suddenly in free- fall. She ran upstairs as fast as she could and burst into David's bedroom.

"Get out!"

"Come on! Mum wants to talk to us."

Jenny turned and ran back downstairs. David followed her, yawning, feet half in - half out of his slippers, fumbling with the belt of his dressing gown, barely awake but still able to sense that something wasn't right.

"Children, Sally's gone," their mother informed them coldly. Nobody spoke. Their father sat staring at the table. He was holding a letter, written in Sally's hand.

"Why?" asked Jenny, the chasm she had fallen into closing over her head.

"Well," her mother continued in the same emotionless tone, "Sally thinks it would be counter-productive for the family if Dad and I started to spend time in New York and so felt that she couldn't support our decision. Given her concerns, we all agreed that we should go our separate ways. Things were said and it became clear that it would be better for everyone if she left as soon as possible. Her brother-in-law came to collect her late last night."

Jenny noticed her father's hand tighten around the letter. "Then don't go! Talk to her, Mum!" she shouted in desperation. "Why don't you talk to her?"

"She's not coming back," said a voice she didn't recognise. She turned and was amazed to see it was her father speaking. "We're just going to have to make the best of it." He looked so tired. "Come on, we'll be late for school."

So Jenny had learnt to do everything. That very day, her mother had been late to pick them up from school. Jane had smiled and hugged and made promises and explained over and over about the traffic and the five-hour time difference between London and New York, but Jenny had already stopped listening. The next day she was late again and by Friday, Jane had 'phoned school and left Jenny a message that a mini-cab would collect them. Within a month, Jenny was ringing the mini-cab firm herself and, left to her own devices, had already learnt how to use the microwave and stack the dishwasher and do all the other things that she and Sally used to do together. She learnt how to organise the chores and the shopping with Karen, the new nanny, and how to order pizzas and DVDs, she even learnt how to tell David what to do without making him angry. She learnt how to reset the answer machine and take messages and where to leave them so that her parents wouldn't miss them, and to explain to strange voices on the telephone that New York was five hours behind London time and that her parents weren't at home. Hardest of all, she learnt how to be alone.

But she never learnt how to cope with what was happening to her parents. She could forgive them for having no time for her or David, but she couldn't forgive them for not having time for one another. At first they'd left for work together, but soon one or other would be gone before the children came down in the morning. Before long they were both gone and there was only Karen to see them off. They came home later and later and rarely together. Their conversations became quicker and harsher and sometimes they didn't have anything to say to each other at all. Without anyone noticing, they stopped going out on Saturday nights.

This saddened Jenny most of all. She had always loved the way her mother would magically transform from *Mum* to *Jane.* She always came downstairs first, looking so elegant and beautiful in Jenny's favourite dress - the black one, which Jane always wore with her grandmother's silver jewellery. Then her father would come down, looking so proud and handsome in his dark blue suit and cuff links and shiny black shoes - the only ones allowed upstairs. Jenny and David would sit side by side in the lounge, waiting for their arrival and beam at their parents as they told them to be good and do whatever Sally said. They would follow them to the door and exchange good night kisses and Jenny would always watch for her father's arm to move up around her mother's waist as they walked away. It already seemed part of a distant memory.

By the time her parents announced their first extended trip to New York, Jenny was almost relieved to hear they were going. Whilst they were away she could feel herself relax. Her relationship with Karen was completely different to that she had had with Sally, who had moved in just after David was born and Jane had gone back to work. Jenny couldn't remember a time when Sally hadn't been around; she really had been pretty much part of the family. Karen was nice enough, and at times Jenny imagined they could almost be friends, but she now took far more responsibility herself for running the home and with her parents away she was able to order things in the way she saw fit.

Within a few days of their going, she was actually beginning to enjoy the responsibility and had to check herself when she remembered the reason why they were in this position.

Nights were still the hardest. They had been since Sally left. Karen would take herself off to her room and Jenny was left alone. She tried to talk to David but he seemed totally unaware of the turmoil the family was in. She said a prayer for Sally every night and often wondered why she hadn't 'phoned or written. She fought constantly against the nagging thought that she was somehow responsible for her leaving. She *knew* Sally couldn't have forgotten them and that there must be a good reason why she hadn't been in touch, but alone in her room the nagging guilt was inescapable and she ached to hear her voice or feel the gentle touch of her careworn hand once more.

"I feel like Kevin Keegan."

"What?!"

"This tangle; makes me feel like Kevin Keegan."

It was the first morning after her parents' return from their latest visit to New York, and Jenny had come down for breakfast already feeling angry and scared about the mood in which they had returned.

"Kevin Keegan – 'England manager."

"Stop talking in riddles; what on earth are you on about now?"

Jenny felt invisible. "Mum, David's staying for rugby after school and I'm going to dance class, are you *sure* it's okay to collect us? It's not a problem if you can't, I can always 'phone for a taxi, it's no trouble."

Jane turned to her daughter and, for the first time since arriving home, she took the time to smile at her properly. "Jenny,

I've just spent two weeks away from you, nothing could be more important than seeing you both tonight. I'll be waiting for you when your dance class finishes, and as soon as you're both done we can go straight out for dinner."

"Are you coming, Dad?"

"Not tonight, darling," replied Dan quietly, before adding, "we've godda nail dis deal while it's still hot," in an appalling New York accent.

Jenny laughed. "You really are rubbish, Dad."

Dan let his eyes drop to the floor. "I know," he said, his voice barely above a whisper. Then, after a short pause, he brightened; "Come on, let's see if we can be early for once. David, are you ready?"

Ten hours later Jenny had had enough. They'd been sat on the bench outside David's school for nearly two hours.

"Try her again," she moaned to her brother.

"What's the point? There's no answer."

"And why don't you ever get changed? You're filthy, Mum's going to go mad."

David, still in his rugby kit, looked down at his mud encrusted legs and shrugged, but before he could respond to his sister's latest attack, their mother's car swung round the corner and pulled up sharply beside them.

"Children, I'm so sorry," began Jane as she reached over and opened the passenger door, "our meeting ran over and by the time I could get away the traffic was impossible. Jump in; you must be freezing."

David opened the back door and climbed in, shedding intractable clumps of the school rugby pitch onto the light beige carpet, before easing back into the embrace of the matching leather seats to enjoy their warmth through his sodden jersey. "Let's go, Mum, I'm starving."

But Jenny stood stock still, unsure of what to do. Then her frustration finally boiled over. "Two hours, two freakin' hours!" she yelled.

"Jenny! Don't you dare speak to me like that!" shouted Jane, feeling her face flush, "do you have any idea of the kind of day. … In the car. Now!"

Jenny didn't move. "Why, so you can leave us somewhere else while you take another *important call from the New York office*?"

"I've had about enough of this."

"You've had enough. *You've* had enough!" Jenny was way past the point of caring. "What are you going to do, drive off and leave us waiting outside in the cold again?"

Jane felt the weight of her awful day pressing her to retaliate but she scraped together her last few crumbs of restraint and willed herself not to bite back. "Come on," she urged herself through gritted teeth, "you can't lose it now." She took a deep breath and tried again; "Please Jenny, I am *so* sorry. … Please get in the car." She looked longingly at her daughter, searching for any trace of understanding. Jenny remained resolute for a few seconds, and then her shoulders slumped. Without a word, she picked up her and David's bags, walked round to the boot and threw them in and then climbed forlornly into the back of the car.

"I really am sorry, Jenny," Jane repeated as she fumbled with her seatbelt. She looked at Jenny in the rear-view mirror, still hoping for some flicker of understanding. "I really have had the most awful day. I should have been here; I made a bad decision."

"'The longer you leave people waiting, the less important to you they are.'"

Jane concentrated on the road, not daring to look at Jenny again, her daughter's rebuke bringing a stinging sensation to her eyes. Her world was unravelling around her and she didn't know how to stop it. She bit her lip hard against the tears as they re-joined the rush hour traffic. What was she doing?

The three of them had eaten dinner in silence, Jenny making no response to Jane's conciliatory smiles and David, school jumper and trousers hiding his true condition, too hungry to notice anything in particular was amiss. The children were weary and so had gone straight to their rooms as soon as they were home. Despite all her maternal instincts, Jane had not gone up to them. They needed time to process their feelings and so did she.

By the time Dan came home, Jane had a clear plan of what had to be done: "We can't be the victims in this; it was our choice."

Jenny listened quietly from the hallway as her parents talked in the kitchen.

"*Our* choice – now there's a thought!"

"What? Don't start talking in riddles again, Dan; I had enough of that Kenneth Keegan nonsense this morning?"

"It's *Kevin.* 'n' were it *our* choice or *tha* choice?"

"Don't do this, Dan; don't make me the bad guy here!" For the second time that evening Jane struggled to keep her anger towards a family member under control.

There was a long pause as Dan tried to work out a way of saying what he wanted to without making things worse. "Look ..." he began cautiously, "Kevin Keegan took 'job o' 'England manager. After a couple o' matches 'e realised 'e wasn't up t' 'job 'n' quit."

"But we are up to the job."

"Well thanks fo' 'vote o' thanks, but it all seems a bit out o' my barrow."

Jane could feel her anger resurfacing. She forced herself to ignore Dan's relapse into his old way of speaking. "It's a bit late for that now, Dan. We've re-mortgaged the house on the back of it not being 'out of your barrow'; so you'd better be up to it, England manager or not!"

Dan's resistance withered under Jane's assault. "Alright then, 'ave your own way - you usually do. What do you want me t' do?"

"We need to concentrate our efforts, even if that means neglecting other priorities, at least until we get back on top of things and if that doesn't work, well, we'll just have to re-group and think of something else."

"Now who's talking in riddles?"

"It's not working because we're not giving it our full attention. One of us needs to go out there and *stay* until they've pulled all the strands together."

"That would be *thee* then, I should reckon," said Dan, recovering a little of his fight.

"No, actually, I thought it would be good experience for you to lead on this."

"But I don't want t' go back t' New York, we've not been back above five minutes."

"I do hate it when you talk like that."

"Like what?"

"In that awful accent."

Despite his best efforts and Jane's constant prompting, Dan often slipped back into his Sheffield dialect when he was frightened or angry. Now he was both.

Half-hoping to goad her, he ignored the criticism. "Why can't tha go?"

"Because I'm needed here with the children."

Dan sighed. It was no use arguing. She had it all figured out. He'd just do as he was told and go back to New York.

Jenny stood stock still in the hallway, unable to move, the

cracks opening all around her once more. First Sally, now this; their father was leaving them to go and live in New York and she didn't want him to. Suddenly the door opened and her mother walked through … "Oh … hello Jenny … how long have you been standing there?"

Jenny turned to her mother and bravely tried to answer but the sobs filled her throat and she buried her face in her mother's breast. Jane pulled her arms tight around her and the two of them stood in the doorway swaying gently from side to side. After several minutes, Jenny lifted her head and looked into her mother's eyes, "I don't want him to go."

"It's alright, Jenny, it's not for long."

4

'Not for long' turned out to be three months and counting and it *wasn't* all right. Dan had been unable to bring the business up to speed and now it looked like they were about to lose the contract that had brought them there in the first place and on which the firm's future depended. Jane had had no idea quite what to expect but when she had heard the mixture of despair and panic in Dan's voice, she knew that she had to come. She finished the last of her drink, carefully pulled her seat upright and fastened her seatbelt. "Well Jane, let's see what kind of landing you're in for this time."

Two hours later, the concierge looked up from his computer screen and observed the woman standing about four feet from the desk. He knew the type; within five minutes she would be asking for the manager, so he waited patiently until she had finished pulling off her gloves finger by finger, pushing them carefully into the deep pockets of her coat - he would make sure that her complaints were not about him. As she took a step closer he addressed her with as much warmth as he could muster; "Good afternoon, Madam."

"My husband is staying here and I have come to join him," she announced.

Her English accent took him by surprise; he'd guessed Upper East Side or even Long Island. The concierge studied the woman more carefully. Everything about her exuded a sense of superiority. Her light brown, shoulder length hair was thick and beautifully styled and he was sure that in the right light it would shimmer and glow. Her make-up, although not newly applied, cleverly highlighted her cheekbones and hid her tiredness. The coat with the deep pockets was obviously cashmere and exquisitely tailored and the soft, brown leather of her handbag matched both it and the leather gloves perfectly. Given her appearance, he was surprised to see the dark stain in one of its corners. He remembered her now; she and her husband had stayed at the hotel last year – he never forgot a customer. This one was a real pain and they'd named her 'Your Majesty'. Her husband had looked really depressed. The concierge could take a pretty good guess why.

"His name is Strives, S-T-R-I-V-E-S. Quickly, please, I've had a long flight and I've still got a lot to do. I'll need my bags sent up straightaway and I'd like some tea."

"Certainly Madam, I'll just check which room he's in."

A long pause followed during which the concierge fought to hide the smile that began to play at the corners of his mouth. "Here we go," he said to himself.

"I'm sorry, Madam, there doesn't seem to be anyone registered under that name."

"Don't be ridiculous; he's been staying here for the past three months."

"I'll check again, Madam, but I'm quite sure there's no *Mr Strives* in the guestbook." Another pause, giving the concierge time to make absolutely certain that only the faintest hint of triumph would be detectable in his reply. "Sorry Madam, there definitely isn't anyone of *that name* staying at the Centurion."

"This is hopeless, fetch me the manager!"

"Of course, Madam". The concierge retreated into the office behind the counter.

"'Your Majesty's' back," he said, grimacing at his boss.

The floor manager looked up quizzically and furrowed his brow in mock concentration. After a few seconds he opened his eyes with a disappointed look. "Oh! And does one require one's presence?"

"What do you think?"

"Great."

The manager stood up with a sigh, composed himself in front of the mirror, stuck his tongue out at his reflection and walked out of the office followed by the concierge.

"Can I help you, Madam?" he said, offering Jane a sympathetic smile.

"My husband and I have used this hotel several times during the last year," (not a flicker of recognition from either of them.) "I've arranged to meet him here, but this person doesn't seem to know which room he's staying in."

"Of course, Madam, what's your husband's name?"

Jane sighed, "*Strives,* S-T-R-I-V-E-S. He's been here for the last three months, surely it's not too much to expect you to know which room he's in!"

The manager checked the guest list. "I'm sorry, Madam, the concierge is correct, there's no one of *that name* staying in the hotel."

"Nonsense!" said Jane, trying to intimidate the manager into acknowledging his mistake. "We always stay here. Is there anyone else I can talk to?"

"I'm sorry to disappoint you, Madam. Can I be of assistance in some way?" asked the manager with a smile so saccharine, Jane had to dig her nails into the palm of her hands to stop herself from reaching over the counter and grabbing him by the lapels. He must know there was some kind of mix up; Dan had to be here, but in spite of her frustration she could feel her confidence draining away. What was going on? She made one last effort to regain control; "No, er …. actually, yes; I'll take some tea - Earl Grey with lemon, *not* cream, boiling water and in a teapot, if it's not too much trouble. I'll wait in the lobby until he returns, in the meantime, perhaps you'll want to check your record keeping; I can't *imagine* what you'd do if there were an emergency. Oh, and have someone bring my luggage across, please; I should think you're able to manage that between the two of you."

"Of course, Your Maj … Madam. At once."

But as she walked away from the desk, Jane could no longer maintain the pretence. She could feel herself becoming increasingly aware of the gaze of the people around her and began to chide herself to 'get a grip'. In one last desperate attempt to shore up her confidence, she found an empty table, removed her coat, folded it perfectly across the middle and draped it over the chair next to hers. Trying not to draw attention to herself, she sat down, put her handbag on the low table in front of her and then, noticing the stain for the first time, lowered it to the floor by her feet. Why would Dan have stayed somewhere else? Where was he? She could feel her face beginning to flush and folded her arms, and then just as quickly unfolded them as she recognised her defensive body posture. "Stop it!" she told herself sternly. "Nobody's watching." She was wrong.

The tea arrived. The waiter had brought milk instead of lemon, but for once Jane didn't complain. She thanked him absent-mindedly and out of habit, lifted the lid of the teapot and began slowly stirring the tea. The familiar movement and the aroma it released had a soothing effect and she began to feel her self-confidence, and with it her poise, returning. She forced herself to block out the distractions around her. She needed to focus, to concentrate: What was going on? Where was Dan? "Come on!" she implored herself, desperate for clarity of thought to return. "Always go back and check." She fished a gin-sodden note out her handbag; it was still legible. She stared at it intently as if by doing so she had the power to reconcile what was written there with what she had just been told – 'the Centurion. Arrive Friday 9th, P.M.' She checked her watch and suddenly remembered Jenny.

"Oh no, not again!" she gasped out loud, fuming at her stupidity as she quickly calculated the time difference: Four-thirty p.m. here, nine-thirty there. "Still time. Do it now, before you forget!" She went back to her bag to pull out her 'phone and then stopped halfway as she remembered its demise. In the pause she glanced round and was surprised to see the waiter still hovering at a respectable distance and so quickly continued the movement downwards to pull out her purse for his tip. … Dollars! She didn't have any dollars. She shrunk back into her chair and stared directly in front of her, the strain of the day threatening to overwhelm her once more. She fought desperately to stay in control, but of its own accord her hand rose to her brow and with her pinched thumb and forefinger she began tapping her forehead. "Come on," she urged herself, "think!"

Suddenly she knew what to do. Staring down the waiter, she stood up and gathered her coat and handbag. As she walked past him, she whispered, "*Lemon* with Earl Grey, never cream – English class: 101." and wandered casually back over to the desk. Her luggage was still waiting. She reached out her hand, rested it on the counter and cleared her throat, thus drawing the concierge's attention away from the computer screen.

"As there appears to be some confusion," she began, rallying all of her self-assurance in a desperate effort to re-establish control of their inter-action, "I've decided to book an extra room until someone finds out where the problem is."

"Certainly, Madam, I'll see what's available but I have to tell you we are extremely busy this week-end." The concierge knew exactly which rooms were available, but still went through the motions of checking. He sucked pensively on his bottom lip and treated Jane to his most anguished expression. "I'm afraid we've only our more expensive suites left this week-end - we are in the middle of Broadway Week."

"And how expensive is expensive?" asked Jane, her mouth tightening as she sensed a scam.

"Four hundred dollars per night, including meals," the concierge smiled back.

"And without meals?"

“I’m sorry, Madam, these suites are only available as part of our full-board tariff. Would you like to speak to the floor manager? Perhaps he could suggest something.”

Jane knew she was being mocked. Out of sight of the concierge, her hand tightened to a fist inside the pocket of her cashmere coat. “Not now, girl,” she told herself, “he can wait.”

“I’ll take it.”

“Certainly, Madam. And how will Madam be paying?”

Ignoring the concierge, Jane reached into her bag again, pulled out her purse, removed a sticky credit card and placed it on the desk. The concierge motioned to pick it up and then, noticing its condition, changed his mind. He read the number from it as it lay on the counter and typed it into his computer. Jane stood in silence, desperately trying to appear as though she had all the time in the world. The concierge picked up the card by its edges and handed it back to her with yet another smile … he *really* was going to get it before long.

“If you could just sign the guestbook, please … Suite 10 07, Madam. I’ll have your things taken up as soon as there’s a bellhop available. Will Madam be needing a replacement carrier bag?”

Jane looked down to where her luggage was waiting. Beside the carrier bag an oily puddle of gin, perfume and mascara was beginning to spread across the gleaming marble floor. “Yes please,” she said with an airy smile, as though this were nothing less than to be expected, and then, as an apparent after-thought, “oh, and could you add the tea to the bill? I need to do some shopping, so I’ll inspect the room later.”

“Certainly, Madam.”

“And is there a cash dispenser in the hotel?”

“Excuse me, Madam?”

Jane sighed. “ A cashpoint – an ATM.”

“Oh, er …. sorry Madam …. ours is temporarily out of order.”

In spite of the inconvenience, Jane was delighted. It was her turn to treat the concierge to *her* most saccharine smile. "You must all be *very* proud of yourselves."

As she turned from the desk and headed to the door, the man in the dark blue suit with the open neck shirt, who'd been sat at the table behind Jane's, coolly reached into his breast pocket and pulled out his 'phone.

"Woman, about forty. Shoulder-length, brown hair, expensive looking coat … British."

"So?"

"Nothin'."

"Got her."

The youth leaning idly against the pillar to one side of the hotel entrance pushed his phone into his back pocket, fixed a pair of tiny headphones into his ears and pulled his scarf over his mouth and nose. He flicked the hood of his jacket over his cap and pulled on the drawstrings, leaving only his eyes visible. He waited whilst Jane fished in her pockets for her gloves and then followed her, head nodding to the music, as she set off along the pavement. After walking about fifty yards, Jane suddenly stopped and turned back. The youth turned to look in the window of a travel agent and watched her reflection walk past him. He waited until she was about ten yards in front of him and then retraced his steps. Jane joined the queue for a cash dispenser. So did the youth. He took out a credit card and pretended to read the number, but his gaze was fixed firmly on Jane's back. He noted her handbag hanging over her right shoulder and guessed the strap to be about two feet long. It would slip off easily when the moment came.

Jane was at the front of the queue. The youth was breathing heavily behind his scarf and he raised his hand to pull it down. "Don't be stupid!" he told himself and scratched the top of his head with his cap instead. She was at the dispenser now. The youth concentrated on the slight movements of her shoulders: "That's her number going in. Now she's checking her balance." He could hear his heart beating wildly, disrupting the rhythm of the music, his scarf was damp with the condensation from his breath. "Wait," he murmured, "any second." Just then, at the critical moment, a car pulled up at the curb. Instinctively he turned; it was nothing, just a cab. "Come on," he told himself, "concentrate!" But his timing had been broken and he was surprised to see Jane turn in the next instant, already putting her purse back into her handbag. Even so, he was still fast enough to reach out and grab her bag by the strap.

Jane froze, unable to either release the bag or fight back. Her eyes widened in terror as the youth pushed her back onto the cash dispenser in a desperate effort to win his prize. Instinctively, her hand tightened around the strap of her handbag, gripping it tight to her chest and pulling the youth close enough to make her turn her head to one side to avoid his wild stare. He was now so close that, in spite of his scarf, she could feel his breath on her cheek. It's warmth made her want to gag but before she could another, larger hand reached over the youth's shoulder and clamped him by the wrist. The force of this second assault was so great that Jane felt the breath being forced out of her chest as she was pushed back even harder onto the dispenser. In a single, graceful movement, the youth's arm was dragged down and then up behind his back. Jane felt his weight being lifted off her as the youth was yanked backwards and then rammed with terrible force into the stone pillar next to the ATM.

"Tha's picked a wrong 'un there, pal," growled a strangely familiar voice.

Another hand appeared, as quick and strong as the first. It

grabbed a fistful of the youth's jacket and threw him to the ground as if he were nothing but clothes.

"Argh, you're breaking my arm, man," yelled the youth.

"Tha'd better shut it reet nah, 'fore I fetch thee 'ead off," said Jane's rescuer, relaxing his grip ever so slightly whilst forcing his knee into the middle of the youth's back.

"Argh," the youth cried again.

"Fetch 'police!" the rescuer shouted at the crowd that had gathered around them.

Jane stood stock still, unable to move, except for her mouth, which dropped open as she stared in total bewilderment at her husband kneeling on top of her assailant.

"How did you know it was me?"

It had taken several minutes before Jane had stopped shaking and several more before she could speak. As she regained contact with her surroundings, she pulled on the blanket around her shoulders and took a sip of the coffee she suddenly realised she was holding. She was sat on the back step of an ambulance. Dan was sat beside her.

"I'd know that coat anywhere," he grinned.

Jane smiled faintly.

"Sir, Mr Strives," came a voice over Dan's shoulder. He rose and turned to the detective, "if you're sure you're okay, we're going to let you go. 'The Centurion' you said?"

"That's right."

"Okay, well someone will be in touch tomorrow. We've been after these guys for weeks; this is their sixth or seventh time. … I'm really glad you're okay."

“Me too,” Dan smiled back, grateful for the detective’s concern.

“The Centurion?” Jane looked up at Dan in child-like confusion.

“Er, yeah, um … there’s a bit of explaining to do.” He reached out his hand to her, which she willingly accepted, but she stumbled as she rose.

“Ma’am, I really do think you should let the paramedic check you over.” The detective was still watching them.

“No, honestly, I’m fine,” replied Jane, “just a bit taken aback.”

“Well okay, Ma’am, I’m sure you’re in safe hands.” The detective smiled sympathetically from Jane to Dan.

“We’re only fifty yards from the hotel,” replied Dan, “I think we can stay out of trouble this time.”

The detective smiled again. “Okay, I’ll wish you goodnight.”

Dan and Jane turned away and began to make their way through the evening throng. As they walked, Dan’s hand rose under the blanket, which Jane still wore around her shoulders and his thumb fastened itself on the belt of her coat. As he pulled her towards him, Jane sighed. Before they had time to speak, they were back at the hotel.

“Good evening, Mr Keegan,” said the doorman as he ushered them inside, “you’re a real hero now.” Dan smiled again. Jane lifted her head from his shoulder with a quizzical expression on her face. Knowing what she was about to ask, Dan stopped and turned to face her.

“Mr Keegan?”

His answer was drowned out by the applause that echoed round the lobby. Jane looked up to find herself surrounded by smiling faces and clapping hands. Her mouth fell open again. There was a movement in the crowd and the floor manager, who had so singularly failed to help before, pushed through the crowd carrying a bottle of champagne in one hand and a huge bouquet over his arm. He pressed the bottle into Dan's left hand, thrust the bouquet at Jane and began pumping Dan's right hand. There were flashlights going off all around them. The manager held up his free hand to ask for silence.

"Mr and Mrs Kee ...". He stopped himself, allowed a knowing smirk to play across his face, and began again. "Mr *Strives* and Ms Whynn," he beamed at the crowd, "as floor manager of the Centurion, may I say what an honour it is to have such a brave and courageous couple staying in our hotel and to offer you an upgrade to our finest accommodation at our expense for the duration of your stay."

As the applause surged again, he leant over to Jane and whispered, "Please accept my wholehearted apology for the confusion earlier. ... I do hope it won't spoil your stay."

"You're only saying that because I'm a lawyer." The manager blanched. "See," said Jane to herself, as she smiled condescendingly at him, "I knew I'd win."

The applause died away and after several more minutes of shaking hands, pats on the back and calls of 'True Brit' and 'Go Limey,' Dan and Jane were finally able to collect the key to their new suite and retreat to the sanctuary of the lift. Jane had clung to Dan the whole time and now he turned and kissed her on the lips. She responded but then suddenly pulled away. "Who on earth is Mr Keegan?"

"Kevin Keegan, the England football manager - the one who wasn't up to the job." Jane laughed out loud but when Dan pulled her back towards him, she resisted again. Dan looked hurt, but it was Jane's voice that was trembling with anticipation.

"Are there any other secrets you need to tell me?"

"Only that I've probably sunk the firm without trace."

"Is that all?" Jane grinned mischievously, "I can fix *that* after dinner."

She leant towards him but now it was Dan's turn to pull away.

“What, straight after dinner?” he asked looking directly into her eyes.

“Well, maybe not straight after dinner.” And Jane kissed her husband.

That night Jane couldn’t sleep. Dan lay quietly beside her as the thoughts whirled around her head as frenziedly as the Broadway traffic ten storeys below. In part she was chastising herself for failing to contact the children. She’d tried ‘phoning as soon as they’d reached their new suite but, overwhelmed by the events of the evening, she’d hung up after only a few rings. Now she wished she’d held on, but even this disappointment, which would normally have generated hours of guilt and self-condemnation, couldn’t prevent her from being preoccupied and overwhelmed by what Dan had told her about New York. The merger itself had hit crisis point and was almost dead in the water. If it failed, it could potentially ruin the business, but more distressing still was the effect that it was having on Dan, and, by extension, the rest of the family. As they’d held one another, he’d wept as though his heart would break, and it was clear that he needed to come home as quickly as possible.

Over the course of the evening she had come to see that only one course of action lay open to her. So, as she lay on her bed, listening to Manhattan through the open window, she’d said her goodbyes. She knew now that she must give up what she loved in order to keep what she loved more and the bittersweet emotion of it forced her to smile even as she wiped a tear from her cheek.

She turned towards Dan and propped her head up with her hand. She looked at him almost as though she were seeing him for the first time; his strong, handsome features, the texture of his skin and the greying hair around his temples captivated her and she was amazed and faintly embarrassed to feel the same nervous excitement she had felt when she'd first met him. She recalled the raging fire in his deep brown eyes as he'd rescued her from her attacker; the memory of his raw, unbridled fury made her shudder whilst at the same time drawing her irresistibly towards him.

She held him close, careful not to wake him. "I nearly lost you," she whispered quietly.

"And I nearly lost *you.*"

Jane was so surprised that she jumped back, her cheeks flush with embarrassment. "I'm sorry, I thought you were asleep."

"I know, too much to think about."

"Do you want to talk?"

"Talk or listen?"

"What does that mean?" Jane asked anxiously.

"It just seems like years since you really listened to me."

"Well, I'm listening now."

"Alright, but are you sure you want to do this?"

Jane rolled back towards him and rested her chin on his shoulder, "I said 'I was listening' …"

Dan turned onto his back and rested Jane's head gently on his arm. "Are you *really* sure? You might not like what you hear."

"Yes, I'm *really* sure," replied Jane, beginning to sound exasperated.

Dan puffed out his cheeks, simultaneously raising his eyebrows and pulling his head to one side as though he were about to take a crucial penalty in a football match or set off down a particularly frightening ski run. "Okay then … it all goes back to …"

Suddenly Jane jumped out bed. Dan threw up his hands in exasperation. "Jenny! I promised Jenny I would 'phone her at Dave's. What time is it?"

Dan reached over and lifted his wristwatch from the bedside table, "Four a.m."

"That means it will be nine in the morning there. Oh no, not again!"

Jane scuttled across to the hotel 'phone and dialled the number quickly from memory, the connection was made within a few seconds. Dave's 'phone rang, but there was no reply.

"Any joy?" Dan asked anxiously. His frustration had evaporated as soon as Jane had mentioned Jenny's name. He'd felt hollow in New York without the children around. He was never very confident on the 'phone but as each new crisis hit the business, he'd found it more and more difficult to speak to them. Now he was as desperate as Jane to hear their voices. Jane raised a forefinger to her lips to interrupt him.

Howdy P-a-a-a-rdna, tha's through t' Dave's. 'e's out 'ridin' range right now, but tha's welcome t' try' is mobile or leave a smoke signal. And remember folks, if tha's trying t' rustle up a great deal on a car, "Tha saves at Dave's." Y'all come back real soon now.

Jane picked up a pencil and rattled it between her teeth as she listened to the answer 'phone clicking past the previous messages, then pulled the 'phone away from her ear as it gave out a long, piercing squeal.

"Urgh!" she threw the 'phone on the bed in frustration, "That man!"

"What?' asked Dan.

"His ridiculous answer 'phone!" Jane shouted into the pillow. She knew she was being unfair, but the overwhelming sense of guilt at forgetting the children, for what was now the third time. pushed her on." Why would anyone leave their answer 'phone on when they knew it was full and they're expecting an important call? He's impossible."

"Try him again," replied Dan gently, "you never know and anyway we could always leave a message."

“There’s *no space* to leave a message! Doesn’t he ever listen to them?”

“Let me try.”

Jane passed over the ‘phone. Dan also knew the number by heart and he dialled it just as quickly. The same rapid connection was followed by the same seven rings and the same ridiculous message. Dan waited patiently through the clicks and was rewarded by the same piercing squeal. He sighed and pressed the ‘end call’ button, walked over to the desk and placed the ‘phone back in its holster. He was suddenly aware of a noise behind him. He turned towards the bed and was amazed to discover that it was the muffled sounds of Jane’s sobs into her pillow. He moved quickly to her side, lifting up her and the pillow together. Cradling them in his arms, he began rocking gently from side to side. After a few minutes he moved her head into the crook of his arm and began to stroke her hair with his free hand. The sobs were beginning to lose their strength and he drew her closer to him. “Hey,” he whispered, “it’s okay.”

“Am I going to spend my whole life letting down the people I love?” panted Jane between sobs.

“Jane, you’ve held this family together; it’s me who should have his head in the pillow. We’ll call them again in the morning. If there was a problem I’m sure Mam would have ‘phoned.”

Jane breathed in deeply and shivered from head to toe. She lifted her head, pulled the back of her hand across her eyes and moved away from Dan. She stood up slowly and walked to the bathroom to wash her face, splashing it with water and examining her reflection in the mirror; her eyes were red and swollen and her face looked tired and drawn. She was reminded of a photograph she’d first seen many years ago of an American woman taken in the 1930s, during the Great Depression. The woman had been staring out from underneath some kind of rough-made shelter, cradling a child in her arms. Jane had felt a deep empathy with the woman, fighting to stay in control of her senses as her world crashed around her. It's significance had further increased when she had discovered Dorothea Lange and her pioneering work as a woman photojournalist: Lange had perfectly captured the mixture of defiance and defeat in the woman's expression, but when Jane turned back to the mirror she saw only defeat. She shivered again and buried her face in the soft towel. She started to weep again, but then breathed deeply and pulled the towel firmly down her face. "Come on," she whispered out loud, "that's enough self-pity for one day." She turned to see Dan leaning in the doorway, arms and legs crossed, staring intently at her. He let his head fall against the doorframe and allowed a slow smile to draw itself across his face.

"Let's have some coffee."

5

Jenny already knew what Dave's house would be like and, although she had only heard of the *renovation* by proxy, she was determined not to be impressed, so she was somewhat taken aback by the immaculate flagstone driveway and the elegant entrance beyond. The original farm had been built around a modest courtyard, with stables along one side, a large two-storey barn opposite and a medium size house for the farmer and his family in between. The stables had been restored but were otherwise unchanged, however the barn and the house had been combined to create a single, large dwelling, whilst the old entrance to the barn had been converted into a full-length arched window, over three metres wide, overlooking the courtyard. It was mirrored by one on the opposite wall, opening up a spectacular view across the valley. Beyond the driveway, where the truck had come to rest, rose a set of perfectly proportioned curved steps. Their shaped reflected the elegant, curved top of a large oak door, above which hung a mariner's lamp lighting the steps and welcoming visitors to the house.

Jenny, who prided herself on her keen eye for design, took all this in as she walked to the back of the car to help Dave with the luggage. She heaved out the largest bags, whilst Dave and her brother raced empty handed towards the front door. "First there wins 'league!" shouted Dave over his shoulder as he leapt up the steps two at a time. Jenny struggled on behind with their cases, almost stumbling as she climbed the steps. She dropped them inside the door just as Dave pushed passed her to gather up the last of the smaller bags.

"'s'up wi' thee?" he teased, "fresh air wreckin' 'lungs?"

"How can such an obnoxious man live in such a beautiful house?" Jenny mused as she entered the main living area. It looked as though it had been taken from a magazine. The stone flags from the steps extended inside the house, forming a large semi-circle between the front door and the polished oak staircase that began about two metres into the living room. Beyond this, the whole of the ground floor had been opened up into a single living area, in which the original floorboards had been rescued and were now polished to a deep, golden glow, contrasting sharply with the lime-washed walls. In the centre of the room was a huge, highly polished, waney edged oak table, showing away the most intricate pattern of knots and grains from deepest brown to golden white. To Jenny's artistic eye it resembled the evening sun chasing along a fast-flowing river bed; as she dragged her fingers along its length, she half-expected her hand to pierce its surface. It was beautiful. In contrast to the table's naturally flowing form, six perfectly aligned matching chairs, stood shoulder to shoulder along each side, as if guarding some great treasure, and she had to admit the whole effect was very impressive.

Behind the table, backed against the wall, was what should have been an equally imposing matching oak sideboard, however it's presence was both figuratively and literally overshadowed by a truly astonishing apparition. It's effect was such that Jenny inadvertently took a step back and let out a startled gasp. She was staring at an enormous … *mirror*, that simply defied description. It was oval in shape and at least five feet wide and four feet tall. The actual mirror itself was mounted in an ancient, deeply patinated leather frame, about three inches wide, decorated with brass studs to resemble a cowboy's belt, or possibly his saddle. At each of the oval's horizontal extremities it disported an ornate brass plaque, the centre of which protruded about three inches from the frame, presumably providing somewhere to hang a suitably over-sized hat. But the mirror's crowning glory, literally, was a set of highly polished, brass-tipped cow horns, spanning almost its entire length and protruding at least halfway over the sideboard. The centre of these had also been housed in intricately embossed leather and finished with a beautifully detailed painted cameo of a cowboy riding the range. Directly below this, at the mirror's base, was another intricately carved two inch brass plaque, announcing to the world that the mirror had been produced in 1919 by the Buck Flynn Co of Santa Fe. Yet none of this expressed the enormity of its impact. It somehow filled her entire field of vision, staring back with such massive self-assurance that even the table seemed cowed by the comparison. Jenny couldn't take her eyes off it; it was the most ridiculous, magnificent, outrageous, unforgettable thing she had ever seen. Where on earth did he get it? She stared at it for an age and then, as a mischievous grin spread across her face, she pressed her hands down onto the sideboard and, pushing through her arms, raised herself about foot from the ground. She lifted her head and true enough her reflection now sported a pair of magnificent horns. She stuck out her tongue and let out a squeal of delight, swinging her legs rapidly back and forth as though trying to run in mid-air. And then suddenly remembering where she was, she quickly lowered herself to the ground, anxiously looking round to ensure neither Dave nor David had witnessed her tomfoolery. And then it came to her.... *ridiculous, magnificent, outrageous, unforgettable* – it had to be – it could only be – this amazing 'thing' perfectly *mirrored* its owner. ... Brilliant, absolutely brilliant - MIRRORED ITS OWNER - what about *that* then Uncle Dave? MIRRORED ITS OWNER! She was definitely saving that one. With a contented sigh and suddenly feeling much better, she turned her back on her new friend and resumed her examination of the room and its contents.

The far wall, which she was now facing, was dominated by a recently blacked wood-burning stove with a chimney pipe reaching up through the ceiling. Beside the stove was a perfectly balanced pile of logs, although there were none in the fire grate itself. To the right of the fireplace, flanked by two matching cavernous chairs to form a separate seating area, was the largest leather settee Jenny had ever seen. She thought the furniture somewhat ostentatious, but was thrilled to see what she immediately recognised as an authentic Native American rug (late nineteenth century, guaranteed original Germantown Navajo) thrown over the settee. Jenny was using a similar design as inspiration for her GCSE Artwork and, ever since discovering them, had been captivated by the beautiful patterns woven with such skill by the Navajo women.

On the other side of the room, beyond the oak table was an archway that led to the kitchen, whose beautifully crafted cupboards appeared to be made from the same timber as the floorboards, although the kitchen floor itself was covered in white-scrubbed flagstones, one of which was inscribed with the date, 1756. Finally, on the farthest wall was a huge, gleaming red and black range, whose colour exactly matched the deep red of the marble work surface, which ran in a horseshoe around three walls before having to give way to an implausibly large fridge.

Jenny walked slowly through the rooms, taking in every detail, unable to resist drawing her fingers along the glistening, smooth surfaces. It was beautiful; everything worked and it was all *so* clean. "It doesn't make sense," she said out loud. Then a magazine lying open on the sideboard caught her attention. She picked it up and stared at it intensely for several seconds before slowly lifting her head and scanning the room again as if looking for something

"What's this?" she asked Dave, who was hanging up his hat by the door (not on the mirror, Jenny noted.)

"What's what?" he replied absent-mindedly.

"This magazine – it's your house."

"Is it?" replied Dave airily. "Oh aah, that's reet; they said summat, now, abaht puttin' on a spread."

Jenny looked at the glossy magazine again, fighting to keep

the smile from her lips. This explained everything: *an up-and-coming interior designer, given a limitless budget and an open brief, transforms a tired and dated country farmhouse into a stunning rural retreat for the new millennium.* - Dave hadn't done any of this; he'd paid someone to show him what good taste was. This on its own was a delicious morsel of information, but Jenny had learnt something far more valuable: Dave had made sure she'd see the magazine – *he cared what she thought!* Now she knew this, victory would be easy and complete!

"It really is a beautiful home, Uncle Dave, thanks so much for letting us spend the week-end here."

"Aah well," replied Dave, somewhat taken aback, "we'll allus be family n' matter what's gone off. I'll put 'kettle on," he added, retreating to the kitchen.

"See," said Jenny to herself, "easy." She wandered round the room, admiring the carefully chosen pieces of art and the skilfully placed furniture, smiling knowingly.

"So tha likes it then?" asked Dave coyly, coming back from the kitchen with three mugs of steaming, milky tea.

"I think it's lovely," began Jenny, but before she could add to her deceit, a roar of *It's MEGA*! drowned her out. She span round in time to see the most enormous plasma television screen descending gracefully from the ceiling in the far corner of what had once been the barn. But where was David?

"Can tha's watch footy on it?" he shouted without giving away his position. Jenny walked over to the back of the massive leather chair positioned strategically in front of the screen. She peered over it and there was David, sitting encased in a huge pair of headphones (Master and Dynamic MW60 Pelletessuta – *can't believe I found exact leather t' match 'Chair – how's that for a bit o' class*), easing himself into the most enormous buffalo hide (Grade A, Prime Winter - *direct from Wyoming – tanned, trimmed and sewn; no cheap tack 'ere, lass!*) hanging over the back of The Chair.

Jenny turned away, not knowing what to be disgusted about first.“ You needn’t think you’re watching television all weekend!” she chided.

“Tha’s reet there, cock,” agreed Dave, “tha’ll ‘ave t’ make time fo’ these, ‘n’ all.” He pushed a button on the side of the large leather cube to the left of The Chair. The top of the cube sprang open on two hidden hinges to reveal a games console, two handsets and two rows of games. “Aye, ‘n’ tha’ll need time fo’ these ‘n’ all.” Dave pressed another button and the tray of games sank mysteriously into the cube to be replaced by two rows of DVDs.

Jenny rolled her eyes and shook her head.

“Eh, ‘n’ if tha’s gaggin’ … tha’ll need these ’n all!”

Dave swaggered round to the other side of The Chair, where he pressed the corresponding button on a matching cube, and this time the lid shot open to reveal a mini bar stocked with crisps, chocolate and fizzy drinks.

“Awesome!” enthused David. “What do all these do?” he asked excitedly, pointing to a row of remote controls, each slung over the arm of The Chair in its own matching leather holster.

“Owt tha wants, young ‘un, but this ‘un’s me favourite,” said Dave passing his nephew a remote control. David pointed it at the television and pressed a button at random. The television failed to respond but the chair back began to recline slowly. He pressed another button and the footrest shot up. He pressed a third and The Chair started to vibrate softly.

“This is totally awesome!” repeated David.

“Dun’t tha want a go, lass?” asked Dave mischievously. “No? Best not any roads, we’ve a couple o’ jobs need doin’ – fo’ kick offs, grub’ll be ‘ere any time now.”

“What do you mean?” asked Jenny.

“From ’supermarket,” replied Dave, his voice rising alarmingly in consternation at his niece’s ignorance, “summat t’eat t’neet ‘n’ snap fo’ tomorra.”

“Speak English!” barked Jenny.

“Snap; fo’ ’walk, tomorra!” exclaimed Dave, by-passing ‘annoying’ and heading straight for ‘excruciating’. “Any roads, *tha pair* can make theesens useful fo’ once; tha can stay ‘ere ‘n’ keep ‘n eye out fo’ ’van. I need t’ call John abaht summat – busy man, me, tha knows. Can’t just drop everythin’ ‘cos *tha pair’s* suddenly rocked up.”

With that, Dave bounded up the stairs two at a time and Jenny, leaving her brother munching crisps with one hand and rifling greedily through computer games with the other, wandered aimlessly back into the kitchen. She felt hungry herself and instinctively reached up and opened a cupboard. To her surprise, it was empty. She opened the next one; apart from an ancient salt and pepper pot, some brown sauce and a suspicious-looking concoction called ‘Henderson’s Relish’, it too was empty. So were all the others. She couldn’t quite take it in; there was no food in the house, and apart from a small stack of plastic plates, a couple of scratched and chipped beer glasses and the three mugs Dave had used for the tea, there appeared to be no crockery either. Further investigations revealed only a battered frying pan, a drawer containing a few odds and ends of cutlery and a bottle opener. The kitchen was virtually empty. Suddenly it dawned on Jenny; Dave never used the kitchen, that’s why everything was so clean. This whole house: the design, the décor, the beautiful fixtures and fittings were a complete sham – Dave never used any of them.

She walked back through the main living area, unnoticed by David, and followed her uncle up the stairs. She could hear him talking from behind the door at the end of the corridor. She knocked tentatively and opened it wide enough to squeeze her head through the gap. Dave was talking animatedly into the ‘phone. Without pausing, he beckoned her in. She tiptoed across the room and, unable to find a clear patch of floor on which to stand, sat down nervously on the corner of the unmade sofa-bed.

Jenny gazed round the room; it was a tip. Most of the floor was covered with discarded clothes, although one corner seemed to be reserved for empty pizza boxes. At the end of the bed was an old doorless, dark wood wardrobe. It reminded her of the beautifully polished one in her grandmother's bedroom. Looking at its battered state, at first she thought that the door must have been lost or broken beyond repair, but then she realised that the wardrobe was so close to the sofa-bed that it had been removed to allow access to its contents. To the side of the doorless wardrobe was a curtainless window. Below this was a three-quarter built self-assembly desk. It was covered in car magazines, half empty cardboard coffee cups, various odd socks and even a pair of faded shorts (at least that's what Jenny hoped they were.) Half-hidden by these were a partially dismantled iPod, all manner of loose change and several rolls of banknotes, bundled together with elastic bands. There was a half-eaten Pot Noodle, piles of unopened mail and dozens of what appeared to be telephone and car registration numbers written around the edges of newspaper pages. These were kept company by all manner of important-looking business papers (Jenny thought she could detect the word 'Summons' on one). Nestled amongst all of this, sat a glass jar with a broken pen and half a blunt pencil in it, a pile of apparently brand-new ordnance survey maps and an unused paint brush on top of an unopened tin of white emulsion paint. The remaining contents of the desk had spilled over onto the floor round about and now appeared to be locked in a life and death struggle with the clothes for control of the bedroom.

On the other side of the room there was a battered armchair, where the clothes were easily winning the struggle and a weary looking bookcase, where the desk overflow was putting up more of a fight. Immediately to her left, balanced on a bedside table that had definitely seen better days, was a very old television with a paint-splattered radio perched on top. The television was positioned in such a way that it could be viewed from either the armchair or the bed. Next to it was a cheap plastic picture frame containing a faded photograph of Uncle Dave and her father as young men, stood outside a garage. With them was a man she recognised as her grandfather, but she didn't recognise the man of similar age standing next to Dave. All four men had linked arms and were grinning childishly. They were covered in grease and dirt and each of them held a can in one hand. She was shocked to see her father there and made a mental note to ask her grandmother about it later.

"Reet then, John, unless there's any probs we'll not see thee later, so it'll be on 'Edge abaht three tomorra … "'n' tha's bringing Meg?""… I bet she would. Alreet then pal, 'opefully 'til tomorra then." Dave laughed and put down the 'phone.

"Is this where you live?" Jenny asked.'" Aye lass, I moved 'ere after tha Dad went off t' finish 'is schoilin'; 'ave only just 'ad it done up."

"No," replied Jenny, "is *this* where you live; in this room?"

Dave hesitated, as if the thought had only just occurred to him, "Aye, lass, suppose it is, most o' time; 'car lot keeps me busy most days."

Jenny's next question was interrupted by the beep of a car horn.

"That'll be 'shoppin'," said Dave quickly. "Come on, let's see what they've fetched us. I'm starvin'," and he made his second hasty retreat of the evening.

"He never checks to see if you're following," thought Jenny to herself.

In no hurry to help with the groceries, she picked up the photo and looked carefully from face to face. How could this be her father? He was always so neat and tidy at home, yet look at him here; face covered in sweat and dirt, grinning from ear to ear, cigarette hanging from the corner of his mouth. There was something else about him that she couldn't quite express; it was her father but it was like looking at a different man. There was a wildness about him, something which scared and thrilled her at the same time - far more reminiscent of Uncle Dave than of the quiet, cautious man who had left for New York three months ago. Dave, too, had a different look. Quite apart from the permed hair and drooping moustache (*definitely* future ammunition), he looked so much younger. But again there was more to it; he looked so much more at ease with himself, as though he weren't trying all the time. She looked round the dingey room again. "I was right" she said to herself, "he doesn't live downstairs; he lives here."

She was completely unprepared for the surge of emotion that rose within her; so far this evening she had regarded her uncle with little more than contempt, but now she suddenly felt the unmistakable bond of family reasserting itself. To her amazement, she actually began to feel sorry for him, living alone in this beautiful house, desperate for people to appreciate his success yet terrified that he would spoil it if he actually used any of it. Frightened and lonely- who would have thought it of big Uncle Dave. "Frightened and lonely," she repeated out loud, that was her father too. She felt a sob well up inside her, but quickly recovered her composure, lest her uncle or David re-enter the room. She looked at the picture again.

"What happened to the two of you?" she asked the photograph and then, after a further moment's consideration, carefully replaced it on the bedside table, wiped her finger along the top of its frame, and turned away to gather together as many of the discarded pizza boxes as possible before following her uncle downstairs.

6

Dan talked. Jane listened. She was in turns fascinated, thrilled and, finally, as the implications of what Dan told her became apparent, appalled at her own shortcomings. It was like listening to a play on the radio, or talking to a stranger on a train; after all these years, she still knew so little about this man whom she loved so deeply. She had often tried to picture Dan before she met him and how close the family had been before he and Dave had fought. As she listened, she was finally able to concede that much of her resentment towards the family had come from their refusal to tell her what had happened. She had always hated being excluded from secrets; even now, her own father still teased her that ever since she could talk it was her nosiness (added to the fact that she was always right!) that had made her such a good lawyer.

As they sat in the window of their suite, their darkened room illuminated only by the city lights, after eighteen years of marriage, Dan finally told her what had happened between him and Dave:

He'd loved the business when they had started out, he'd even skipped college for most of his last year to take over from his brother on the spanners. Dave was quicker, but both of them knew that it was Dan's patience and attention to detail that brought the cars up to scratch. Even so, Dave had still forced him to go in and do his exams, but although Dan had done well he was sure that he would never need them. Within the first two months of 'proper' trading, they'd already outgrown the lock up and so, after a few weeks searching, had moved onto their first commercial pitch on Barnsley Road. *That* only lasted another six months as their reputation spread rapidly across the north side of the city, leaving them unable to meet demand for their cars.

Their cars – each and every one checked personally by Dave or Danny, as he was then, before the keys were proudly handed over. Dave's philosophy was simple: "Would we sell this car t' Dad?" If the answer was "No," then the car didn't make it onto the forecourt. Of course they were sharp, no one was sharper, but they never, *never* sold a nail.

When they'd had to move further out onto the new pitch at Ecclesfield and taken on John, their father's neighbour and friend, Danny had felt like a king. It was John who had first interested them in cars, always tinkering with them in his garage across the road. There wasn't anything Uncle John didn't know about cars and he always found the time to show the lads what he was doing. Be that as it may, he'd hated working at Stephenson's - everybody knew they were crooks - and John had no time for them. When they'd gone under he was glad, even though he hadn't a hope of being set on again at his age. But after a couple of months on his allotment he was bored and so, although he'd been apprehensive about working for the lads, when Danny asked him to help out over a busy period he'd said he would give it a try.

From the very first day, John had loved it. He'd forgotten how much he enjoyed the early mornings, when he had the house to himself, breakfasting on tea and toast over the racing. Almost immediately he'd re-connected with the minutiae of working life: the feeling of his rough work jacket on his neck as he pulled it over his heavy shoulders, the snap neatly packaged in grease-proof paper and tucked up inside the same old battered tin, sidling out of the house whilst it was still dark and carefully pulling the door to and locking it so as not to disturb Christine all added up to the same thing - he mattered again.

He felt a pride in himself once more as he greeted the other early starters as they passed on street; sometimes just a nod, at other times a brief comment on the weather, neither party breaking stride - too busy to stop and chat. As key holder, he was always first in and last out. The weight of the keys in his pocket and the chill of the workshop, which hit him as he stepped inside, checking the windows and lights last thing, locking the door and pulling it hard just to be sure, all added to his sense of belonging and making a difference. This was what was expected, this was what he did, this was what gave his life meaning and purpose and order.

But the cherry on the cake for John was the lads. They were so respectful and attentive, making him tea and fetching the sandwiches at lunchtime or asking him for advice about the cars they were offered. It was he who'd started them off in the business and, "Now look at 'em," he would say to Christine as they drove past the pitch on a rare day off. John had a renewed pride in his own work, too. Working on older cars, which relied less on computer analysis and more on the knowledge of the mechanic, reminded him how much he'd learnt over the years. Despite the vague feelings of embarrassment, and although he would never have mentioned it to another soul, even at his age, he couldn't suppress the sense of honour and respect when Danny, who still worked in the shop when they were busy, came to him with a problem.

"You'll not find that in your manual," he would tease, "I should never 'ave let *tha pair* anywhere near a set o' spanners." Then Danny would watch attentively as John showed him the way round the problem.

John had known Danny all his life. They'd never been able to have children for themselves and John and Christine had always treated Danny as they might their own son. For his part, Danny loved to wander into their house as though it were his own, never knocking but always welcome. Perhaps because they had no children of their own, the house was immaculately clean and the cupboards were always full of treats. Of course they were kept there for him and Dave, but Danny never comprehended this, he just thought of Uncle John and Antie

Christine's house as his own magical hideaway, where he could always find what he was looking for.

It was John, too, who had first instilled a sense of pride into the boys about their work. "If you do it right, you only do it once," he would chastise them as youths whenever they tried to take short cuts.

"But no one'll know when 'cover's on," Dave would argue.

"*You'll* know, 'n' *I'll* know 'n' that's why it 'as t' be right. Now strip it back 'n' do it properly, cocky little so 'n' soes! 'should never 'ave let *tha pair* in 'ere in 'first place."

The boys would wink and grin at one another in youthful conspiracy, but they always did what Uncle John said and, when it was finished, their bantam chests would swell and their eyes blaze with pride as he looked over their work and declared, "Now *that's* a proper job."

John was as committed to the business as the boys. Whenever he saw one of their cars on the street he would always stop and look it over. Christine would smile and shake her head in mock disapproval as he furrowed his brow and listened intently to the idling engine and then 'tut' and raise his eyebrows if his workmanship were being abused. The day when the lads had made him workshop manager and given him his own apprentice, he'd come home and cried in front of his wife for the first time since they were told that they would never be parents.

Dan had always enjoyed a special bond with John, but his *most* treasured memories of that time were of his mother, or, best of all, his father, 'droppin' in.' Dave was usually out buying and neither of them stayed for long. His father was his usual taciturn self and Audrey's concentration soon wandered, but as he showed them round their latest acquisition or the newest gleaming example to make it to the forecourt, he could still sense their pride in what he and Dave had achieved. Audrey would usually bring something to eat - a packet of cakes or a curd tart from the pork shop and tell them not to be late or their tea would spoil. Their father, on his way home from an early or on his way to the bookies on a day off, always needed an excuse. Often it was a message from their mother about meals or shopping or some other domestic arrangement and it usually ended with a complaint, either about them, "Treatin' 'place like an 'otel" or, less vehemently, about their mother's fussing, always finishing with a plaintive, "Tha knows what she's like." Then he would wander over to the workshop and talk to John, who would carry on the conversation with his head under a bonnet or lying on his ancient wooden creeper beneath a car. Dan never really knew what they talked about; he didn't really want to. He was content with the idea of his father and John being together in the workshop, in their own little world of cars and greyhounds and lads who had done well for themselves. Given what was to follow, Dan would always be grateful for those times.

After an hour or so, Jane began to feel hungry and they rang for room service. Fortified by croissants, bacon and more black coffee, Dan continued:

It was enough for me, but Dave was always so restless, always moving on to the next thing …". His voice tailed away and Jane silently finished the sentence for him.

Dan smiled wistfully. "I never really believed this was a good idea;" he nodded at New York through the window, "opened too many old wounds."

Jane could feel the knot tightening in her stomach and took a deep breath and smiled nervously. Knowing what she was thinking, Dan reached for her hand across the table and squeezed it gently, "Anyway, I was saying…"

Dave had had a new idea; it was time to expand the business again, but this time they were going all in. They'd gone as far as they could with the car lot, but Dave knew a *far* faster way to shift stock - a car auction! The old one, the one they'd used when they were starting off, had gone under; bloke who owned it got into a tangle with his VAT, so there was a gap in the market that was as clear as day to anyone with half an eye for the business. Everyone was trying to off-load trade ins, there were plenty of lads just crying out for one, Dave couldn't believe no one else had thought of it. He'd spied out a huge abandoned industrial site down the East End, which they could pick up for next to nothing, there were no worries about planning permission and the start-up costs were almost non-existent. It would mean some serious graft to begin with, but they had no ties and this would set them up for life.

"Come on Danny boy, this is what we've worked s' 'ard fo'. Wi' my charm 'n' good looks 'n' tha 'ead fo' figures we can't go wrong."

In this mood, Dave was irresistible, so Danny hadn't even tried. But from the outset there were problems. The first was John: "'ow can we check on 'quality o' cars passing through?" he'd asked when Dave broke the news.

"Not our problem anymore; 'buyer beware!'" was Dave's off-hand response. He was annoyed that Danny and John hadn't shared his enthusiasm.

"But that's not what you lads 'ave built 'business on."

"Times change, Johnny boy!"

Danny had seen John bridle over the lack of respect and so it had come as little surprise when a few days later he'd asked for his cards. Dave had ushered him into the office with gratingly off-key courtesy and offered him a seat.

"Nah den, what's all this about?"

"I've done my whack. It's time t' let some o' these young uns 'ave a go."

"Well, if that's 'ow tha feels..." replied Dave, not trying to dissuade him. "Any roads, don't worry theesen we'll see thee reet."

John stood up quickly, before replying with stiff and unnatural formality, "That's not necessary, thank you. You've always paid a fair day's wage for a fair day's work. If it's all the same, I think I'll just take my cards now and be on my way,."

"Suit theesen," replied Dave flatly.

There was an uncomfortable silence whilst Dave looked through the top drawer of his desk and pulled out a plain brown envelope containing John's P45 and a few other documents. Dave slid the envelope across the desk and, without a word, John picked it up and crumpled it into his jacket pocket. He held out his hand across his desk and, meeting his gaze, Dave shook it firmly. Danny turned and left the office in disgust.

"It's just business, John," said Dave less confidently, but still with the steely edge to his voice that he used when forcing through a deal.

"I know, lad," responded John, his usual gentle manner returning, "it's just not my kind o' business, that's all. I'm sure you'll be fine."

"No hard feelings?"

"Don't be s' daft, lad; I can still gi' *tha pair* a clip if needs be."

"Well if tha does need owt ..."

"I won't," John replied sternly and then, his gentleness returning for a second time, "I'll see you later lad."

John released his hand and Dave smoothed down his jacket and sat back down at his desk. Then John turned to Danny, who had stepped back into the office and watched in silence as Dave and John had said good-bye.

"'bout time tha stopped faffin' around wi' 'onest folks' cars 'n' all."

Danny smiled. "Thanks," he replied meekly, holding out his

hand, “thanks for everything,” and as John grasped his hand he suddenly pulled him close and held him in his strong embrace. He could smell the engine oil on John’s jacket; his heart was breaking. “Sorry,” he whispered and stepped back.

John let go of his hand, smiled wistfully and turned towards the door. With his hand on the handle he looked over his shoulder, “Eh, ‘n’ don’t *tha pair* be forgettin’ t’ call in ‘next time you’re at your mother’s or you’ll ‘ave your Antie Christine t’ answer to.” Dave smiled briefly and nodded, whilst Danny closed his eyes, bit his bottom lip and quietly shook his head, but neither brother spoke again as John quietly shut the office door behind him and left the pitch for the last time.

“Come on, Danny Boy, we’ve a business t’ run ‘ere.”

“Why was John’s papers in that envelope?”

Dave began leafing through a brochure that had been lying on his desk for weeks, “Mmm?”

“Did tha plan this?”

“Don’t be s’ daft!” replied Dave curtly. “Come on, I need them figures fo’ t’neet. I ‘aven’t got time fo’ tha t’ be goin’ off on one. Tha’ ‘eard ‘im; ‘e’ll be fine.”

Danny sat back down at his desk, staring at the columns of figures in front of him, hardly able to comprehend what had just happened. None of it made sense, but if this is how it was going to be from now on, John might not be the only one asking for his cards …

Dan stopped again as though weighing up whether or not to proceed. Jane was terrified of what might come next, the parallels between then and now were becoming so obvious and her heart was filled with foreboding. Her pinched thumb and fore finger moved to cover her mouth and behind them she bit hard on her bottom lip. "If I say one word," she said to herself, "the whole world will shatter like a pane of glass." So, she waited, staring at the remains of their breakfast, hardly daring to breathe. After an age, Dan began again. She lifted her gaze and breathed a deep sigh of relief, her world still intact:

Dave had been right about the car auction and never missed an opportunity to let Danny know: "I can't fathom what tha were mitherin' abaht - tha'd 'ave t' be a reet gorm not t' see this 'ould make money. We've a licence t' print 'stuff."

Danny had to agree that things were going well. They'd had to add a second sale to stop the lot from overflowing with cars and there was a queue of dealers wanting to sign up for a regular slot. But it wasn't the business Danny was mithering about; it was their father. The fall out between Dave and John had really knocked him back and he seemed to have aged so quickly since his own retirement. Danny had noticed how he'd begun to drift off whilst he was visiting and how rarely he was leaving the house or using his car.

"Should never 'ave bought it off a couple wrong 'uns like *tha pair*. Pedals are in 'wrong place, 'n' what's wi' them electronic 'andbrakes? Why can't they just leave well alone?" he would complain whenever Danny tried to broach the subject.

"Why don't you let us pick you up a nice little automatic from the auction?" Danny had suggested tentatively. "You don't need anything big anymore." But their father would have none of it and would go off complaining about computers putting honest blokes out of business and car companies lining the government's pockets; you'd no idea who to trust anymore. Danny knew when to stop listening. He also knew the real reason his father had stopped using the car - he was scared.

Then, one afternoon, whilst his father was tying up beans in the back garden, he'd suddenly doubled over in pain and fallen to his knees grasping his stomach. He'd looked up to ensure that

Audrey hadn't seen him and half-staggered, half-crawled back into the house. He was slumped over the kitchen table, still holding his stomach, when she found him.

"What on earth's the matter?"

"Nowt. Don't start carryin' on, makin' a fuss! 'just a spot o' indigestion, I'll be fine in a minute." But it patently wasn't. Audrey 'phoned the doctor's and, as an old friend of the receptionist, was given an appointment at the end of the evening surgery. To make matters worse, his father didn't argue. Danny left work early to take them. One look at his mother's face told him how anxious she was, and as he held her in his arms he could feel the fear passing from her to him. When he saw his father still slumped over the table, he had to fight down the panic that threatened to overwhelm him.

"Nah den, what's tha playin' at, draggin' me out o' work on a sale day?" he tried to joke.

"Sorry, son." his father replied earnestly.

Between them, Danny and Audrey managed to walk him to the car, his jacket draped over his hunched shoulders, his hand and forearm never leaving his stomach. The surgery was empty by the time they arrived and they were ushered straight through to the doctor's rooms.

"I think we need some help here," said the doctor calmly after a short examination, "I'd like you to go for some tests." Danny felt the colour draining from his face and he fumbled for his mother's hand beside him.

"How long will it take for those to come through?" asked Audrey.

"I think I'd like you to go across to the Northern General as soon as possible," replied the doctor evenly.

Audrey and Danny tried to keep up the pretence of small talk as they drove across town, but each of them knew the game the other was playing. As they approached the hospital, the conversation dried up, driven out by the suffocating fear, which seeped into every corner of the car. They passed Dave and Danny's first pitch and their father smiled to himself with an air of contentment completely at odds with the pain etched across his face. Danny caught the smile out of the corner of his eye but couldn't think how to ask him about it, so he glanced instead through the driver's mirror at his mother behind him, and when she saw him she smiled back like a frightened child trying to reassure her parents. Danny responded in kind, hoping it would give her encouragement.

They waited for an age in the ante-room of the assessment unit, not even sure that anyone knew they were there, and the only words spoken were from Audrey to Danny, rebuking him again for parking in a disabled bay. Eventually they were ushered into a small, non-descript room and Danny's father was told to lie on the bed. Audrey sat on the chair beside him, brushing her hand gently along his forearm. His other hand rested on his stomach beneath the blanket with which the nurse had covered him. After twenty minutes or so, a young woman dressed in jeans and a sweatshirt, with a mobile' phone protruding from her back pocket, entered the booth and introduced herself as 'Cassie,' the doctor who would be examining his father. She noted the look of alarm on Danny and Audrey's face and sighed inwardly. She half-thought to tell them her age, but knew it would make no difference, so she set about winning their confidence by the professionalism and care with she always went about her work.

After a few cursory questions, Cassie pulled back the blanket and gently undid her patient's trousers. She could see how much pain he was in and regretted having to add to it, but there was no alternative and so, warning him to tell her if it became too intense, she began her examination. Within a few seconds she had identified the source of the pain but didn't allow a moment's concern to cross her face. She carried on her investigation for a further five minutes, gently prodding and pushing around the abdomen. Allowing herself a momentary glance at Audrey, she smiled kindly in response to her child-like expression of appreciation for the care she was taking with her husband.

"I think we need to run some tests. We'll keep you in tonight and find something to ease that pain."

"Drop of Bell's 'll be out o' 'question, then?" asked Danny's father, responding to the winsomeness of the young doctor.

"I can see we're going to have trouble with you!" she responded lightly and then immediately checked herself. "It's too early to speculate on the cause of the pain, it could be a dozen different things, that's why we need to do these tests as soon as possible. I'm going to go and look for a bed for you. Is the car park alright?"

Danny's father smiled and then immediately winced.

"How long will it take?" asked Audrey anxiously.

"I'm afraid it might take a little while, but I'll come back as soon as I have some news. In the meantime, I'll order some painkillers."

"Lovely girl," said Audrey as soon as she'd left.

"Give over, Mam," cut in Danny gently, before she could continue with her matchmaking.

"Well, if that's the way you're going to speak to your mother, you can go and move the car so they've somewhere to park your father."

Danny felt the relief wash over him as the normal perspectives and proportions of life returned. "Alright, I'm going," he sighed, "I'll be back in a minute." He leant over and kissed his mother. "I'll not be long Dad."

Once outside, he turned on his mobile 'phone and was greeted by four messages from Dave. He sighed and held down the number three button.

"Where's tha' bin? We're startin' in 'alf 'n 'our 'n' nowt's ready."

“Dad’s in hospital.” There was a pause on the other end of the line.

“’tha sure?”

“Course I’m sure. What, tha thinks I’m messin’?”

“Alreet, calm down,” said Dave slowly, thinking and speaking at the same time, “… what abaht … if tha stays there fo’nah … ‘n’ I’ll tell Graham t’ sort out ‘lots fo’ t’neet - as a one off, like? Make sure tha’s back in time t’ ‘elp settle up though; we can’t be gettin’ behind this month, not wi’ extra nights startin’. ‘n’ tell Mam if I get a minute, I’ll gi’ ‘er a bell - can’t promise though, not wi’ this lot kickin’ off. Got t’ shoot, it’s absolutely rammed in ‘ere t’neet ‘n’ we’re nowhere near ready.”

He hung up before his brother could reply. Danny stood stock still, staring in disbelief at his ‘phone; there were a thousand questions racing through his mind, and he was terrified of every answer, but none of these could draw his attention away from one simple, devastating truth: Dave hadn’t even asked about their father.

Danny drove round and round the winding hospital grounds looking for a parking space. After ten minutes he’d had enough and returned to the disabled bay he’d first used. He hurried back to the examination room but by the time he arrived, his father and Audrey had gone. He almost bumped into Cassie, who told him that they’d been lucky and found a bed in transit on the next floor. He ran up the stairs and along the corridor and was breathing hard by the time he found Audrey staring at a noticeboard beside the entrance to the ward. After another ten-minute wait, a friendly nurse came out and told them that the doctor had given his father some painkillers, so he was a bit drowsy, but they could come in and see him now. He looked so much better propped up under the pristine white sheets that Danny could almost believe that there was nothing seriously wrong, but when a nursing assistant came and asked him if he needed anything, his father only shook his head, trying not to let Audrey see him wince.

"How long has this been going on?" she asked, the annoyance obvious in her voice.

"Don't start again! I've told you, it's probably nowt but a bit o' indigestion."

Audrey looked at Danny and shook her head in exasperation; he could be so stubborn at times, but before she could say anything else, a nurse came in and gently told them that it was time to leave.

"Any roads, lad, it's time tha were back at work, 'n' not leavin' it all t' thee brother. … Tha can drop thee mother off on 'way past."

Danny understood perfectly; his father was in pain and needed to rest, but he was also thinking of Audrey. He didn't argue. "Come on Mam; 'e's in 'best place now 'n' your tea'll be spoilin'."

Audrey understood too. She picked up her scarf and handbag from the bed and bent over to kiss her husband tenderly on the forehead. "I'll ring later. Good night, God bless." Danny leant over and touched his father gently on the arm. "See you tomorra, Dad."

"Don't tha be leavin' it all t' our Davey," his father repeated. Danny smiled back, then, feeling the tears well up in his eyes, he turned quickly away, took Audrey gently by the elbow and led her off the ward.

Danny didn't arrive back at the pitch until after ten. Despite his protests, his mother had insisted on giving him his tea and he'd had to drag himself away. Dave did little to hide his annoyance. "Is 'e sorted?" he snapped, momentarily lifting his head from the pile of papers scattered across his desk. "This is a reet carry on this. Tha can't just be lakin' off whenever it suits - we've a business t' run 'ere tha knows."

" 'n' that's our Dad lyin' in hospital, so shut it! I thought tha were gonna call Mam. … Tha can be a selfish chuff sometimes."

Dave was completely taken aback by Danny's outburst. "I'm lost wi'out thee t' sort 'paperwork," he said plaintively. He looked up again, this time leaving the papers untouched, "'ow's Mam?"

"Nearly as scared as me."

"Gi' o'er, 'e's as strong as 'n 'oss that 'un. Tha' don't do thirty years in 'rollin' mill if tha's not made o' summat tougher than that. 'e'll be back givin' thee jip 'fore tha knows it. 's up wi' 'im, any roads?"

"Like tha cares."

"Eh, 'e's my dad 'n' all."

"Aah, that why tha didn't bother t'ask after 'im earlier?" Danny paused, took a deep breath and then added quietly, "They're not sure, they're runnin' some tests."

"Aah, well, like I say, 'e'll be out 'fore tha knows it."

Danny stood stock still, trying to come up with the right reply. He couldn't and so simply responded, "'ere, let me 'ave them figures." He sighed and sat down wearily at his desk, shaking his head at the mess of papers Dave had handed to him. He stared at them as if he'd never seen their like before. "Come on," he urged himself, "keep it together," as he forced himself to start adding up the night's takings. Neither spoke again.

Jane looked down furtively at her watch. "Dan," she interrupted him gently, "it's 5.30; we must make some calls."

"I know," he replied calmly. He wasn't angry with her, just the opposite in fact. He knew she didn't want to interrupt him, but she was torturing herself about missing the children last night *and* she was worried about meeting with The Client that afternoon. He loved her for her willingness to be torn in different directions.

"Are you sure that's alright?" she asked tenderly.

"I'm sure, but if I don't do this now, I'm not sure I ever will. Five more minutes …."

Jane smiled. She leant forward and simultaneously rested one elbow on the table and her chin on the palm of her hand, her fingers folded over her mouth. Dan smiled back, took a deep breath and continued:

Their father's strength never did return. There appeared to be a grim inevitability hanging over the family during the next few months. Audrey fussed and clucked over the boys in-between visits to the hospital, but Danny could see how wearing the whole business was for her. Dave, on other hand, seemed totally unconcerned. Depending on the news from the hospital, he would veer wildly from one point of view – "they're amazing them doctors, wish my lads knew 'alf as much abaht motors"- to the other – "they 'aven't a clue that lot; Dad'll show 'em, don't worry theesen abaht *that*."

Danny could neither comprehend nor accept how his brother remained so completely obsessed with the business, putting in longer and longer hours and constantly bragging about how much money he was making when there were so many more important things going on. How could he be so selfish? It was only after their father's death, when he was away at university, that Danny was able to appreciate that this was Dave's way of coping with the situation – to immerse himself in things he knew and could understand. It took even longer to acknowledge that, in his own way, Dave had been thinking of the family and that his fixation with money sprang from a deep need to ensure that he could provide for everyone after their father had gone. Finally, only after having had children of his own, Dan was able to admit that their father would have approved of Dave's intentions, if not necessarily his behaviour.

On a rare joint visit to the hospital, at Dave's instigation, the brothers had tried to persuade their father to 'go private,' but he would have none of it, chiding them for wanting to waste their money after he'd paid his stamp all these years.

"Any roads," he asked, waiting for a nurse to pass within earshot, "who's gonna look after me better than these lasses?" The nurse turned and smiled and Danny let his gaze fall to the floor. The doctors and nurses had taken excellent care of both of their parents, particularly Audrey and although he would have done anything to help his father, he recognised that they'd made a mistake in suggesting a move.

Walking down the stairs after visiting time, he and Dave had argued, his brother accusing him of being afraid of standing up to their father. Danny had told him to grow up and try to see someone else's point of view for once: money wasn't the answer to everything, no matter how many people you had to walk over to make it. Stung by the inference, Dave had responded by telling him that at least someone was taking responsibility and trying to stay on top of things instead of moping around all day, neither use nor ornament. They'd parted on bad terms; Danny was cut to the core, but not even Audrey was allowed to find out why.

Following this latest fall-out, Dave seemed to become more obsessed than ever with expanding the business. He took on more and more staff and, in an effort to 'go regional,' began to place adverts on local tv and radio. After great deliberation he finally settled on *'Tha saves at Dave's'* as his catchphrase and before long it could be heard across the city as children raced around the schoolyard, imitating the roaring engines and screeching tyres that served as the backdrop to Dave's unique Yorkshire-American voice-over.

Danny found himself under more and more pressure to keep up with the never-ending flow of paperwork. He moved to an office at the back of the lot and changed his routine, getting in before anyone except the cleaners and finishing at two, before Dave started checking the preparations for the now nightly auction. This allowed him to pick up Audrey in the afternoon and go over to the hospital together, then he would return towards the end of the auction to begin working through the accounts.

Danny was self-taught and the combination of his ever-increasing workload and caring for his parents was exhausting. On the one occasion he had brokered the idea of passing on the accounts to a professional, Dave had dismissed it out of hand, telling Danny that no one outside the family need ever know their business and, any roads, how could some poncy college kid be expected to know the motor trade like Danny. So he struggled on, trying not to let his parents see how tired he was or just how much the fall out with Dave had hurt him. But they did. To Audrey, it was almost a relief to have something else to worry about, and in her own gentle but determined way she took every opportunity to smooth over the obvious ill-feeling between her boys. Their father, too, was aware of the tension between them, although, unlike Audrey, he never discussed it; after fighting his own daily battles, he no longer had the strength to sort them out and so fell back on the faith that family ties would see them through in the end.

As the spring days lengthened, their father was allowed to return home. By now everyone except Dave seemed reconciled to his prognosis. Audrey was hoping to give him one last summer to enjoy in his garden before the end and Danny moved his old armchair out onto the concrete slab behind the house, allowing him to relax in the afternoon sun, when John would come round and they would talk and smoke until their father became cold or the pain grew too intense.

To Danny's surprise and relief, Sunday became Dave's day with his parents. Audrey still insisted on doing a roast, but, other than that, he could use the time to catch up on the backlog of work that had accrued during the week. As the days lengthened, if he were well enough, Dave would take their father and Audrey out to Highfield to watch the cricket. Dave's newly imported American truck was high enough to allow his father to watch the play over the dry-stone wall that surrounded the ground. He would sit there in the warmth, drifting in and out of the game, criticising the umpires or occasionally praising one of the youngsters until he nodded off and his barely touched ice-cream would melt and fall into his lap. The first time it had happened he had barked at Audrey as she'd tried to clean up the mess but, as spring turned to early summer, he barely stirred as she carefully wiped down his coat and hands, finishing with the gentlest of brushes across his face with her handkerchief.

It was during these rides out that Dave had first had the idea of moving out to Highfield. He'd never been able to concentrate on the game for long and his attention would soon drift off towards the hilltops surrounding the village. As the weeks passed by, little by little, despite having sat beneath them for longer than he could remember, Dave became mesmerized: the familiar peaks and edges appeared so strong and permanent, looking down benignly on the lives of the cricketers and their spectators, their gigantic mass unmoved by the tiny problems below, yet somehow able and willing to absorb the troubles and worries that beset them all. Although he'd never be able to put it into words, and, even if he could, it didn't really make much sense, somehow Dave knew deep within himself that these hills would one day become his friends and here, finally, he had found what he was looking for - a place to breathe and to rest.

One Sunday, for no particular reason, he'd driven his parents home the long way, skirting the reservoir above the village and out onto the moors. As his truck climbed the long hill, passing the squat, windswept church, he'd spied an ancient stone-built house and barn. Without speaking, Dave had stopped the truck and stepped down onto the empty lane. The house seemed inhabited but badly in need of repair and the barn looked neglected and unused. He leaned over the weary gate guarding the path to the house and stared; in that moment he had known that this was going to be his home.

To his surprise, an elderly farmer wandered out from the barn. "Now then, young 'un," he greeted Dave in that cautiously friendly manner so common amongst the locals, "thinkin' o' goin' into farmin' or just tryin' t' wear 'inges out on that gate?"

"Only if tha's sellin' up."

"Why are you interested?"

"Maybe, if 'price is reet."

"Mmm," responded the farmer thoughtfully, "'n' what's a city lad like you want wi' a place in 'middle o' nowhere?"

Dave immediately sensed a deal was possible and ignored the farmer's question, "I'll tell thee what, 'ere's me card, gi' us a bell if tha thinks on. I'll see thee later." Dave climbed back into the truck, unable to keep the 'Now *that's* what I call a deal' grin off his face.

"You look pleased about something," said Audrey suspiciously. She loved her son with all of her heart but she was well aware of, and not entirely at ease with, his reputation as a ruthless businessman.

"I think I've just found me new 'ouse, Mam. … Eh, tha can both come out 'n' stay on me country estate 'n' enjoy fresh air …" His voice tailed away as he remembered his father's cancer. "Tha'll love it, Dad," he went on, recovering his conviction, "we'll 'ave them cucumber sandwiches 'n' tha can take pot shots at 'pheasants on 'lawn." His father smiled, not at the joke but at the thought of how well his lads had done for themselves. It made everything easier.

7

By July, Audrey had finally conceded that the 'one last summer' would not be spent at home. Their father was moved to St Francis' hospice on the far side of town and Danny spent more time than ever ferrying his mother back and forth, with the inevitable effect on both the business and his health. Dave tried not to criticise, but Danny knew he was unhappy with his performance, so he began to stay at work after the others had gone; the last thing he or anyone else needed now was another argument between the two of them, there was still more than enough ill-feeling left over from the last one. So Danny pressed on, ignoring the tiredness that made his body ache so much that at times he thought it would explode. He wasn't eating and couldn't sleep, but by now even Audrey was failing to notice how ill he was looking. On more than one occasion, he'd fallen asleep at his desk and was woken by the cleaners in the morning. He'd simply rinsed his face in the bathroom, poured himself some fresh coffee and picked up from where he'd left off the night before.

By August, their father was so ill he could hardly speak and he began to lapse in and out of consciousness as the painkillers took hold. The end wasn't far off and Dave, Danny and Audrey began to visit together. Dave was still full of ideas about the business and plans for his new house. He would talk endlessly about how good the fresh air would be for their father and how he could stay there until he'd recovered - perhaps they could even build their own apartment for them in the barn. Danny and Audrey no longer had the energy to contradict him and turned their attention instead to the rows of stately detached houses lining the road out of the city towards the hospice. When Dave eventually ran out of things to tell them about his new house, he would start counting the number of cars with a *Strives* sticker in the window. The thought of all these well-to-do people buying cars that had passed through their auction filled him with delight, like a child listening to an adult praising his painting or telling him how well he'd performed in the school play. Danny wondered where this constant need of approval came from and where Dave would ever be able to find it. "She'd better be special," he would murmur to himself, as he tried to imagine the woman who would have to win him round.

Finally, Audrey began staying over at the hospice and even Dave stopped attending the auctions in the early part of the week when things were less hectic. Then one Friday afternoon, Danny took the call from his mother. "It's time," was all she said. "Come as soon as you can and bring David."

Danny sat for a moment pressing the 'phone against his forehead and then wearily pushed himself to his feet and walked over to Dave's office in the main block. He wasn't there, but Christine said he'd left a message to 'phone him if anything urgent came up. Danny lifted the 'phone off the secretary's desk and dialled his brother's number. No reply. His 'phone was turned off.

"Where is 'e?" Danny asked impatiently.

"He said he was going to lunch 'wi' a couple o' big wigs,'" replied the secretary, mocking Dave's way of speaking when he was trying to impress.

"Where? Where is he?" asked Danny curtly.

"At the Cutler's Hall, I think. He said he would be there until four and to send one of the lads to pick him up."

Danny turned without replying, swept out of the office and ran over to his car. He fumbled the key as he rushed to start the engine and, ignoring the seat-belt warning alarm, sped off towards the city centre to find his brother. It was a typical, busy Friday afternoon and almost immediately Danny was stuck in traffic.

As the queue crawled to halt, he reached for his 'phone and pressed re-dial but there was still no response. He checked his watch and groaned in despair. The pressure building in his head and chest was unbearable. For a second he thought he was going to pass out. Grinding his teeth and scraping his fingernails backwards and forwards across his scalp, he let his head fall down hard onto the steering wheel. He sat there motionless and then as the rage finally pushed him over, he raised his hands and grabbed the steering wheel and began shaking it with all his might. "Aargh! Aargh! Aargh!"

After what felt like an age he opened his eyes and looked up. The traffic hadn't moved. He was trapped. There was nothing he could do. Not when he was stuck in traffic.

Suddenly the dam burst and as despair swept over him he let his head fall to the steering wheel once more. The tears broke through his defences and accompanied by the snot from his nose fell unchecked onto the steering wheel and down to the floor. He was sobbing uncontrollably. The drivers of the cars around him could see it plainly. He didn't care.

Eventually he let out an anguished sigh, bit hard on his lip and shook his head inconsolably from side to side. And then, to his own amazement, calmly, decisively and irrevocably, before the tears could begin to well up in his eyes once more, he made up his mind. He knew what to do. He pulled the back of his hand across his nose and eyes, sat up straight, took a deep breath, looked over his shoulder and accelerated into the bus lane. He was out. And within seconds Danny was cannonballing the car under the huge arch of a disused railway line, ignoring the screeching tyres and blaring horns of the traffic joining from the right.

At the end of the road was a junction, which guided the traffic onto a one-way system, Danny ignored this, too, and drove straight on, sticking to the bus lane. He did the same again at the next set of lights, praying that he wouldn't hit anything, following the bus lane into the heart of the city. At the top of an incline, he swung the car left onto a wide-open road and accelerated along a set of tram lines before screeching to a halt outside the main doors of the Cutler's Hall, pulling up half on the pavement and half over the double yellow lines. Despite leaving the engine running, he still had the presence of mind to turn on the hazard warning lights and then leapt out of the car and up the steps in front of the Hall. He almost ran into Dave in the foyer.

"Ay up our kid, bit up market fo' thee in 'ere in't it? Dear me, there's some reet brass up there t'day. Tha shoulda tagged along; bit o' 'igh life mighta done thee a bit o' good for a change. Eh, 'old up, take a butcher's at these beauties." Dave reached into his jacket pocket and pulled out a handful of fat cigars. "Finest Cuban, these – no cheap tack, 'ere, our kid … not fo' 'Strives lads! Come on," he slurred, fumbling in his pocket for a non-existent cigarette lighter, "someone round 'ere must 'ave a light. Eh, 'old up, 'as tha come in that poncy motor o' thine? Course tha 'as - that'll 'ave one. Come on …". He paused momentarily and furrowed his brow, squinting down the steps towards Danny's car, as if trying to comprehend its sudden appearance outside the Hall. He shrugged his shoulders, "Can't enjoy a decent *Corolla* on tha todd," he returned to his previous theme, "that toffee-nosed lot up there don't know nowt abaht owt. Come on, our kid; thee ''d me still know 'ow t'enjoy ussens." He reeked of alcohol and was swaying precariously.

Barely able to contain his fury, Danny could only snarl, "It's Dad. Why the chuff is thee 'phone turned off?"

Dave's mood changed instantly. "I'll fetch me stuff," he replied.

"Forget it, just get in!" snapped Danny, already turning away and heading back down the stairs, but when he turned back Dave was nowhere to be seen.

By this point, despite all his best efforts, Danny was struggling to maintain a grasp on the reality that was unravelling around him. Not knowing what to do, he simply followed his instincts and dashed back down the steps towards the car. He breathed a huge sigh of relief when he saw that there was no one around and quickly climbed in and began revving the engine. There was still no sign of Dave. "Come on, come on!" he hissed, checking nervously in the rear-view mirror, "What's tha doin'?" He fought down the desire to jump out of the car again; gripping the steering wheel as hard as he could and pressing his foot down repeatedly on the accelerator, his whole body was trembling with emotion. Unable to wait any longer, he yanked open the car door, jumped out and ran back up the steps and into the foyer. He found Dave on the stairs, holding firmly on to the banister, descending cautiously.

"What the chuff's tha been doin'?" Danny yelled, turning back the way he'd come.

"Eh, tha don't just walk out on these people, tha knows," lectured Dave as he followed his brother unsteadily back down to the street.

Outside, Danny glared at his brother over the roof of the car and, even in the panic that was consuming him, found a second to make sure that Dave saw him shake his head. Dave ducked down and climbed in, relieved to be out of his brother's sight. Danny followed suit, then, slamming his door, releasing the hand brake and ramming the car into gear, he looked quickly over his shoulder and pulled straight out into the path of an on-coming tram.

The driver, having only just pulled away from the stop, had had time to anticipate Danny's mistake but couldn't prevent the tram from sliding into the wing of his car, flinging it backwards along the tram tracks and spinning it through 180 degrees. Nevertheless, neither brother was injured and Danny was out in an instant, already dialling 999 on his mobile 'phone. "I'll need 'police 'n' an ambulance straight away. It's an emergency, please 'urry!"

Dave spent some considerable time fighting with the passenger-side air bag, and then clambered unsteadily out of the car. "What's tha done that fo'?" he asked angrily.

"Shut it 'n' phone fo' a taxi!" Danny barked back. He had known in an instant that this was the quickest way to sort this out; he could deal with the police, whilst Dave went on ahead to the hospice, then he'd join them as soon as he'd done.

Dave, meanwhile, stood swaying uneasily and swallowing hard. His head was spinning, partly from the crash but mostly from the Master Cutler's hospitality and for a moment he thought he might be sick.

He took a deep breath and steadied himself and the nausea passed, but his general confusion remained, compounded by Danny's latest instruction. He furrowed his brow and grimaced, mumbling, "'ow am I meant to shut it *and* 'phone fo' taxi?"

He shrugged his shoulders and smirked and then began patting his pockets in search of his 'phone. "I'd like t' order a taxi but I've been told t' 'shut it!' Eh, can tha use that sign language ov'r 'phone?" He stifled a laugh. "Must o' left it up there," he finally concluded, patting the last of his pockets and squashing the cigars. "Oh, that's not 'elpin'. … Eh, Danny," he shouted to his brother, "thought tha were goin' t' fetch that cigarette lighter; shake theesen! … I'll be back in two ticks - left me 'phone …" he waved his arm in the general direction of the Hall, but as he turned back towards the foyer, Danny flew across the pavement, grabbed him by the collar and spun him round.

“Tha’s not goin’ anywhere, tha drunken gob-end!”

For the second time in as many minutes, Dave’s mood changed in an instant; with a dexterity completely at odds with his condition, he instinctively reached up and grabbed Danny’s wrist, simultaneously forming a fist with his other hand and pulling it back ready to strike.

“No!” yelled Danny. “Leave it!”

The two brothers stood locked together, eyes searing into one another, each waiting for the other to make the next move. For what seemed like an age, they remained motionless, like two bronze statues frozen in combat and then, finally, Danny’s shoulders slumped. He relaxed his hold on Dave’s jacket, the blaze in his eyes already fading, and in spite of his brother’s iron grasp, he slowly lowered his hand.

“It can wait … we can’t d’ *this*, not now - not wi’ everythin’ that’s goin’ off.”

Dave didn’t move.

“Look, I were out o’ order,” Danny continued, barely above a whisper, “I shouldn’t o’ grabbed thee, I’m sorry … it’ll just ‘ave t’ wait. Can’t tha just go ‘n’ sit in ‘car ?... *I’ll* sort taxi …please … ‘am askin’ thee.”

Dave blinked several times and then slowly lowered his fist and let go of Danny’s wrist. “Mardy chuff,” he hissed, pulling his head up sharply and narrowing his eyes, “s’up; not ready fo’ thee big brother yet? Still ready t’ give out orders though. Allus knows best this ‘un, allus ‘as; tha can ask anyone. Knows best, does least - too busy bein’ taxi service ‘n’ playin’ goody two shoes for ‘is mam. No wonder ‘e’s always been favourite.”

But the dam had burst and the rage that had threatened to overwhelm Danny was spent. “Yeah, whatever,” he responded, still holding his brother’s gaze, “’ere you do it if it’s that important.” He held out his ‘phone to Dave, who hesitated before sneering and snatching it out of his hand, “Whatever tha says, Mummy’s Boy.”

Dave turned and swaggered back over to the car, making sure that Danny could see he had no intention of 'phoning until he was good and ready, but after a few seconds he turned away and made the call. Danny watched on silently, already reproaching himself for his loss of control. He sighed deeply and turned away and was suddenly aware of the crowd of onlookers that had gathered. He didn't care, he just wanted it to be over. "Seen enough?" he asked no one in particular and then, noticing Dave was now sitting on the steps, head resting on one of the stone pillars, and not really knowing what else to do, he, too, wandered aimlessly over to the car. By the time he reached it, he was completely calm.

In times of extreme stress, once the initial burst of adrenalin had played out, Danny possessed an amazing ability to become completely detached from his circumstances, and, knowing there was nothing else he could do for the next few minutes, and that any attempt at reconciliation with Dave would only make matters worse, he stood silently surveying the consequences of his brother's selfishness and thinking back over everything that had led to this moment. Leaning back on the undamaged side of his car, he thrust his hands deep into his trouser pockets and casually crossed his legs. He looked across to the sturdy cathedral on the opposite side of the road and up into the pale blue sky beyond and smiled wistfully, the tranquillity of the late afternoon reflecting his own serenity. Quietly and calmly, without any great emotion, he finally acknowledged what he'd known ever since the day that he and Dave had argued on the hospital stairs – it was over, it was time to move on.

Entirely lost in his own thoughts, he began to wonder what he would do when all this was behind them and whether or not he would even stay in Sheffield. To his surprise, he was suddenly overtaken by a desire to travel and see the world beyond the narrow confines of his early life - he might even consider a change of career. In total contrast to what was going on around him, he could feel the excitement of it beginning to build within him, but then quickly rebuked himself as the sound of an approaching siren forced him to re-connect with the present reality. Reluctantly, he acknowledged to himself what came next and with a deep sigh turned to Dave, "Tha'd better 'phone Mam 'n' all, 'n' tell 'er what's gone off - don't even think abaht tellin' 'er abaht this carry on; that stays between thee 'n' me, 'reet?! Just tell 'er no one's 'urt 'n' we'll not be long. And *don't* upset 'er!"

By now, the tram driver had come down from his cab and was pulling at the crumpled wing of Danny's car in a vain attempt to relieve the pressure it was exerting on the tyre. The conductor, having checked the passengers and, seeing no one was hurt, now stood watching his partner with an air of bored familiarity. "Not in a 'urry were you?" he asked with no great concern. Danny turned and fired a glare at the conductor but before he could find a suitably biting response to accompany it, an ambulance swung round the corner and pulled up beside the tram.

"Everyone here okay?" the paramedic asked briskly. Danny nodded his assent and the paramedic moved off with the conductor to check the passengers, most of whom had stayed on the tram to see what would happen next. Seconds later a police car pulled up and Danny, now totally re-engaged with the urgency of the situation, ran over to it and wrenched open the driver's door.

"It were my fault," he blurted out, "I shouldn't 'ave parked 'ere 'n' I weren't payin' attention. Look, 'ere's me licence. Can tha 'urry? Me fatther's seriously ill in 'ospital 'n' we've t' be there, urgent."

"All in good time, lad … take a breath," replied the portly, grey-haired officer as he slowly squeezed himself out from behind the steering-wheel, "… all in good time."

He walked round to the back of the car, showing little interest in either Danny or the accident, wearily lifted the tail gate and took out a warning triangle and a fluorescent jacket. He closed the tail gate, slowly pulled on the jacket, walked about ten metres back from Danny's car and fastidiously set up the triangle. Then he sauntered back to his own car, reached for the driver's door and, with his hand on the handle, paused and unenthusiastically surveyed the scene around him. He puffed out his cheeks and shook his head at one more example of the shortcomings of an unthinking and ungrateful public, before opening the door and pausing again to let out an even deeper sigh and shake his head for a second time. By now, it was crystal clear to all concerned that he'd seen it all before, none of it came as a surprise, and, most importantly of all, he had no intention of do anything in a hurry. Having given his audience time to fully absorb his message, he leant in and picked up his notebook and radio from the dashboard, then stood up tall to indicate that he would do his duty regardless, and slowly surveyed the scene once more.

Danny had seen this a dozen times before as a youth – the deliberate slow-timing, accompanied by the officer's studied refusal to acknowledge the presence of those around him until he was good and ready. He knew the drill and recognised his powerlessness against it; everything would be done to the same steady rhythm, forcing whatever was happening in the world and the people in it to conform to the officer's will. The more he tried to fight it, the longer it would take, so, mustering every last ounce of self-control, he thrust his clenched fists into his pockets, clamped his jaw shut and waited. But before the officer spoke again, a taxi pulled up and Dave set off unsteadily towards it.

"And where do you think you're going?" asked the officer sternly

"Did tha not 'ear 'im? Me fatther's sick - we're not 'angin' round 'ere just 'cos that chuff of a tram driver can't be bothered t' look where he's goin'. 'as tha got nowt better t' do? Dear me!"

Danny's heart sank. This was just what the officer had been waiting for.

"Mate o' yours?" he asked, turning to Danny.

"Brother - 'e's tellin 'truth, though," added Danny despairingly.

"Is he now? So it's not the drink talking then? Right, well if his lordship's got a pressing engagement, we'd best not detain him. We'll start with you, I think, Sunshine. *You*," he looked directly at Dave, "aren't going anywhere 'til *I'm* good and ready. In the car!" The officer nodded to Danny, indicating that he should get into the passenger seat, whilst he guided Dave into the rear.

But Danny had been wrong about the officer; having established who was driving and breath-testing Danny, he listened in silence as Danny explained the situation, then rushed through their statements as quickly as possible.

"Right, *you'd* better be off then," he ordered Dave with a slight nod of his head.

"Cheers boss 'n' when tha's ready fo' a new set o' wheels, call me first; I'll sort thee out wi' summat a bit special - *Tha saves at Dave's,* tha knows." With a knowing wink and a double click of his cheek, Dave reached over and handed his card to the officer, who glanced at it briefly before slipping it into his jacket pocket.

The officer turned back to Danny, raising his eyebrows and shaking his head. "He's a character, your brother," he said light-heartedly, but Danny's glare quickly removed his smile. It only took another ten minutes to sort out the remaining details and Danny was amazed when the officer told him that he would see to his car and that he should get off as quickly as possible.

"Thanks," Danny responded with genuine gratitude, "I just need t' 'phone me mam 'n' order another taxi 'n' I'll be off. Thanks again." As he walked away from the officer's car, he reached into his pocket for his 'phone and his world finally fell apart. He lifted his hand to his forehead and slumped down by the side of the road.

"Alright son?" asked the officer, whose long years of experience had prompted him to keep watching.

"gave 'im me 'phone, didn't I?" replied Danny, still staring into the gutter. Then he suddenly lifted his head, his eyes filled with renewed hope, "Can I borrow thine? I'll pay thee for it."

"Sorry, son, can't do it," replied the officer sympathetically, "more than me job's worth." He paused, "What about a lift, though, would that help?"

Danny felt a tear trickle down his cheek but left it untouched as he looked up into the officer's face, "More than tha could ever imagine."

Within twenty minutes, they were turning into the drive of St Francis'. As the car pulled up, Danny released his seat belt and thanked the officer again for his kindness.

"No trouble, lad. I hope he goes on alright."

"Thanks," replied Danny, leaping out without closing the door. He crashed through the entrance doors and ran along the corridor to his father's room. But as he turned the corner he was stopped in his tracks by the sight of Dave with his arms wrapped tight around their mother. Audrey wasn't immediately aware of his presence, but when she realised he was there, she lifted her tear-stained face and held out her hand to him. Danny touched it for an instant and then, without acknowledging his brother, walked past and into his father's room. He was surprised to find a care assistant there, straightening his father's bed. When she recognised him, she smiled kindly and whispered, "I'm so sorry you missed him, I'll leave you alone."

As the door closed behind her, Danny took his father's hand and lent over and kissed him on the forehead, before falling to his knees beside the bed. He held his father's hand tight against his forehead and wept.

After five minutes the door opened quietly, “I’m sorry you missed him,” said a gentle female voice. He turned his head, wiping his face on his sleeve as he did so and was surprised to see that it wasn’t the care assistant. Instead he found himself looking up into the face of the Chaplain. She’d visited his father several times over the past few weeks and, although Danny was deeply suspicious of anything to do with organised religion, he’d appreciated her gentle concern for his father and the family. “He was waiting for you,” she said in the same soft, even tone. She hesitated momentarily and then added, “He’d want you to know, he made his peace with God.”

“Thank you,” replied Danny rising from his knees, “I know ‘e appreciated what you did fo’ Mam.”

She offered him her hand and he took it willingly. He was desperate to fall into her embrace but, despite her slight motion towards him, he forced himself to take a step back. “Thank you,” he repeated, slowly letting go of her hand and reaching for the door handle. “If you need anything …” she began,

“Thanks, perhaps if you could ‘ave a word wi’ Mam …” Before she could reply, he’d left the room. He closed the door quietly behind him and fixed his stare at the end of the corridor.

“Daniel?” His mother had never seen such a look on his face in his entire life.

“It’s alright, Mam,” he replied, without altering his gaze for a moment. She moved towards him but as she did so he began to walk away, her tear-filled eyes following him in stunned silence.

“*Why* didn’t you ‘phone, love?”

Danny stopped, turned in his tracks and looked straight at Dave, who bowed his head, reached into his pocket and silently handed back his ‘phone. Averting his own gaze, Danny took it and turned to leave. “I’ll call later, I’ve a few things t’ sort out,” he said coldly, now staring straight ahead once more. Audrey’s whole body was shaking and Dave had to reach out to stop her from falling. He held her tightly in his strong arms, watching his brother walking away. He knew, at that moment, that he would be alone for the rest of his life.

Dave hardly saw Danny over the next few days and when he tried to engage him in conversation, he was met by a flat, monotone response that made it clear that Danny wasn't interested in talking to his brother. For Danny himself, the days between his father's death and the funeral passed by in a blur. As usual, his efficient organisation ensured that everything 'went off fine' and it was only later, when distance from Sheffield gave him some relief from the heart ache, that he was able to piece together any memories of his father's funeral and its aftermath without breaking down once more. Day after day, for weeks on end, he went back to the awful journey in the hearse, with Audrey holding each of their hands, Danny and Dave staring out of opposite windows. He could still feel the weight of his father's coffin on his shoulder and picture the sea of faces in the chapel, which all seemed to merge into one great expression of grief as he delivered the eulogy. He recalled the warm glow of the September sunshine and going out alone into the garden to harvest the last crop of beans. He remembered their warmth on his hands as he pulled them easily from the frame. He gave them to John and asked him to keep an eye on his mother. He remembered driving out to Highfield, he in one car, Dave in another, and Audrey scattering their father's ashes beside the bench on the tops where they used to sit and drink tea and watch the summer sun turn the reservoirs silver and gold.

Finally, he remembered how he'd told Audrey he was leaving. She understood and he loved her more than ever for it. He knew she didn't want him to go, but she also understood how things were between him and Dave. It hadn't crossed her mind for a moment to abandon the search for a reconciliation between her sons, but she also knew how deeply Danny had been hurt by his brother's actions. So, rather than risk losing her son in the same summer as she had lost her husband, she chose to add to her pain and wait, knowing that the moment would come when she would at last have a chance of reuniting her family. Their father always said that she was the wisest and bravest person he'd ever met. He would have approved.

Jane knew the rest of the story:

Danny had been wondering what to do with himself ever since the funeral; his heart hadn't been in the business ever since they'd moved to the auction and John's quitting had only confirmed his misgivings. Finally, the terrible events surrounding his father's death had extinguished any faint hope he'd had of rescuing the situation and he'd come to realise that leaving was his only option. However, it was John, who always read him best, who'd finally convinced him of the need to 'use the brains God had given him.' So, much to his own amazement, he'd begun to contemplate returning to full-time education. To begin with, he found the idea ridiculous and terrifying in equal measure but, as the summer drew to a close, the thought grew steadily and after a couple of conversations with the family's solicitor, Danny began to seriously consider the possibility of studying Law.

In one sense, it didn't matter where he went or what he did; he just had to go. There was no way he could be around Dave anymore, but if he were going to leave, he might as well do something that really interested him. So, one warm October afternoon, having finally made up his mind, he'd driven Audrey out into the hills above Highfield and told her his plans.

He'd first chosen Exeter because it seemed so different from anything he'd known and, like so many Sheffielders, the thought of living closer to the sea had always fascinated him. Now that there was so much he wanted to forget, he was more grateful than ever for the distance between himself and his old life. He began his access course late, but after recovering from the shock of being away from the daily round of business, and despite having thrown up with the terror of his first day 'back at school', he eventually became accustomed to his new surroundings and actually started to enjoy himself. By the turn of the year, he was starting to feel genuinely at ease in this strange world and from the beginning of his degree course, Danny had impressed his tutors and fellow students with the quiet, measured way he approached his studies. His willingness to learn from others and gentle, self-deprecating humour made him a popular member of the faculty and it wasn't long before he came to Jane's attention.

Jane herself was four years older than most of the other under-graduates, having set out on a one-year world tour and become intoxicated with Africa along the way. Her nineteenth to twenty-second years had been spent teaching in the poorest regions of Mozambique. Such waywardness had driven her mother to a state of distraction, which was regularly communicated to her in wickedly funny letters from her sister. Of far greater importance was the pride she'd seen in her father's eyes when they'd been out to visit the sun-baked school full of shining children. She had caught him brushing a tear from his cheek as her students had flocked to her as they entered the school compound. Later he had swept them up and held them enthralled with stories of England and the War, when he was a boy and the time when Winston Churchill, no less, had come to tea. Her mother had spent the week 'tutting' and trying not to touch anything before finally pleading with her to come home. Her father smiled wryly and whispered, "You'll know when you've tortured her enough."

Three years was more than enough and to the secret delight of her father and further dismay of her mother, she opted to abandon the well-worn family path to Balliol and chose Exeter instead to read Law. "Why Exeter? You've never even been to Cornwall," her mother had protested. "Why do you have to be so contrary? Sometimes I think you only do these things to annoy me. I don't know how I'm going to explain *this* at the bridge club? It was hard enough explaining how you went straight from school into the diplomatic service."

Jane had smiled conspiratorially at her father, who nearly choked on his afternoon scone. "Who knows what's round the corner?" was all he would add to the conversation and, despite his wife's constant hectoring, he steadfastly refused to make their daughter see sense. It sometimes crossed Jane's mind that he was actually enjoying the whole business.

She had excelled at Exeter, her drive and intelligence sweeping all before her. In her own mind at least, she could have had any man there, but she chose 'Dan,' as he had become known. Her mother had gone apoplectic; "Sheffield! That's worse than Mozambique! Why do you have to do these things?"

But her father had known why in an instant. He and Jane had always enjoyed a humour and warmth that totally eluded her mother, now his daughter had found the same in her soon-to-be husband. They'd married in their third year. Audrey, John and Christine had travelled down to Hampshire for the most beautiful wedding they could ever have imagined. Jane's mother tried her hardest, even managing to compliment them on their accents; "Isn't it wonderful that we can understand almost everything you're saying." John had had to stuff a *vol au vent* in his mouth and pretend to choke, but later on he'd pronounced that Danny had done very nicely for himself and declared Jane a smashin' lass – totally wasted on him! Audrey had brimmed with pride the whole day at her lawyer son and his beautiful bride, but even matriarchal Yorkshire pride couldn't prevent her from shedding a tear when Dan declared in his speech that his only regrets were that his father and brother couldn't be present.

Dan hadn't seen Dave for three years. His rare visits home always seemed to coincide with his brother being away and although he'd made a couple of brief stopovers at their mothers, there was never time to visit the new house. The pattern continued after they were married. Jane had already decided that Dave wasn't worth the effort and although she had warmed to Audrey immediately, she made herself a promise never to be indebted to this man who, even though he never spoke of it, had so obviously hurt her husband so deeply.

They had passed through law school together, Jane beating Dan by one mark on their final paper (although she could never quite remove the nagging doubt that he had let her win.) From there, the obvious move for both of them was to the City. Dan's aptitude for the intricacies of corporate law had long been acknowledged and Jane's drive, quite apart from her influential family connections, enabled her to develop almost any potential merger to a successful conclusion. Promotion, children and Surrey had followed in quick succession and by the time she reached her mid-thirties, Jane had achieved all her goals. She had her career, her husband and best of all, her children. It was time to launch out on her own.

The children! Not again. She grabbed for Dan's watch; two hours she'd been listening to him - *more* than two hours. That made it after eleven in England. She reached for the 'phone once more and dialled again from memory. Once again she was greeted by Dave's voice on the answer 'phone, but this time she hung up immediately.

"Let's go and find some fresh coffee and then make some calls about the business," said Dan gently, "Like I said, I'm sure Mam would have 'phoned if there was a problem."

8

David hadn't moved from 'The Chair' when Jenny came back down the stairs, but her uncle was already staggering towards the kitchen, loaded down with carrier bags. "Come on then, I thought tha were domestlocated one," he shouted over his shoulder.

Jenny shook her head in despair. "What about David, has he lost the use of his legs?"

"Ooh-ooh-ooh," responded Dave, feigning shock at Jenny's sarcasm. "Any roads, lad's shattered; 'e's been fightin' them aliens while tha's been lakin' abaht."

Ignoring him, Jenny walked to the front door. She pulled it open and looked straight into the deepest brown eyes she'd ever seen. "Oh, er, hello … sorry, I didn't know there was anyone there … thanks," she said awkwardly, brushing her hair away from her face.

The tall, dark-haired owner of the eyes reached out and offered her a handful of plastic carrier bags loaded with groceries. She tried to take them from him, but their hands became entangled in the handles. Mortified, Jenny tried to pull her hand away but only succeeded in tearing one of the bags, causing its contents, mostly tins of beans as far as she could tell, to tumble onto the doorstep and roll back down the steps towards Dave's truck. Jenny stood stock still in the doorway, unable to move, transfixed by the … plop … plop … plop … of the tins rolling down the stone steps into the still night air.

"It's okay," shouted the youth as he scurried after the tins, "I've got them."

"Nah den young 'un, what's *tha* playin' at?" chided Dave, straight into excruciating pitch as soon as he came back through the doorway. "I'm not payin' thee t' be faffin' abaht wi' my shoppin'. We're after waitin' for us tea 'ere, tha knows … tha can forget a tip, 'n' all."

Jenny watched on helplessly as the youth scurried around the driveway, gathering up the tins. "It was my fault, Uncle Dave," she stammered. Dave stopped in his tracks. He turned back to his niece and then to the hapless youth and then back to his niece once more, before treating her to his most mischievous grin accompanied by a knowing raise of his eyebrows.

"Oh no," thought Jenny, "this can't be happening."

Dave almost didn't say another word. He gathered up the remaining tins, carefully balanced them on top of the other bags, picked up his load and walked back into the house. "I'll leave thee t' finish off 'ere, Jen lass; money's on 'side," he shouted over his shoulder, but he just couldn't resist adding, "I'm sure 'e'd rather 'ave thee payin' 'im. Eh … might get a bit o' discount!"

Jenny's face flushed with anger and embarrassment.

"That's … er … £235 exactly," said the youth hesitantly.

Jenny didn't move.

The youth stared at her.

"If I make one more move, I'll fall down a crack and never stop falling," she said to herself.

"Er … £235, please," the youth repeated.

Jenny stared back.

The youth waited. "… £235?"

"Do something!" Jenny implored herself. After keeping her waiting for what seemed like an age, her feet finally obeyed; without a word, she turned and fetched the money from on top of the sideboard.

"Thanks," he said, with a smile that made Jenny's heart race as he handed over the change and turned to go.

"I'm sorry about the beans and my uncle and everything," she suddenly blurted out.

The youth turned back. “Don’t worry about it,” he replied, with another smile Jenny thought sweet enough to match his eyes.

“My name’s Jenny!”

“Bye Jenny, see you around.”

“I hope so,” she whispered, waiting until he was out of earshot. She forced herself to turn back into the house and gently closed the door. She leaned her head back on it and sighed; in spite of everything, things were suddenly looking better.

“Reet then, Davey boy; pizza ‘n’ beans it is then!” shouted Dave from the kitchen. He’d been looking forward to continuing his niece’s interrogation, but now the shopping was here the need to address his stomach’s concerns about his throat’s well-being took precedence. David, locked in hand to tentacle combat, didn’t respond.

“Looks like thee ‘n’ me on jankers then, lass.”

“What?”

“Come on then, I’ll unpack ‘n’ tha can start peelin’ ’beans.”

“What?!”

“Op’n some tins, lass, let’s ‘ave ‘em in ‘oven.”

Jenny smiled knowingly. “And have you used your range recently?”

“Not for a while,” replied Dave confidently.

“Well, you’ll know then that solid fuel stoves like these take hours to warm up.”

“Oh, do they, Miss Fancy Pants?” replied Dave, totally unperturbed.

Jenny let out an exasperated sigh. “Look!” she scolded him, “Cold, stone cold!” She stood in front of the oven with both hands on what were supposed to be the hot plates, “Now what are we going to do, suck on frozen pizza all night?"

"Aye, it's a thought. Or … we could just use my brand new ACP Menumaster microwave oven: direct from 'US o'A, 'n' only a few mile north o' 2K, including tax *and* shippin'. Now *that's* what I call a deal."

Dave theatrically swung open the door to a small utility room at the back of the kitchen and there, on an old painted table, stood a large cardboard box with a picture of a microwave oven on it. "Look, I know what tha's gonna say 'n' tha'd be wrong abaht that 'n' all! I've looked into it proper like - MFS18, this; 'll run all day long on 240 volts* don't worry theesen abaht that … . Takes a *fourteen* inch plate 'n' all. Like I said; no cheap tack 'ere, lass!"

"Sorry," Jenny said quietly; she had no idea what her uncle was talking about – it just seemed to be what was expected.

"Aah lass, not me first rodeo this, tha knows; tha'll 'ave t' be up a lot earlier than that t' catch t'old Uncle Dave out. … Any roads, don't just stand there gawpin' at us, gi' us ''and wi' this beast!" Between them they carried the cardboard box into the kitchen and placed it on the work surface. He handed her a knife, "I'll tell thee what; tha can do 'onours, seein' tha's come all 'way from 'Smoke just fo' grand openin'."

"No thanks, you can do it; looks like you've gone to a lot of trouble."

"Ti'n't nowt special, lass. Let's get it unwrapped sharpish 'n' sort tea out; stomach's *still* mitherin' abaht 'throat bein' cut."

Dave cut along the tape on top of the box and pulled open the two halves of the lid. Jenny carefully lifted out the packaging and Dave took hold of the oven. "I'll 'old big begga' 'n' tha can

---

* Close, but no cigar this time, Dave! Whilst he was right to ensure that the MFS18 could handle the 240 volts used by British mains electricity, and not just the American 120, US electrical products typically operate at 60hz, whereas British run at 50. So, his new pride and joy still wasn't compatible. But let's not spoil his moment of triumph. Yet!!

pull on 'box," said Dave swinging it round. The box came away easily and Dave placed the oven back on the work surface with great ceremony. He stepped back to admire the gleaming machine. "Look at that bad boy; nah den, that is a piece o' kit. Tha can do some *reet* cookin' on that, lass."

"I don't think so, Uncle Dave," replied Jenny trying not to laugh.

"Eh, 'old up, lass! Thee Na'nan tells me tha can do a reet Sunday roast. I've ordered 'meat 'n' everythin'. Tha's not gone all women's lib on me, 'as tha?"

"It's not that. Look!" Jenny slowly unwound the cooker's electrical lead and began casually swinging round the plug.

"What's that?" asked Dave in alarm.

"That, t'old Uncle Dave, is an American plug and unless you've thought to order an adaptor, we won't be using *this* bad boy tonight."

"Where's me tea?" asked Dave, crestfallen.

"On the table, where you left it half an hour ago," chided Jenny, still smiling.

"Oh, 'n' tha's not enjoyin' this. Reet chip off t'old block, this un."

Jenny could have been offended, but she felt in such good spirits that she only responded, "Surely you're not telling me that *two* women in this family have gained the upper hand over the great Dave Strives?"

"Ah well, perhaps if I saw a bit more o' *tha pair*, I'd 'ave a chance o' knowin' what I were up against."

Jenny was about to respond in kind but then thought better of it. "I'll fetch your tea. It'll be cold by now," she added, returning to the kitchen with all three mugs.

"Be reet, lass," replied Dave, grateful for once for Jenny's conciliatory tone. He slurped his tea noisily. "Uurgh!" he shouted, spitting it back into the mug.

"I told you," laughed Jenny, "it's been there nearly an hour."

“No sugar!” exclaimed Dave, slamming down the mug in front of the microwave.

He reached up into the cupboard and then suddenly froze. A sly grin spread across his face. “Sorted!” he proclaimed triumphantly, lifting down a bag of sugar. “They’ll ‘ave thought on abaht ’plug; I bet they’ve left adaptor inside wi’ ’instructions. No cheap tack ‘ere, lass tha knows!”

He stood facing the microwave and, after a rapid survey of the control panel, eagerly pressed the door release button. The door flew open, destroying any last hope of rescuing their supper and scoring a direct hit on his mug, sending its contents flying across the kitchen before smashing it to pieces on the stone floor. Dave stood in silence, cold, unsweetened tea dripping down his Official PRCA· Wrangler 3MWZ jeans.

“Reet then …” he said after an agonising silence, during which Jenny thought she’d explode, “we’ll be off down t’ John’s then. ‘just got to nip upstairs fo’ summat. Tell that lump o’ lard t’ start gettin’ ‘is coat on; John’ll not want t’ be kept waitin’ fo’ *tha pair*.”

Five minutes later, David and Jenny were stood outside the front door, waiting for Dave. He eventually hurried out, pulling on his authentic, first nation, buckskin jacket and brushing lint off his clean jeans. “Must sort out ‘advert fo’ ‘new cleaner. Trouble is, no one round ‘ere’s interested, ‘n’ ‘buses from town are nowt but useless.”

“Why don’t *you* tidy up? After all, it’s only one room.” Jenny was feeling confident after her victory in the kitchen.

· Pro Rodeo Cowboys Association

"Dunno, lass, never seem t' find 'time - always workin'. Nah den, what's tha think tha's up to?" David was climbing up onto the running board of the truck. "Shanks's pony t'neet, young 'un!" Dave proclaimed to the world at large. "Must be them aliens – kidnapped 'is brain!" he added as an aside to Jenny, with a knowing smile and shake of his head. "Eh Davey, 'ave a butcher's in that pile o' 'oss muck ov'r wall, see if they've 'id it."

David started off towards the wall and Jenny grinned; it felt nice not to be the one on the wrong end of her uncle's teasing for once. Although she hated to admit it, she was hurt by the way he and David so often excluded her with their childish humour. David's ridiculous attempts at a Sheffield accent only added fuel to the fire, and for a split second she allowed herself to revel in her brother's discomfort, but then half way across the driveway he suddenly realised his mistake and with a bewildered expression turned to her for reassurance. The innate goodness she saw there instantly recalled her promise to her mother to look after him and she began chiding herself for being dragged down to her uncle's level. She looked around, desperately searching for a way to rescue the situation. "Come on," she laughed light-heartedly, "last one to John's is a northern nancy boy," and with the graceful elegance of a trained dancer she turned on her heels, vaulted over the gate and began running down the hill.

"Come on, Davey boy, we're not 'avin' that!" shouted Dave as he charged towards the gate, but as he drew nearer he thought again and at the last second veered off towards the much smaller gate to the side of the driveway. He yanked it open and David followed him through at the gallop as they both raced down the hill after Jenny, who was already disappearing into the night.

Suddenly Jenny stopped. "Wait …" she gasped, half turning to face the boys, "what about Mum's 'phone call? We won't be back in time."Dave caught up and stood bending forward, resting his hands on his knees and breathing heavily. A look of uncertainty crossed his face. “Well,” he panted, ‘there’s allus ’answer ‘phone, if that’s any use.”

“Okay.” replied Jenny brightly and without checking to see if they were following, she set off again, running down the hill with all her might.

This time, Dave made no attempt to follow. Instead, he stood in total bewilderment, watching his niece disappear. *He* hadn’t forgotten about the ‘phone call but, after his lack of success with their evening meal and misadventures with the Menumaster, he was happy to put as much distance as possible between himself and the kitchen. *He* was in no hurry to speak to Jane, but why wouldn’t Jenny want to speak to her mother, even if it were only to have a good laugh at his expense? She knew they wouldn’t be back in time if they went to John’s, so why was she in such a hurry to get away? He couldn’t figure it.

Despite all his bravado, somewhere in the depths of his consciousness, Dave was aware of his limitations. John had always been Plan B and Dave knew that John knew that he was likely to be called upon. So, when Dave had ‘phoned from upstairs to say he ‘might o’ ‘it a few snags’ John was already prepared. None of this was of particular concern to Dave, he’d half expected something to go wrong – it usually did – but he’d had no idea of how he was going to get Jenny away from the house given Audrey’s promise that Jane would be ‘phoning. Just now, when she’d suddenly remembered, he’d braced himself for Plan B to unravel as quickly as Plan A. But now this! She didn’t seem the least bit bothered. Perhaps it was part of an even *more* devious plan to undermine him.

Dave had been delighted, flattered and, to be honest, quite overwhelmed when Jane had asked him to look after the children. On the odd occasions they’d met, she had been cool and aloof, and it was clear to Dave that she didn’t think much of him, so she must have been desperate to call. This was his chance to show her she was wrong and he needed to do a good job. Well, that was okay, how hard could it be? Audrey had offered to help but Dave wasn't having any of it; he was going to do this his way. And anyway, there was always John.

Even so, the intensity of Jenny's outbursts up to this point had definitely knocked him back. She really was a bit of a firework this one, and although he'd tried his hardest to make the two of them feel welcome, as far as he could tell, she'd spent most of the evening looking down her nose at him. He had no idea what Danny and Jane had told her about him, but it couldn't have been very good. The fall out with his brother had hurt him even more than the loss of their father. He missed his father every day, but at least he wasn't haunted by the feeling that he was somehow to blame. He sometimes wondered what Danny made of it all - probably not a lot. Dave wasn't surprised that they'd more or less lost contact since he'd moved on, in fact it was something of a relief. Once Danny had settled down, being so far away, there was even less chance of them seeing one another, particularly given Jane's opinions. Fair enough; Jane could please herself, but he'd been quite unprepared for how much it would hurt not to be involved with the children as they grew up. On the other hand, being with them now and taking on the responsibility for their well-being was quickly reawakening his emotional commitment to his niece and nephew. Davey was a great lad, even for a *plastic piggy* - a bit gormy, fair enough, but then who wasn't at his age? And as for Jenny, her strong will and fighting spirit was a family trait and most likely the reason why they sparked off on one another all the time. It made him laugh to think that they were so alike. But at the same time she also made him feel uneasy and he just couldn't shake off the nagging suspicion that she was somehow keeping notes, almost as if she were collecting evidence against him. He readily admitted that he was enjoying having her and Davey around, but she did make him nervous and he wasn't sure that he altogether trusted her. So, what was she up to now?

Alternating between skipping, leaping and running down the hill, Jenny could feel her whole body relaxing. She was a good runner and she was relishing the cold February air rushing through her lungs. She felt a great wave of relief wash over her. Truth be told, she didn't want to speak to her mother; she was terrified of what she might hear and so had literally jumped at the chance of putting some distance between herself and the 'phone. With each step away from the house she felt the burden of responsibility and the nagging sense of guilt slip away and she began to shriek and yowl as she ran. She sprinted round the corner, knowing that John's house was almost in sight. Accelerating again, she was drawn on by the solitary streetlight at the end of John's road. The steepness of the hill was pulling her faster and faster until she could believe she was flying rather than running. She forced herself to slow down as she reached the streetlight, taking a dozen tiny steps as she fought against the hill. As she successfully turned the bend, she let out a squeal of delight. And then ran straight into a boy riding his bike in the opposite direction.

Still musing over his niece's behaviour, Dave had continued watching until Jenny was out of sight. All this *Uncle Dave* carry on and the complications it brought with it was unknown territory for him. Up until today, as a rule, his life had proceeded with the minimum of forethought or reflection. There was just him, the car lot, his Mam, John and Meg and the hills, and that was it. His life was simple and straightforward - just how he liked it. Things weren't meant to be this complicated and he could easily have started to feel out of his depth. But in total contrast to his niece, he was blessed with the capacity of the natural optimist never to let things he didn't understand trouble him for long. So, looking up to the stars, he let his anxieties about his niece and her mother follow his breath away into the clear night air. He filled his lungs with Yorkshire's finest and with a shrug of his shoulders, turned to David and shouted, "Come on, Davey lad, she's at it again!"

Not waiting to see if David were following, he hurled himself down the hill after Jenny. He too felt the cold air rush into his lungs. He rarely ran anywhere anymore and was carrying more weight than he cared to admit, but now he was tearing down the hill, he felt the same inexplicable joy that all adults feel when given the chance to cast off their responsibilities and briefly revisit the wild abandon of their childhood. By the time he hit the point where the hill fell away more steeply, he too was flying. The long tassels on his coat streamed out behind him and he whooped and hollered like the Native American he took himself to be. He had the same terrifying feeling of his legs running away from him, and not helped by the leather soles of his snakeskin boots, had an even greater struggle than Jenny to slow down, but by the time he reached the streetlight he had just about managed to regain control. He stuttered to a halt, just in time to stop himself falling over his niece as she disentangled herself from the bike.

"Not again!" he panted between laughs. "When's tha gonna stop throwin' theesen at 'local talent? 'n' 'im vicar's lad 'n' all."

Pretending she hadn't heard, Jenny sat down on the curb and concentrated on trying to pick out the grit from the grazes on her hand and brush the worst of the dirt from her jacket. Averting her gaze for as long as possible, she eventually looked up imploringly at her uncle. "*Please* don't say anything else," she thought to herself, "this is bad enough without your gloating." She should have put him in his place after the microwave fiasco, but having let him off the hook she was defenceless against the inevitable taunting.

“Come on, lass,” said Dave, surprising them both with the concern in his voice, “let’s ‘ave a look at thee.” He crouched down beside her. “Is owt broke? Can’t see nowt. Jeans is ripped but then what’s tha expect comin’ up ‘ere in city gear? … ‘n’ what abaht thee, young un?” He turned his attention to the cyclist, “Tha needs to look where tha’s goin’ … ‘could do wi’ some better lights, ‘n’ all. Eh, I tell thee what, I know a bloke who could do thee a reet deal; I’ll let thee ‘ave ‘is number tomorra neet. Come on then, who’s worse off, thee or ’bike?” Dave picked up the bike and began to cast an expert eye over it. “Nowt much wrong wi’ this,” he announced, gripping the front wheel between his legs and straightening the handlebars.

“Thanks,” said the cyclist, gingerly taking off his helmet, ‘I’m really sorry.” For the second time that evening, Jenny felt herself blushing and half-turned away as if to examine the newly discovered tear in the side of her jeans. “It’s okay,” she replied, “I should have been looking where I was going.”

Dave held out his hand and, carefully avoiding her grazes, pulled Jenny to her feet, allowing her to see the boy more clearly. She was sure she recognised him, but how could she, never having met anyone from the village other than John?

“I’m Jenny,” she said, trying not to wince as she surreptitiously wiped the palms of her hands on her jeans. She held out one hand in the business-like manner she’d seen her mother adopt whenever she’d needed to regain control of a situation.

The boy took her hand limply, “I know,” he replied, “my brother told me.”

“Your brother?”

“The delivery boy … from the supermarket.”

“Oh … that’s nice,” was all Jenny could think of saying, as her newly recovered confidence evaporated.

“Hey, hey, Jen lass, brothers feetin` ov’r thee now!” chuckled Dave.

“Oh why, don’t you just grow up?” snarled Jenny, her contempt immediately outweighing any appreciation of her uncle’s earlier concern. Without another word to anyone she turned on her heels and headed off towards John’s, trying not to limp. “His brother’s going to have a real laugh when he hears about this,” she muttered to herself.

“Is she alright?” asked the boy, gazing after her.

“Bit o’ altitude sickness; nowt t’ worry abaht!”

9

Jenny was seething as she marched down the road, but even as she approached John's house she knew that her anger wouldn't last. Despite her uncle's loathsome behaviour, she had to admit that he had a point. At her mother's insistence, Jenny had attended an all-girls school, and for the last three and a half years David had been pretty much her sole source of young male company, so the thought of staying down the road from two such attractive boys certainly caught her attention. But all that could wait; Jenny knew that the real reason she couldn't stay angry was the thought of going to John's.

John's cottage was at the end of a small, terraced row on the upper side of the highest street in the top village. It was the same size as all the other cottages, but as it was at the end of the row its carefully tended garden stretched around three sides, allowing access to a garage at the back, on whose roof John had fixed up a small wind turbine. Jenny could just see the top of it from her bedroom at Dave's.

The front of the house was simplicity itself: to one side was a green door, covered by an unassuming, double pitched porch, next to a small sash window sheltering beneath a sturdy stone lintel. There were two identical windows on the first floor and above these was a beautiful stone roof. The whole arrangement was topped off with a stumpy, stone chimney that never seemed to stop smoking. Jenny smiled at the neat, simple cottage as if greeting an old friend.

They'd been to John's several times before. The occasions on which the children had stayed with their grandmother always seemed to coincide with one of her bus trips out to Highfield and Audrey insisted that they came along. As a young girl Jenny had spent much of the journey staring out of the window, watching excitedly for the urban landscape to peter out and make way for the rolling hills and clear open skies, which offered such an enticing contrast to her usual, somewhat prosaic, suburban surroundings. Springtime was her favourite, when she and David would compete to count the new born lambs skiddling between the dry stone walls that chequerboarded the valley. But as she'd grown older she'd lost interest and started to pay more attention to her grandmother's musings. It didn't take long for her to begin to piece together what had happened after her father had left home:

In the early days, Dave had often slept over at Audrey's or booked into a hotel after an auction, rather than facing the long journey home to a cold, empty house. For several years, as Jenny vaguely remembered it, the place had remained pretty much as he'd bought it – sitting snugly in a dip in the hillside, but tired and characterless inside, whilst the barn and stables remained badly in need of repair. He seemed not to know what to do with it, but when Audrey had told her that he was planning to have it 'done up', Jenny had shuddered at the thought.

In truth, the village and its hills had not offered the solace he was hoping for, and for the first time in his life, Dave had been lonely. Danny had been his best friend as well as his brother and, as he'd never found the right girl, he was left with no one to come home to. But Dave was as sharp as they came and he'd kept a close eye on business affairs in the village. When the cottages had come up for sale, he'd bought the lot, sitting tenants included. As each of the tenants had moved on or passed away, he'd renovated the empty cottage and then re-leased it at a much higher rent.

He'd done well, in fact he'd done *very* well, but he was

always an attentive landlord. Whenever a cottage was to be re-let, he'd asked himself the same question; "Would Mam and Dad 'ave been 'appy 'ere?" As a consequence, the cottages' green livery always looked freshly painted, their stone walls were scrubbed white and the pointing was kept clean and smooth. Dave had never had a complaint from his tenants and he hoped that his father would have approved. "After all," Dave imagined him saying, "tha'd 'ave t' be a complete chuff t' rob a man 'n' 'is family fo' roof ov'r 'is 'ead."

John's had been the last cottage to become empty, and after its occupant had moved on Dave had ensured that the outside was renovated to match the others but, to the surprise of the post office regulars, he'd made no changes to the interior. The house had stood empty for a few months and then John had moved in. Audrey, who never missed the opportunity to praise her boys, had told Jenny of Dave's generous offer: John could live there rent-free whilst he renovated the interior himself. After it was finished, Dave charged John far less than the other occupants, even though his cottage was in by far the best position.

Opting to disregard her recent ignominies, Jenny opened the green picket gate and started up the narrow garden path to the front door. She was still hoping that the rest of the evening might help fill in a few more gaps in the story of this wonderful man and his mysterious past. As she approached a dog began to bark, and before she was halfway up the path a laughing black and white face peered round the door and Meg, the most beautiful border collie imaginable, leapt out. She ran to Jenny and jumped effortlessly into her arms.

"Hello girl," laughed Jenny, "have you missed me?" Meg

busied herself licking Jenny's face and hair, but as soon as John appeared in the doorway she ran back to his feet and then back to Jenny and then back again to John, as if trying to make as many laps as possible between the two of them before they met.

"Hello lass, how are you?" asked John with his usual gentle concern.

"Oh, a little worse for wear," she smiled. "I don't think I've made too good an impression with the locals."

"What do you mean?" asked John.

"Well, apparently I've managed to upset both the vicar's sons *and* ruin my new jeans at the same time," sighed Jenny, approaching the door.

As she came into the light, she hesitated. John was one of her favourite people in the whole world and she had the greatest respect for him. Her problem was that she never quite knew how to behave around him, or even how to greet him. With Dave, there was never an option; he'd stopped halfway across the footbridge at the station and almost suffocated her and David in an enormous bear hug. Her grandmother, too, was always demonstrative in her affection. It could hardly have been more different to the restrained demeanour of her own family these days – she couldn't remember the last time she and her mother had hugged or kissed. Her Sheffield family were completely overwhelming in their public displays of affection and, even though she found it extremely embarrassing, she couldn't deny that part of her enjoyed the physical contact, even if Dave's coat did smell of dead animals. But John was different. It was obvious that all the Strives held him in the highest regard, but it was equally clear to Jenny that there was an unspoken acknowledgement amongst them that he was somehow set apart. Whenever they gathered together they were always playing and teasing one another in their boisterous, over-loud manner, but when John was around they were calmer and quieter and altogether less conspicuous. Jenny had decided that he was a good influence on them, especially on Dave.

Try as she might, she simply couldn't understand Dave and John's friendship. To Jenny, the two men had almost nothing in common. Dave's relationship with the world around him, particularly his new life in the country, seemed completely superficial - a crutch to prop up his fragile self-esteem. Of course, she recognised his move out of the city as an attempt to show everyone that he had made something of himself, but he never seemed truly at ease there. Despite the daily declarations of his love for the outdoors, the countryside seemed to chafe on him like a pair of ill-fitting boots. As far as she could tell, the whole thing was just a backdrop for his *born wi' a plastic spoon in me gob* show. Like the stones they skimmed across the reservoirs, it was a relationship a mile wide and an inch deep and if Dave were to slow down, even for a moment, he would sink without trace.

John, on the other hand, was the most genuine man she'd ever met. He seemed almost to have grown out of the land. The roughened texture of his hands and the craggy features of his thin, drawn face seemed to be part of the landscape. You couldn't say that John loved the countryside; it was more like he *was* the countryside.

In Jenny's mind, the two of them couldn't be more different: Dave was loud and flash – John modest and self-effacing; Dave loved show – John valued usefulness; Dave was always buying over-priced trophies he didn't really need (*no cheap tack 'ere lass!*) – John spent his days rescuing and repairing things. Dave was always in a hurry – John was always calm; Dave was forever striving, whilst John appeared totally at ease with himself and the world around him.

She could see why Dave was drawn to John; he was so many of the things that Dave sub-consciously aspired to be, but why, as was evidently the case, was John so fond of Dave? It made no sense, but unlike her uncle, she could never let go of the things she couldn't understand and so had made up her mind to find out the truth. That was why she'd pressed Audrey so hard when her grandmother had pointed out Dave's generosity to John.

"Why does Uncle Dave let John pay so little rent?" she had enquired as casually as possible.

"I think he was just trying to help out a friend. He's always been very generous like that, ever since he was a boy."

"But how did they meet?"

"I don't actually know, your Uncle David never said."

"But the other tenants have to pay market value," Jenny had prodded, using a phrase she'd picked up from her mother.

Abandoning David to his search for things beginning with 'D', Audrey had turned to the seat behind to examine her granddaughter. "And when did you become so interested in your uncle's business?" she asked suspiciously.

"It's not that …" replied Jenny hesitantly, "… I was just wondering why Uncle Dave and John were such good friends."

"Why don't you ask him?"

"Oh, I don't know … it doesn't matter. Let's just go home."

But it had mattered and although Jenny forgot about it for long periods of time, she always returned to the subject whenever she visited Sheffield. Of course, she had no intention of asking Dave, but she was equally determined that she would find out the truth. She'd had several opportunities to talk to John when Audrey and the children had 'popped in' on him during their visits to Dave's house. Secretly, their grandmother longed for the children's appreciation of Dave's success as much as he did, so it suited Audrey to show off her son's generosity. And anyway, John's house was just across the road from the bus stop.

John was always pleased to see the children and would usually have something magical to show them; some wild animal he'd rescued and was nursing back to health or antiquated piece of engineering he was renovating. Best of all, if the weather held, he would invite them along for a walk down the lanes with Meg. It was during these walks that Jenny had tried to find out more about John, but he was far too sharp for her, and anyway, she had too much respect for him to try to trick him into telling her something he didn't really want to. So, she'd waited, taking every opportunity to enjoy the company of this quiet, dignified man, who seemed to understand so much yet give away so little, and as she waited, she mulled things over, looking for clues.

Jenny took the final few steps to the door and tentatively held out her hand. John was about to take hold of it when he noticed the grazes. "What *'ave* you been up to, Jen lass?" he asked in his gentle Yorkshire brogue.

"Oh," sighed Jenny, "just falling for every boy in the village."

"Come on, let's see if we can clean you up a bit before that uncle of yours starts with his daft jokes."

"Think it's a bit late for that!" replied Jenny, hoping that her annoyance with Dave might divert the conversation. "He's determined to embarrass me in front of those …". Her voice trailed away but it was too late; John had already picked up her interest in the boys and had instantly understood.

"Oh dear, am I that obvious?"

"Don't you worry, lass, your uncle's only messin; he can't do any real harm; he'd' have Meg to answer to for start offs!"

Jenny loved John's house; although it reminded her of something from a children's novel, it was a *real* house, for a *real* life. Almost nothing in it was new, yet everything worked perfectly and, unlike her uncle's house, everything was in use. Nothing was for show in John's house. The front door led straight into a tiny living room, where a small fire burned in the grate, in front of a single stone slab that served as the hearth.

Jenny knew that John had found the slab in the garden when he was levelling the ground. It was so typical of him to make such good use of it. Above the fire place was a huge stone lintel, which John had dressed himself, using an ancient chisel that he'd also dug up outside.

In the recess to the left of the fireplace was a small bookcase, straining under the weight of well- thumbed books, showing the reader how to tie flies or keep dry-stone walls to the correct batter. This made perfect sense, but of far greater interest to Jenny was a whole collection of reference books, whose spines suggested that Africa had played some significant role in the long-buried past of this wonderful, mysterious man. She ached to ask him about them but could never quite find the courage to do so.

In front of the bookcase was a wooden chair, with wooden arms and thin green velour cushions tied to the frame with even thinner beige cords. The cushions were old and faded and had moulded themselves to the shape of John's long, angular body. Jenny knew, because she had seen him, that if John sat in the chair and stretched out his long legs, his feet would reach the exact mid-point in front of the fire.

On the other side of the fire from John's chair was Meg's basket. Jenny loved to imagine the two of them sitting in silence on a winter's night, as the wind whistled round their roof top, John warming he feet and reading his books about Africa and Meg gazing at her beloved master.

Directly in front of the fire was a 1930s-style leather settee. Underneath their neat, beige covers, the arms were worn colourless and the settee's cushions sagged when Jenny sat on them. On the wall behind the settee was a map of the area around Highfield, whilst over the lintel hung an old, pitted mirror. The floor was covered with a well-worn beige carpet, which was given extra protection by a rubber mat directly in front of the door. And that was it, this plain simple room, where John spent his evenings with only Meg and the sound of the wind on the tops for company.

On the far wall was a second door that opened onto a small lobby, giving access to the stairs. Jenny had only been upstairs once, when Audrey had insisted that the children were given 'the Grand Tour'. The furnishing and decor followed the same plain, simple pattern as the ground floor but the two bedrooms held a wonderful secret; each had a real fire. John used the smaller bedroom and on cold winter nights, at around nine o'clock, he would carefully place his book face down on the hearth, climb out of his chair, and with Meg threading herself repeatedly between his legs, ascend the stairs and light a fire in his bedroom.

"How cool is that;" Jenny had asked in wonderment, "to fall asleep to the light of an open fire?"

Beyond the downstairs lobby was the kitchen. Like Dave's, the floor was made up of flagstones, but here, despite having been scrubbed just as white, they were used and worn. There were three large cupboards around the walls and a large oblong table in the middle, where meals were both prepared and eaten. Beyond this was a simple painted door and a further sash window looking out onto a vegetable patch that took up most of the back garden and made regular contributions to those meals. Below the window stood an ancient pot sink and between the two hung a pair of equally ancient, deeply patinated, brass globe taps, the likes of which Jenny had only ever seen in tv costume dramas. She liked to imagine the sink and taps arguing with one another like two cranky old women over who'd been there the longest. She loved them. She loved everything about John's house.

Finally, on the right-hand wall, maintaining a dignified distance from its squabbling neighbours, stood an even older but newly blacked range, imperturbably blowing wood smoke out onto the road through its chimney. And to top it all, on one of its two hot plates was a huge aluminium saucepan, from which was coming the delicious smell of stew.

"Take off your jacket and let's see if we can clean you up a bit," said John, turning on the taps and pulling out a first aid box from one of the cupboards. He found some cotton wool, wet it under the cold tap and carefully began to bathe Jenny's scratches. At first, she pulled back at the stinging sensation, but the water soon began to soothe her hand and wrist. Then John washed the wounds again, carefully brushing out each tiny piece of grit, before finally drying off her arm. Just as he finished, Dave and David poured through the front door.

"Where's 'walkin' wounded then?" shouted Dave playfully from the lounge.

"Leave her alone," replied John, "there'll be no supper here for troublemakers!"

"Well then if there's no *supper* for troublemakers, we'll 'ave no *trouble* for suppermakers. NO TROUBLE FOR SUPPERMAKERS! - what abaht that 'un, Davey lad? NO TROUBLE FOR SUPPERMAKERS." Dave could hardly have been more pleased with himself, but to his surprise Meg jumped out from under the table and positioned herself threateningly in the door way, growling softly.

"Alreet, Meg, I were only messin lass.'

Meg backed towards the sink and when she felt Jenny's legs she turned and rubbed her flank reassuringly against them, never for a moment taking her eyes off Dave. John looked down, "It's alright, girl, we're all friends here," he said gently, "he's only havin' a bit o' fun with his favourite niece."

Almost convinced, Meg lay down at Jenny's feet, her long hair tickling her toes, still looking threateningly over her shoulder at Dave. John smiled conspiratorially at Jenny, who smiled back; there was more than enough help here to put her uncle in his place should he continue badgering his niece.

"Is tea ready then? I'm gaggin' 'ere, runnin' around after *tha pair* all neet," shouted Dave, even though by now he was standing in the kitchen doorway.

"First things first. I'll see to my visitors and then sort out 'locals once *they're* comfortable." Dave grinned, pleased to be identified as a local in front of David and Jenny.

"Right," said John purposefully, turning away from the sink, "stew and roast potatoes - who's hungry?"

"Me!" shouted everyone, raising their hands in unison and rushing for the chairs.

"Funny, I didn't hear the music stop, did you Meg?"

Under the table, Jenny could feel the border collie's tail wagging enthusiastically. John smiled benignly, then took the tea towel hanging from the range and wrapped it round the handle of the saucepan. He lifted it carefully off the hot plate and placed it down on a wooden chopping block in the middle of the table. He went back to the oven and returned with a bowl of steaming roast potatoes, followed by a loaf of freshly baked bread. Although everyone was desperate to dive in, no one made a move until John had joined them. Then, as was his custom, he quietly bowed his head and thanked God for His provision and as the 'Amen' sounded, Dave and David made a dash for the food.

"Come on, Jen lass, fill thee boots," laughed Dave, but Jenny needed no encouragement; John's cooking was famous locally, and she hadn't eaten since she and David had shared a chocolate bar at the station.

'Champion!" cheered Dave through a mouthful of stew and bread, "I'm glad t' see tha's been takin' me advice." Everyone laughed.

Jenny felt so safe here in this warm, welcoming house, where almost without thinking she lay aside her responsibilities and cares. Even her uncle was almost bearable when John was around.

They ate their fill of stew in a state of happy contentment and afterwards Jenny helped John clear away.

"What's fo'afters then, Chief?" asked Dave patting his spreading stomach.

"Your favourite," declared John proudly, revealing a large jelly in the shape of a rabbit, "*and* custard to top it off."

Dave and David cheered and Jenny couldn't resist joining in. This was one of the best meals of her young life and she was determined to enjoy every moment of it. After the jelly, they drank giant-size mugs of scalding, sweet tea and Dave produced an enormous bar of chocolate, which they all complained about, but squeezed down, nonetheless. Jenny cleared away and she and John began the washing up whilst Dave and David pored over a huge map, which her uncle had produced from the same, seemingly bottomless, pocket as the chocolate bar.

"Reet then, Davey lad," said Dave, suddenly sounding very severe, "tha mustn't mess abaht on *these* 'ills. There's plenty 'ave come a cropper out 'ere before now. 'ill walking's 'serious business, tha knows, 'n' thee Mam'll not want *tha pair* gettin' into bother. … We need t' take us time 'n' plan this proper." At the sink Jenny rolled her eyes and passed another plate to John.

"Now, I've a lot o' experience o' this sort o' thing 'n' we all know abaht John, but we don't want t' start *tha pair* off on summat too demandin', so we'll not 'ave t' go chewin' off more than we can bite." Jenny cast a quick glance at John, who allowed the faintest of smiles to pass across his face.

"So, 'ere's plan: we're gonna walk from ours on a circuitous route that passes through 'athersage. This'll let *tha pair* see what tha's been missin' stuck in 'Smoke. By my reckonin' it's abaht twenty-five mile." It was John's turn to raise his eyebrows.

"Cool!" responded David, "How long will that take?"

"Well … what it is Davey lad … is we need t' take into account *tha pair's* lack o' experience, we all know that, but there's 'difference in altitude between 'ere 'n' there t' consider ‘n’ all; lotta folk don’t realise. So … all things being equal … I reckon abaht … eight ‘our’, give or take.”

Jenny nearly dropped the plate she was washing. “Eight hours! Yeah, like that’s gonna happen!” she sneered without bothering to turn round.

“Don’t tha *ever* gi’ o’er wi’ mardiness?” snapped Dave, embarrassed that his carefully made plans for the day were being undermined in front of John.

“It does look a bit far for February, Dave,” said John calmly, “I don’t think we’ll be back before dark.”

Jenny had been watching ‘The Boys’, as she had started to refer to Uncle Dave and her brother, in the reflection in the kitchen window. To this point, Dave had expressed himself with complete confidence but now that John had spoken, she could see that he was starting to waver. “What’s tha reckon, then?” he asked respectfully.

“Well, I think it is a great route, but I wonder if it might be better just to do the first part.”

“’ow can we do that?” asked Dave.

“Well, why don’t you three set off like you’ve planned and, as I’ve a few jobs round and about, I’ll park in Hathersage and when I’ve done walk out to meet you? We can still have our snap on Stanage … I think that’s a great idea … then we can all walk back down to the Land Rover and drive back together.” Jenny thought she was going to cry.

“Will Meg be alright?” asked David nervously.

The dog’s ears shot up at the sound of her name. “What do you think, lass?” asked John, Meg suddenly appearing at his side, “Do you think we can manage a walk out to Stanage?” Meg ran round and round in circles, wagging her tail wildly and everyone laughed again.

“That’s sorted then,” said Dave cheerily. “We’ll meet thee on ‘Edge fo’ ‘snap around two. Butties are on me. Now, Johnny boy, is tha certain tha knows ‘way?”

"Well if not, I'll look out for that jacket of yours!"

"That reminds me," said Dave, "we've still *tha pair* t' kit out."

"Oh please, Uncle Dave," pleaded Jenny, "we'll be fine."

"Your uncle's right," said John patiently. "You need to be wrapped up properly this time of year; it always amazes me how much colder it is on the tops."

"OK," replied Jenny after a moment's hesitation, "I'm sure we can find something that won't be too embarrassing. After all, how bad can it be?"

Dave stared at his niece and his friend in bewilderment. How was it that every suggestion of his was met by such hostility yet one word from John and everything was sorted? He sighed inwardly, but immediately cheered up at the thought of the walk tomorrow. This was his chance to show David and Jenny *his* country and how well he knew it; it was going to be a great day.

Jenny and John returned to the washing up, whilst Dave tried to explain to David how to plan a route and use a compass. By the time they had finished, it was eleven o'clock and, after thanking John one last time for his hospitality, at a much slower pace than they'd descended, the three Strives set off back up the hill.

"John's so cool," said Jenny, half-hoping to goad her uncle.

" Aye, 'e is, lass," replied Dave, "but, t' be fair, it's a bit off givin' us 'same fo' dinner *and* puddin'."

"What do you mean?" asked David.

"Rabbit, lad;" laughed Dave, "stew fo' us dinner 'n' jelly fo' us puddin'." The children's eyes grew wide as they took in what their uncle was telling them.

"That's not funny, why do you always have to try and spoil everything?" snapped Jenny, marching off ahead.

'Aye, lass, but it's true!" Dave shouted after her with great relish.

Unsure whose side he was on, David followed his sister at a

distance, not daring to turn round but taking great care not to lessen the gap between them. Not another word passed between any of them as they marched single file back up the hill, leaving only the wind whistling over the hills to drown out the sound of the ringing 'phone.

10

As with most teenagers, Jenny's mood could change in an instant, and the blissful serenity she had enjoyed at John's had rapidly been expunged by her uncle's clumsy attempts to undermine his friend. She couldn't bear the thought of anyone criticising John, least of all a puffed up, pretentious bully like Dave. And, like most teenagers, to accompany her fits of self-righteous indignation, she was prone to volcanic over-reaction towards those closest to her. So, by the time she'd hung up her coat and marched into the lounge, she was ready to erupt. But suddenly she didn't know what to do; this wasn't her house and she was at a loss as to how to show her uncle the absolute disdain in which she held his childish competitiveness. At home she would have stormed off to her bedroom, but here she didn't even know if this were allowed or what effect it would have if she did. So, she walked over to the leather settee and threw herself down, hoping that her contempt would communicate itself to her uncle. Almost as she fell, she noticed, for the first time, the flashing light on the answer machine and her anger instantly evaporated. The panic that replaced it almost took her breath away; there had to be a message from her mother and, if so, what was it? Jenny was terrified that things had gone badly in New York and that her parents had … . She couldn't even form the thought in her mind. She had to escape.

"Is it alright if I go to bed?" she asked meekly.

Dave looked at her suspiciously, "Don't tha want t' see if thee Mam's 'phoned?"

Jenny hesitated. "No … not really. I'm really tired and anyway it's too late to 'phone them back. Would it be alright if I left it 'til the morning?"

"Whatever tha wants, lass," replied Dave with a tenderness, which, for the second time that evening, surprised them both.

Jenny stood up and headed for the stairs. “Good night, Uncle Dave.”

“Good night, lass.” he replied with a gentle smile.

“Tha can forget that ‘n’ all,” he added, suddenly raising his voice. Halfway up the stairs, Jenny looked round, her face frozen in fear, but to her relief Dave wasn’t talking to her. Her brother was just making himself comfortable in The Chair and it was to him that her uncle’s reprimand had been addressed. She turned and climbed the rest of the stairs as quickly as possible, hardly daring to breathe, and before she’d closed the bedroom door behind her the tears started to flood down her cheeks. She fell down onto the bed and began to sob uncontrollably.

Downstairs, Dave was persisting with his stern uncle routine. “Bed for thee, young ‘un. We’ve some reet tops t’ cross tomorra ‘n’ I don’t want thee laggin’ behind; tha’s in for a reet shock when tha sees what tha’s in fo’.”

David reluctantly pulled off the headphones and began dragging himself out of The Chair as slowly as he dared. “Five more minutes?”

“Five more *seconds* ‘n’ tha‘ll be in bother.” Feigning anger, Dave took a few quick steps towards his nephew, but David hurdled easily over The Chair and ran up the stairs laughing. “Thou’s about as fast as t’ Wednesday’s defenders,” he shouted over his shoulder.

“I’ll be seein’ thee in ‘mornin’,” replied Dave with mock severity.

“Good night ye Blade.”

“Bed! Tha little Glory Hunter.” Still chanting for the Blades, David closed the door to his bedroom, oblivious to the sobs of his sister a few metres away.

Waiting until he heard the click of his nephew’s door, Dave allowed himself a smile and said out loud, “It’s goin’ alreet this, ‘n’ tomorrow’s gonna be a belter.” He looked over at the answer machine and thought about listening to his messages, but the truth was he didn't really know how to operate it and he was worried about deleting something important. Anyway, Jane's message might lead to all kinds of trouble, so what was the point? Jenny could sort it out tomorrow. "Right then, that's me, then," he said out loud, his accent far less pronounced now that his audience had dispersed. He locked the doors and turned out the lights, "Piece of cake this parentin'; don't know what all 'fuss is about."

He ran up the stairs two at a time but as he reached the landing some hitherto hidden instinct made him stop in his tracks. He crept over to Jenny's door and inclined his head towards it. He was completely taken aback by the sound of her sobbing. "Now what?" he asked himself, and then added as the truth dawned on him, "She can't still be mitherin' abaht 'stew!" He waited for an age, weighing his options. What would Danny and Jane do? He had no idea. It was hard for a city girl to appreciate country ways … perhaps he'd better have a word. He knocked gently on the door. On the other side Jenny quickly dried her eyes.

"Alreet, Jen?" he whispered, half hoping she wouldn't hear.

"I'm fine, Uncle Dave; just give me a minute, can you?" She ran over to the sink and looked in the mirror. Her cheeks were red and her eyes bloodshot. She quickly splashed cold water on her face and buried herself in the thick towel. She stood up straight, brushed her hair from her face and took a deep breath. "For goodness sake, girl," she told the reflection in the mirror, "pull yourself together, he can't see you like this. … Come in."

Dave entered the room nervously. "Alreet, Jen lass?" he repeated.

"I'm fine, just a bit tired."

"I know tha's a bit upset but sometimes tha just 'as t' accept these things 'appen, 'specially in 'country."

Jenny looked up, furrowing her brow, "I know, but it feels like I'm about to fall down the deepest hole and I'll *never* stop falling."

“I didn’t know tha were that mithered. Tha should ‘ave said summat.”

“I didn’t think you’d understand.”

“Well, between thee ‘n’ me, I’d not ‘ad it fo’ years ‘fore I met John. I’m not that bothered me sen but ‘e ‘as it all ‘time. Out ‘ere, tha just ‘as t’ try ‘n’ fit in, lass.”

“But I don’t want to *fit in,*” said Jenny, finally allowing her feelings to surface, “it’s not right, they belong together, everyone can see that.”

“What … stew and spuds?”

“Eh? No! Mum and Dad, of course.”

“Er, yeah, course they do, but what that’s got t’ do wi’ ‘price o’ bread?”

“What?”

“Eatin’ rabbit.”

“I don’t understand.”

“Rabbit stew - I knew tha wouldn’t be keen; wish I’d not mentioned it now.”

What ? … what are you talking about?”

“Tha’s mitherin’ theesen abaht eatin’ ’rabbit. I don’t blame thee; I reckon John were out o’ order, me sen, givin’ roadkill t’ city folk.”

Jenny smiled and then started to laugh. “Is that why you thought I was crying?” she asked through her tears.

“Er … well I know ‘ow tha feels abaht animals ‘n’ that, ‘n’ tha’s ‘ad a lot on thee mind ‘last couple o’ days, what wi’ comin’ up ‘ere, ‘n’ that. I reckon this brought it all t’ ’n ‘ead. … What’s up wi’ thee Mam ‘n’ Dad, any roads?”

Jenny took another deep breath and fighting back the tears and the giggles, just as her parents were returning to their hotel, she began to tell her uncle all about the last few months. Once she started, she couldn’t stop. Dave sat in silence, not knowing whether to be more amazed about what had been happening to his brother or that Jenny would think to share it with him.

“Well,” said Dave when she finished an hour later, “no wonder thee Mam were desperate.”

“What do you mean?”

“Nowt, lass. Look, I’ve known thee father a lot longer than thee ‘n’ ‘e’s as tough as they come. Thee Mam’s no push ov’r ‘n’ all. If anyone’s gonna sort it, them two can. I’d offer t’ ave a word, but it’s not up t’ me.” Then he smiled and Jenny smiled back. “Now, ‘best thing tha can do is shut thee eyes ‘n’ try fo’ some kip; big day tomorra … . Does tha want owt’ t’ drink?”

“Could I have some milk please?”

“What, warm, done in ’microwave?” They both smiled again.

“Cold milk will be fine.”

Dave went back down to the kitchen and headed towards the huge fridge. Suddenly he paused and turned to look at the range. A sly grin spread slowly across his face and, forgetting the fridge, he walked over to the utility room where the MFS18 sat in dark disgrace. He unlocked the door at the far end and disappeared. A few minutes later he returned with an armful of logs and some firelighters. He dropped these in front of the range and began to carefully stack the logs in the grate at bottom of the oven. He stood up and patted his pockets - no matches! He began rifling through the drawers, slamming each of them shut in turn and then, in frustration, turned and stood staring down the range, as if by doing so he could force it to spontaneously ignite, “Tha’ll be goin’ back, ‘n’ all, ‘fore tha knows what’s ‘it thee!” Then, after a few more seconds, like the sun appearing from behind a sullen cloud, the sly grin slowly returned. Still smirking at his resourcefulness, he picked up his car keys from the sideboard and opened the front door. In his stockinged feet, he walked gingerly down the steps towards the car. He groaned as he felt the damp seeping through his socks; he'd wanted to wear these tomorrow, and so he pulled them off and threw them back through the doorway. As he reached the bottom step, the front door of the house swung slowly to, and if he’d been concentrating he would have been able to hear the distinct 'click' of a Yale lock. But Dave's attention was elsewhere; ignoring his freezing feet, he climbed into the truck, put the key in the ignition, pressed in the cigarette lighter and rubbed his hands together in excited anticipation. Thirty seconds later, the lighter was glowing brightly. He grabbed it quickly, relocked the truck and tottered back up the steps. He went to push the door open but its failure to respond caught him by surprise, causing him to drop the cigarette lighter onto his foot.

"A' ya'!" he hissed under his breath, hopping about on the porch, holding his foot and trying to blow it.

"Funny time o' day to start with a bit o' dancin'! They do 'ave some strange habits these country folk," said in a voice in the darkness beyond the gate.

"Am I glad t' see thee?!"

John opened the small gate to the side of the drive and walked through as calm and relaxed as a man who saw these things everyday (and given that he saw Dave most days, this was probably true.) Meg was by his side. When she saw Dave hopping around, she instantly forgave him his earlier misdemeanours and ran to him and began licking his injured foot.

"At least someone's got some symphony. As tha brought tha keys wi' thee?"

"I usually do if I intend to lock up."

"No, my keys."

"Oh, yeah, I've got them here," replied John patting his pockets.

"Well come on then 'n' stop faffin'; one foot's burnin' 'n' t' other 'un's freezin'."

John pulled out his keys, opened the door and followed Dave inside. "What were you doing, anyway?"

"I'm *tryin'* t' light this chuffin' cooker."

"Silly me. … Let's have a look."

John walked over to the range and nodded approvingly at Dave's careful arrangement of firelighters, kindling and logs. He produced a flint stick from his pocket and in one swift movement struck a spark, which glowed momentarily and then grew rapidly into a small, steady flame. "Smashing; that'll be red hot by morning. Just don't forget to put some more logs on it before you turn in and pile it up with coal. Then tomorrow pile it up again first thing."

Just 'job," said Dave gratefully, "I'll put Davey boy on it in 'mornin'.

"Right, I'll see you on 'Edge for us snap." Without another word, John walked back through the open door and in a moment he and Meg had disappeared into the night. Dave smiled as he locked up again. John was the one person he didn't mind besting him – sometimes.

"Nah den," he sighed, returning to his original task, "where's that milk?" He poured out a large glass and carefully carried it upstairs. He knocked again on Jenny's door but there was no reply. So, he opened it tentatively, whispering her name; Jenny was asleep, fully clothed on the bed. He placed the milk carefully on the bedside table, went back downstairs and returned with the buffalo hide from The Chair. He carefully drew the hide over her and brushed her hair away from her face, then he leant over and kissed her tenderly on the forehead. "Good night, lass," he whispered quietly, "don't you worry about anything. It'll all be fine."

As he closed the door, Jenny opened her eyes and smiled sleepily. "I like you better without the accent, uncle," she whispered and then immediately closed her eyes and fell into a deep sleep.

Jenny never could say for certain what woke her the next morning. It may have been the daylight creeping around the edges of the curtains with its strange, luminous quality that she recognised but couldn't place; it may have been the muffled voices rising from the courtyard, or it could just as well have been the chill she felt creeping up her bare legs left uncovered by the buffalo hide. She furrowed her brow as she tried to remember how it had come to be here and why she was still fully clothed. Suddenly recognising the animal skin for what it was, she threw it off in disgust and climbed shivering up the bed and under the duvet. The sensation of the cold, fresh sheets through her clothes made her pull the duvet tight around her shoulders, but the moment she closed her eyes she was shocked out of her reverie by the remembrance of her conversation with Dave the night before and she immediately promised herself that there would be no further shows of weakness.

Unable to settle, she propped her head up on her arm and concentrated on the voices she'd detected coming faintly from the courtyard below.

"Hi 'ave halways taken a keen hinterest in the hanimals my sen, halthough my hexecutive role in 'company stops me riding as much as hi would wish." The voice sounded like Dave's, but she could hardly make out what he was saying. She jumped up and out of bed, ran over to the porthole window overlooking the courtyard, prised it open and just as quickly jumped back under the duvet, pulling it tight around her shoulders once more.

"The stables 'ere har fully restorated 'n' so now Hi'm on 'lookout for 'right hanimals." The rapid breathing before every other word sounded like a nervous child delivering its lines in the school play. "Perhaps you would like to come round one hevening 'n' watch the NFR 'ighlight show on 'Cowboy Channel."

"I'm sorry … what's that?"

"National Finals Rodeo! On my satellite television; hi hoften tune in the 'hevening after tea; 'elps reveal 'stress. 'as thou not seen 'dish?"

"Sorry?"

"Satellite dish! Raven 2.4 Orbit. *No cheap tack 'ere thou knows!*" Jenny bit down hard on the duvet to stop herself laughing out loud.

"Yes … er … we had noticed it …" said a female voice. "… I'm afraid we are quite busy in the evenings, what with the surgery and everything."

Unable to resist, Jenny crawled back out of bed and crept over to the window. By pressing her head against the glass, she could just look down and see Dave stood on the drive, hands clasped firmly behind his back, looking up into the imperious faces of two magnificent hunters peering over the gate.

"No probs. Hi can record it 'n' drop it hoff. You can let me 'ave 'DVD back next time you drop by."

"I'm afraid we don't have a DVD player."

"Eh?! Oh … reet, course not; busy people like thou sens wouldn't 'ave 'time t' shop around fo' howt like that - Hi could see thee right if thou thinks on. Eh, 'ere's an hidea; Hi'll record it 'n' tha can come round one hevening 'n' Hi'll send out for a takeaway. We could 'ave barbeque – proper Texan like, no cheap tack."

"Er … yes, well we'll have to check our diaries. Anyway, must press on; need to stretch their legs."

"Habsolutley, wouldn't want t' 'old thee up. We're hoff ov'r 'tops hour sens later; me niece 'n' nephew's hup from 'Smoke? Mam 'n' Dad's big shot lawyers, did hi mention it?

"Yes, I think you did. Anyway, times pressing, so bye for now Mr Strives."

"Eh, we might meet up - hi'll keep an heye op'n fo' 'osses. Reet thoughtful o' thee t' stop 'n' chat. Cheerio fo' now."

Jenny would have sworn that Dave tugged his forelock but he probably only waved. She ran back to the bed, laughing and whooping. Oh, this was so cool; even better than the magazine. “Just wait until he starts,” she told herself, completely forgetting their conversation from the previous evening, “he’ll never win now.”

Suddenly she jumped back out of bed and ran to the window for a third time. “Yes!” she shouted clapping her hands together rapidly and jumping up and down with glee. “Even better!” In her anxiety to see whom Dave was talking to, she hadn’t taken in what was so glaringly obvious; *it had snowed*. Now they wouldn’t be able to go on Dave’s stupid walk. Only ten minutes gone and it was already a brilliant day. She pulled on her dressing-gown over her clothes and ran downstairs.

“Who were you talking to?” she called to Dave as he came through the door, stamping his feet.

“Aah, wouldn’t tha like t’ know?” said Dave proudly. “Now them’s proper country folk; doctors both on ‘em. Live up in that big old farmhouse next t’ ‘pylon. Tha’ll not meet many folks as classy as them, ‘am tellin’ thee.”

“Right,” said Jenny thoughtfully, “friends of yours?”

“Course they are!” said Dave, sounding affronted, “We allus neighbour up these parts. They ride down at ’week-end ‘n’ pass time o’ day. No stuck-up types round ‘ere tha knows.”

“They’re only doctors; it’s no big deal.”

“No big deal! I suppose tha knows all abaht that ‘n’ all … I’ll tell thee abaht them two; too classy t’ ‘ave a DVD player. What’s tha make o’ that then, eh?”

Jenny puffed out her cheeks and raised her eyebrows. “That is pretty classy, to be fair,” she said, turning away to hide a grin.

“Aah, ‘tis ‘n’ all. Come on, any roads; thee brother’s been up ‘ours - almost emptied ‘Chair, ‘n’ we’ve a reet load o’ gear t’ sort out ‘fore we set off. I‘ve scraped ’snow off ’truck, so tha’s five minutes t’ sort theesen out, s’ jog on!”

“We’re not still going are we?”

“Course we are. Bit o’ snow not stop proper ‘illsmens ‘avin’ a blow. Come on, we’ll see thee in ’wagon.”

Jenny clenched her fists and sucked on her teeth. “Aargh,” she seethed under her breath, “he really is impossible.”Even so, she hurried back to her room to wash and change. Five minutes later, she stomped back downstairs and dragged her brother out of The Chair by his coat. “Come on, you! You’re spending far too much time staring at that TV. If I have to suffer, I don’t see why you shouldn’t.”

“What have I done?” asked David in bewilderment.

“Just put your shoes on; we don’t need him telling us we’re making him late,” snapped Jenny, the stress and anxiety of the previous evening beginning to resurface. David shrugged and picked up one of three drinks cans from besides The Chair. He shook it and frowned before tipping his head back to drain its last few drops. “How many of them have you had this morning?”

David only shrugged again, but before she could upbraid him further her uncle swept past them, “Reet then, last one in ‘truck eats yella snow.” David stuffed his feet into his shoes and ran out of the house followed reluctantly by his sister. Dave patted his pockets to ensure that he had his keys and pulled the door to, but just as he turned towards the steps, the ‘phone rang. He stopped in his tracks and looked across to Jenny, “Tha want to answer that? It might be thee Mam.”

Jenny hesitated, unable to look away. She bit her lip and waited, motionless, willing the ‘phone to stop ringing. For a moment it felt as though the whole world was holding its breath, but then the ‘phone went dead and Jenny breathed again. “Oh well,” she said, trying to feign disappointment, “it couldn’t have been them or they would have left a message.” She turned on her heels, walked briskly to the truck and climbed in, her gaze fixed firmly on the snow-covered hills the whole time.

Dave reversed the truck out onto the deserted road with studied care, and after leading his passengers through the safety procedures for travelling in bad weather at high altitude, he pulled away, taking them even further up the hill from the top village. He smiled knowingly as the powerful four-wheeled drive dug the Fulda Yukon tyres through the centimetre of light snow to the asphalt surface half-hidden beneath. "Now let's see 'loudmouth from 'yard start wi' 'is *needin' t' get a grip* wisecracks." (Dave had been the butt of several unwelcome jokes following his 1400-mile round trip to Germany to have the tyres factory-fitted!)

Unaware of her uncle's foresight, Jenny was staring intently in the direction of The Doctors' house and the pylon next to it silhouetted against the brilliant snow and the piercing blue sky. Her gaze was fixed firmly on the two horses wandering across the field in front of the house, nuzzling through the snow for the remnants of last year's grass. In spite of everything, she smiled. Dave watched her in the driver's mirror, taking careful note of the excitement on her face and the way she craned her neck to continue looking for as long as possible. "So, tha reckons tha can get 'better o' t'old Uncle Dave then, does tha lass? Well, we'll see abaht that," he murmured under his breath, making sure she didn't see him.

Eventually, a small copse blocked off Jenny's view and soon after the truck plunged down the far side of the hill, leaving the horses to their foraging and taking the family back towards Highfield. Jenny continued to stare out of the window, grateful for the distraction of the snow-covered countryside. From inside the warmth of the truck, the black and white landscape took on a magical appearance and in spite of the gnawing condemnation for not having answered the 'phone and her embarrassment at having revealed so much the previous night, she was surprised to find the Christmas card scenery drawing out of her a child-like excitement that she thought had gone forever. Although she hated to admit it, she was actually beginning to look forward to walking through this beautiful place; if nothing else, it would be a welcome distraction from the nagging guilt and dread that crept up on her whenever she allowed herself to relax.

A surprise right turn took them away from the village once more and along a narrow pass, eventually leading to a series of hairpin bends as the road crossed the heads of the streams that filled the reservoirs far below. The road finally straightened itself up and passed through a canyon of dark green conifers, giving only the occasional glimpse of the open moors beyond. The quietness of the newly fallen snow seemed to have worked its way into the truck and no one had spoken since they'd passed The Doctors' house. It felt as if they were alone in the world, which at that moment was just how Jenny would have wanted it.

"Fifteen minutes from 'centre o' town, who'd o' thought it?" Predictably, it was Dave who roused them from their thoughts. "Some reet sledgin' round 'ere, Davey lad, 'n' 'whole place to ussens."

"Cool. Can we go today?"

"Doubt it lad, tha'll be shattered after 'walk. Any roads, 'be dark by 'time we get back, 'specially if *tha pair* don't get a wiggle on."

"Aah," moaned David.

"We might make a bit o' time tomorra - *if* tha behaves theesen."

"Yes. Get in!" David sat back and grinned; staying at Uncle Dave's was surpassing all his expectations.

After what seemed an age, the road eventually led them out of the forest and up over the tops, on a course running parallel to the reservoirs. They crested a hill and passed a sign by the side of the road.

"Strines," read David out loud, "hey, Uncle Dave, sounds like Strives."

"Hey, hey," laughed Dave, "Strines 'n' Strives; who'd o'

thought it….. Eh, 'old up a minute …". He paused as if rehearsing something in his head, muttering under his breath and nodding his head, before finally drawing himself up in his chair and proudly announcing, "One chicken too many. ONE CHICKEN TOO MANY! - What abaht that 'un, Davey lad? ONE CHICKEN TOO MANY!"

"Where?"

"What?"

"Where is there a chicken?"

"There i'n't one - not a real 'un any roads."

"I don't understand."

"Dear me, Davey lad, what they teachin' thee in that posh school thee Mam 'n' Dad's shellin' out fo'; "The *N*! Look, if tha swaps ''N' fo' 'V', tha's got Strives; one chicken too many!"

"But there aren't any chickens!" David was beginning to panic.

"Fo' goodness sake, gormy; the *N* in Strines; like 'n 'en … 'en – lays eggs, like a chicken. Tha don't need 'N', so there's one *chicken* too many. Wish I 'adn't o' bothered"

Even David shook his head at this.

"Does tha get it finally?"

"It's not worth it, David."

"Oh, 'ello princess," replied Dave, grateful for the distraction. "Decided t' join us?"

"What on earth are you going on about?" Jenny sneered in the tone she used when trying to impress other people's stupidity upon them. It was the first time she had spoken since they'd set off and despite the initial excitement of the horses and the peaceful repose of the snow-bound countryside, she'd been unable to maintain the pretence of her own innocence or shut out the thought that for a second time she had abandoned her mother when she needed her most. Now sensing an opportunity for redemption, she leapt to her brother's defence.

"Do you know what, *Uncle* Dave; if you take away the 'N', then you have to add a 'V' to make Strives," she explained as clearly as possible. "'N' and 'V' – make 'envy'. How appropriate!"

"Tha's quite a tongue on thee, when tha wants 'a'n't tha lass?"

"At least I don't put on ridiculous accents to try and impress the neighbours."

Dave reddened with anger and tried desperately to find the right response, but something held him back. He remembered their conversation from the previous evening and somewhere in his mind he made the link between the fears Jenny had expressed then and the sudden change in her mood this morning. "Only trying t' better me sen, lass. We weren't all born wi' rich parents, tha knows; some on us 'ave 'ad t' graft fo' what we 've got."

"Well, well done big Uncle Dave. … Idiot!" Jenny hissed under her breath as she turned to look back out of the window, hoping to give the impression that nothing inside this ridiculous vehicle could be of the slightest interest to her.

But she was in the wrong and she knew it. She bit hard on her lip and forced herself to calm down. Over the course of the journey, the accusations had grown deafening and she was feeling condemned to the core. Any calming influence that the countryside had begun to exert had been slowly and mercilessly eroded away by the realisation that she had betrayed her mother by refusing to answer the 'phone. First Dave's announcement that they wouldn't be home from the walk until after dark, followed by his pathetic attempts to belittle David had finally pushed her over the edge. It was no wonder she'd been unable to resist the anger and shame ready to explode inside her. But her outburst had only made matters worse. Desperate as she was to tell this ridiculous man what an embarrassment he was, no matter how angry he made her, it was her job to keep things together. Her mother was depending on her; to cause any more trouble would be a further betrayal. She looked across at her brother and was immediately condemned to the core once again by the look of hurt and confusion on his young face. She turned away to stare back out of the window and caught a momentary glimpse of herself in the darkened glass. “Idiot!” she repeated, not sure if it were directed at Dave or herself.

11

The rest of the journey had followed in stark contrast to the gentle calm that had marked out its beginning. A sullen silence hung over the truck's interior and even David recognised that it was better to keep quiet. He was glad when the truck finally pulled up in Hathersage and jumped out as soon as they'd stopped. Escaping the suffocating atmosphere, his natural good humour instantly returned and he casually sauntered over to a shop window displaying a bewildering array of outdoor equipment. "Cool!" he announced, looking back towards Jenny.

"Whatever," she replied mournfully, climbing slowly out of the truck.

"'old up, *tha pair*!" shouted Dave sternly from inside the cabin, as he carefully placed the disabled licence in the windscreen. The sullen silence had eventually worn away his optimism as well. He'd tried his hardest to maintain his patience towards his niece, but had eventually run out of steam. Now he was sulking as badly as her. He'd been looking forward to the trip to Hathersage ever since he'd heard they were coming to stay. The journey should have given him the chance to tell them all about the Dale Dyke Dam and the Sheffield Flood, and Ladybower and the Bounding Bomb, quite apart from the Youth Hostel sign, with its picture of Little John, and stories about the open-air swimming pool and how he and their father used to cycle out here as lads. There were so many interesting things they could have learnt, if only Jenny hadn't spoilt it; he knew she was upset about her parents, but she really could be mardy. And anyway, why did she have to take it all out on him? He was only trying to help. He sighed to himself and then suddenly raised his voice and announced, "I don't want t' 'ave t' come lookin' fo' *tha pair* when tha gets lost. 'old up a minute!"

He went around to the back of the truck and opened the tailgate, sat down on the shelf, pulled off his cowboy boots and, to the children's amazement, began to take off his jeans.

"Uncle Dave, what are you doing?"

"Just wait there 'n' 'ave a bit o' patience." Dave pulled down his jeans to reveal a pair of incredibly close-fitting running tights from which Jenny quickly averted her gaze. He proceeded to unzip a large boot bag, from which he ceremoniously extracted the most enormous pair of silver walking boots and began to put them on.

"What on earth do you need those for?" asked Jenny impatiently.

"Never tha mind, lass. Leave this t' me." With a great show of care and attention, Dave pulled his foot up onto the tailgate and, ensuring that it was correctly stationed, began lacing up the boots. "Do it reet 'n' tha'll only do it once," he lectured, but the anti-heel-lift lacing that he'd practised endlessly at home now deserted him and instead of a neat surgeon's knot accompanied by the top to bottom cross-lacing he was expecting, he was quickly faced with an unmanageable tangle that pretty much summed up his morning. He pulled, twisted and tugged at the lace, but it simply refused to obey. The combined effort of holding his folded leg on the tailgate whilst simultaneously wrestling with the lace was beginning to take its toll and beads of sweat began to form on his crimson forehead. Thankfully, neither his niece nor his nephew was paying attention and whilst he would normally have taken great offence, on this occasion, he was happy to let it go. Making the most of every available second, he pulled furiously at the knot with both hands, hoping against hope it would come undone before they realised what was happening. But it was too late; Jenny turned back from the shop window. Having endured for years her brother's hapless attempts to tie his own laces, she recognised Dave's predicament in an instant.

"Thought I'd *knot* get better o' t'old Uncle Dave," she mocked mercilessly. "Eh, what abaht that 'un, Davey lad? *KNOT* GET THE BETTER OF T'OLD UNCLE DAVE!" David started to laugh uncontrollably and had to cling on to a convenient street sign for support.

Dave was speechless, but the harder he pulled the worse the lace became entangled. If he could have freed it, he would gladly have used it to strangle his niece, but realising he was only making matters worse, he finally admitted defeat and quickly shoved the whole mess into his boot before surreptitiously tying the other lace in the more traditional manner.

"Let that be a lesson t' thee; I were so busy stoppin' *tha pair* wandering off 'n gettin' lost I wasn't concentratin' – *that's* what 'appens when tha can't do as tha's told, so let's 'ave less on it before tha gets theesens into some proper bother. Don't just stand there gawpin! Come on! We're runnin' late 'cos o' this tangle 'n' we've some reet gear t' sort out if *tha pair's* gonna manage on them tops."

Still furious, he climbed down from the tailgate and reached into the truck's cavernous flat-bed for an enormous waterproof holdall. He pulled out a huge silver padded jacket, threw it on and zipped it up. To finish the picture, he topped himself off with his cowboy hat. Jenny stifled a giggle. "Tha can forget that 'n all young 'un," barked Dave to his nephew, "'ow many times; no cheap tack fo' 'Strives! There's some proper gear up 'ere. Let's be 'avin' thee." Dave strode out purposefully, laces flapping behind him, theatrically ignoring the shop window in which David had been looking. The boy turned and followed his uncle like an obedient sheep dog and was soon at his heel. Jenny followed on, as far behind as she dare, hoping that nobody would associate her with the two of them.

The distance gave her the opportunity to fully take in her uncle's appearance. He did look truly ridiculous, with his enormous padded jacket and spindly legs, clad in their running tights. Add in his huge boots and he looked like one of the Mr Men. She would have to think of a name for him; 'Mr Know-It-All,' perhaps, or 'Mister Wannabee,' or 'Mr Annoying Middle-Aged Uncle Who Really Needs To Grow Up And Find Himself A Wife, If Any Woman Would Be Stupid Enough To Have Him'. 'Annoying Middle-Aged Uncle'," she repeated, "– he's an ANNYMU!" She smiled to herself, her anxiety and guilt temporarily displaced by the returning feelings of superiority encouraged by her insight into her uncle's neediness.

She followed The Boys uphill along the main street for about a hundred metres, before they climbed the steps into a large outdoor equipment shop housed in an imposing stone building that looked like it had once been a bank. Just before they went in, Dave reached inside the pocket of his silver jacket and pulled out a large pair of sunglasses, polished them on his sleeve and nonchalantly put them on.

"Reet then, me old rascal, let's 'ave some decent service fo' tha number one customer for a change," shouted Dave across the large display area, his customary bravado unmistakably back in place. The half dozen people in the shop turned towards him as one. "'ow much tha gonna con me out o' t'day, then?" he asked loudly, walking briskly up to the counter and holding out his hand to a bewildered shop assistant. "'e's a reet lad, this un, pretendin' not t' know me; should do, I paid 'rent on this place last month."

Jenny cringed; *why* did he have to be so loud? She looked round desperately for cover and found it by bobbing down behind a rack of coats to look at a price tag. In doing so, she almost knocked over a shop assistant searching intently for something on the floor. As teenage girls are wont to do, in an instant Jenny, took in the girl's appearance; she was probably about nineteen or twenty and looked extremely fit. She wore no make-up but her glowing golden complexion suggested that she spent much of her time outdoors. Her most striking feature was her beautiful jet black hair. Jenny was impressed. They smiled at one another sympathetically and Jenny whispered, “Sorry!”

“Are you with him?” hissed the girl, jerking a thumb at Dave.

“’fraid so.”

The girl gave her another sympathetic smile. “See you later,” she hissed again, and dragging along the coat rail as camouflage, she began to creep towards the stairs. When there was no cover left, she took a deep breath and made a dash for it. Before Dave could turn, she was away, climbing the stairs three at a time, as fast as her legs would carry her. Jenny smiled at the girl’s escape, admiring her pluck, but her frown soon returned as she heard her uncle’s voice ringing out once more around the shop. She flung herself behind another clothes rack and waited.

“I need t’ kit these two young ‘uns out, for a blow s’afto - twenty-five mile ov’r ‘tops,” announced Dave with great solemnity, looking round to make sure that everyone was suitably impressed.

“Er, *two* young ones, Sir?” the shop assistant asked hesitantly.

Dave looked over his shoulder. David was right beside him, but he couldn’t see Jenny anywhere. “Now where’s she gone? Funny age that ‘un; up from ‘Smoke fo’ week-end. Mam ‘n’ dad’s big shot lawyers,” he added turning back to the assistant. “Reet then,” Dave’s accent was more pronounced than ever. “Let’s kit this ‘un out first. We’ll sort *Face On* out later. We need top gear fo’ ‘tops. Heh, heh! TOP GEAR FO’ ‘TOPS! - What abaht that ‘un, Davey lad? Is anyone servin’?”

Jenny watched from her hiding place as shop assistants shot off in every direction. Some suddenly remembered orders that needed chasing, others rapidly headed to the furthest parts of the store to check again whether or not the few remaining customers had everything they needed. It was like watching a hawk scattering a flock of pigeons or a leopard terrorising a herd of zebra, and in true predatory style Dave homed in on the most vulnerable and separated him from the group. The hapless, young Saturday boy was innocently stacking shelves when Dave descended on him.

"Reet then, young 'un, meet Davey boy, *our* young 'un. We need 'im kittin' out from top t' toe wi' proper gear. Can tha manage it?"

"Yes Sir," said the boy eagerly, "where would you like to start?"

Dave needed no further invitation. He was off, charging around the shop, picking up waterproof coats, fleeces, hats, gloves, base-layers and anything else that might be needed for a Himalayan expedition. "The works, lad, 'n' no cheap tack; only 'best fo' Davey boy - tha buys cheap down 'ere, tha pays big up there!" he pronounced to the shop at large, nodding towards the street.

Despite his age, the assistant was well-trained and had a good grasp of the store's merchandise. He tried to steer Dave in the right direction. "How often will you be using the equipment, Sir?"

"What chuffin' difference does that make? Just bring us top o' range."

"But you could end up spending money you don't really need to, particularly if the customer is still growing," the plucky young assistant persevered.

"Look young 'un, no offence, but I reckon tha's a bit wet behind 'ears fo' this job. Fetch us 'manager, there's a good lad." Dave turned and winked at David, who smiled back nervously. Sensing the impossibility of his situation, the assistant retreated and returned shortly afterwards with a large-framed man in his early forties, sporting a thick red beard and a healthy outdoor glow.

"Is there a problem, Sir?" he asked politely.

"Well, no offence young 'un, but what it is see, Boss, I'm not sure 'lad 'ere quite knows what we're after; perhaps tha'd better 'andle this."

“It’s okay, Jonathan,” said the manager kindly, “I’ll look after Sir’s needs.” Dave puffed out his chest and grinned as the manager carefully surveyed the mountains of clothing and equipment around David. “Of course, Sir should choose whatever feels right, but I do wonder if some of the choices are a little excessive.”

“What’s tha mean by that?” For the first time since they’d entered the shop there was note of uncertainty in Dave’s voice and his volume was noticeably lower. “What’s *tha* think, Davey lad?” Totally bewildered, David smiled weakly and shrugged his shoulders. “Fat lot o’ use, thee!” chided Dave, increasing his volume again. “Young ‘uns!” he added with a ‘tut’. “What’s ‘crack then, Boss?”

“Well Sir, for young people we do have an excellent range of mid-priced equipment; it’s very popular for the D of E.”

“Oh aye; fo’ off-roadin’ ‘n’ that – young ‘uns probably still flyin’’P’s. Eh, I’d like t’ see ‘em take on my left ‘ooker – that would be worth ‘entry fee. No dual controls on that stallion, eh Davey lad?”

Again David could only smile wanly but before his uncle could pounce, the quick-witted store manager came to his rescue. “Ah, Sir … I think you might be thinking of the *DVLA* …”

“Oh, aah, reet … well, tha’s expert - I’ll ‘ave t’ take thee word for it. … So what’s ‘D of E when it’s at ‘ome then?”

“The Duke of Edinburgh Award Scheme, Sir; as part of their challenge, young people have to complete an expedition.”

“*Nah* tha’s talkin’, fella. ‘ear that, Davey; *expedition* – that’s us alreet! ‘n’ tha reckons ‘Duke of Edinburgh’s in on it? Well if ‘e’s wearin’ it, we’ll not go far wrong - *definitely* no cheap tack there, lad!”

‘It would certainly suit your needs, without appearing …” the manager hesitated, “… to be spending money … just for the sake of it.”

“I know just what tha means there, old pal. Can’t stand them posh city folk, come out ‘ere, think just by buyin’ all fancy gear makes ‘em some kind o’ expert. … Alreet then, tha’s ‘boss, show us ‘ropes … SHOW US ‘ROPES! Heh-heh! What abaht that ‘un, Davey lad? SHOW US ROPES!”

The manager patiently sorted through Dave’s collection, replacing most of it with more modestly priced items. After five minutes, David was sent to the changing rooms to try on a variety of sizes of under-layers, shirts, jackets, walking trousers and waterproofs and in the lull, Dave remembered Jenny. “Jen lass, where’s tha bin?” he shouted at the top of his voice.

Jenny had been considering making an appearance but to make the point that she couldn’t be hailed like some disobedient terrier whenever her uncle felt like it, she shrunk back behind the clothes rack. And anyway, she’d found a far better way of passing the time and didn’t want her game to end just yet: it had dawned on her that every item of clothing that Dave was wearing had been bought in this shop. It was *The House: Part Two*; just as he needed an interior designer to create a home for him, he needed these people to show him how to dress. It was pathetic and comic in equal measure.

Jenny had identified each item of clothing Dave was wearing, even down to his sunglasses and was sneaking around the shop to find out how much they had cost. Her challenge was to find out the full cost of Dave’s outfit before she was spotted. So far she’d found:

Scarpa Freney XT GTX silver boots @ £299
Rab Neutrino Endurance silver jacket @ £225
Ron Hill Men’s Stride Flex Pants @ £50
Oakley Carbon Blade Black Iridium Polarised sunglasses @ £348
and
Extremities Ice Climbing Gauntlets XCR @£100

(admittedly, sighted back of the truck, but still permitted under new 2005 regulations.)

She was just setting off to look for Sealskinz Waterproof Cold Weather Mid Length Sock @£40, when, for the second time in the last ten minutes, she nearly stumbled into someone.

"Oh, hello again, who are you hiding from?" It was the supermarket delivery boy.

"Not again!" said Jenny out loud. The boy looked hurt.

"Oh … er … I didn't mean to say that. Well, I mean, I thought it … but not like you think I thought it."

The boy looked puzzled and amused but Jenny was becoming more and more flustered. "Look," she snapped, "just forget it, okay?" and choosing the lesser of two humiliations, she abandoned her cover.

"Where's tha been, lass?" asked Dave cheerily. "Too much t' take in in't there? Quality shop, this; all 'proper gear."

"Whatever you say," sighed Jenny wearily.

"Reet then, let's fit thee up wi' summat a bit better than that skinny thing tha's wearin'."

Jenny looked round and out of the corner of her eye caught sight of the delivery boy, still staring at her from the far side of the store. Pretending she hadn't seen him, she looked down at her favourite denim jacket. She and Jane had bought it together in Covent Garden on a day out in London for her birthday and it had immediately become one of her most treasured possessions. The memory of it brought all her anxiety and embarrassment to a head, and suddenly she didn't care anymore. All her frustrations concentrated themselves in the direction of one unmissable target; "Well at least I don't look like some wanabee freak!" she hissed at her uncle.

Dave's whole face flushed with rage at the thought of being spoken to like this in front of the shop assistants. "Tha'll 'ave what tha's given 'n' be grateful, tha cocky little so 'n' so. Thee Mam 'n' Dad's gonna be reet chuffed when they 'ear abaht this carry on." Pierced to the core once again by this further reminder of her mother, Jenny tried desperately to restrain herself. "Alright, I might be able to find a jacket that's not a *complete* joke, but that's it."

"Suit theesen, lass; tha can be as cold as tha likes as far as I'm concerned. I'm abaht finished wi' *tha pair*."

They stomped off in different directions, growling at one another under their breath. It was as though they were engaged in some strange trial by combat: finder of the most annoying jacket to the other, triumphs.

Dave walked over to a head-high rail of bright orange padded jackets, which seemed to glow in the light of the window behind them. He flicked over the price tag on the first jacket, nodded approvingly and pulled it roughly off its hanger. There was a tearing sound and Dave froze. "Oh great," he moaned, "that's 'er fault. She'll 'ave t' 'ave it now."

At the other side of the shop, Jenny was having even less success. "They're all hideous," she complained to herself. "You owe me for this, Mum." Eventually she screwed up her face and carefully unzipped and pulled down a padded black jacket with white fur trim round the hood. She held it out in front of her and sighed, "£150! Most expensive walk I've ever been on. What a waste! Still, if he's determined for me to buy something, it's this or nothing."

She walked purposefully back to where the manager was waiting, just in time to meet her uncle resolutely holding out the orange jacket in front of him.

"Nah den, thee, try this un 'fore I change me mind," Dave growled.

"You're joking right?"

"'s'up wi' thee? I'm not shelling out me 'ard earned cash on cheap tack just 'cos tha wants t' go poncin' abaht like tha's in some sort o' fancy southern fashion show. 'undred and ninety quid in 'sale, this. Get it tried on!"

"If you want to look like a walking satsuma, you wear it!"

"Well tha'll 'ave t' 'ave it now, 'cos it got ripped pullin' it off ''anger 'cos o' thee."

"If you're too clumsy to be left in such a *classy* shop on your own, then maybe we shouldn't have come in," retorted Jenny, treating her uncle to her most sarcastic smile.

"I've just abaht 'ad it with thee 'n' tha condensating attitude." snapped Dave. "Don't know why I said tha could come in 'first place. Thee Mam 'n' thee's always been too good fo' me."

"Well at least we agree on something!"

Fearing that they might come to blows, the manager bravely stepped in. "Please don't worry about the damage, Sir, I'm sure we can come to some arrangement if the coat isn't suitable. It was very good of you to even mention it."

"Stay out on it, sunshine; she's 'avin' 'coat whether she likes it or not."

"Don't you ever understand anything? I'm not wearing it!"

"Uncle Dave?"

"What's *tha* want?" snapped Dave.

"Leave him alone; *he's* not done anything."

"Aah, tha's reet abaht summat, any roads. Don't know 'ow 'e puts up wi' 'avin' a stuck-up madam like thee for a sister. No wonder 'e's always 'appy t' see me; only one in this family wi' a sense o' 'umour."

"Uncle Dave!"

"Well perhaps that's because you're the only one who doesn't have to put up with you!"

"Uncle Dave, can I come out yet?"

"Well, tha'll not 'ave t' put up wi' me fo' much longer 'cos thee Mam'll be back day after tomorra 'n' tha can clear off back t' London 'n' stuck up folk down there, where tha belongs."

"Uncle Dave, please, I need a wee."

"You've always been jealous of Mum and Dad; no wonder Dad left as soon as he could."

Dave looked apoplectic. “Oh, ‘n’ I suppose tha knows all abaht it.”

“Yes, Mum told me everything.”

“Aah, I bet she did.” When he was this angry, Dave’s conversation slowed to allow him to emphasise every syllable. He tilted his head back and sneered, “Thee ‘n’ that toffee nosed Mam o’ thine make a reet pair.”

“Uncle Dave, I’m desperate!”

“What’s *tha* mitherin’ abaht. Come out ‘ere!”

David struggled out of the changing room, clothed head to toe in layer upon layer of varying sizes of outdoor clothing. He was wriggling from head to toe and the sweat was running down his face from underneath the three hats on his head.

“What’s tha wearin’ that lot fo’?”

“You told me to try everything on,” explained David desperately.

“Not all at ‘same time; tha looks like ‘Michelin Man.”

“But you said we had to wrap up properly for the tops.”

“Not even tha would think o’ wearing three pairs o’ keks at ‘same time!”

“Er … there is a staff toilet he could use,” interrupted the manager, his voice reflecting sympathy for the boy and concern for the merchandise in equal measure.

“Can tha ‘old on, lad?”

“Ooooh, can we hurry?”

“Jonathan, could you show the customer to the staff toilets. Quickly please!” The Saturday boy led David away, waddling across the shop followed by the anxious gaze of the manager and his sister.

“Be reet,” said Dave, but as his eyes met Jenny’s he couldn’t prevent a mischievous grin from spreading across his face. Jenny couldn’t help herself either; she started to giggle and quickly averted her gaze from her uncle’s. She put her hand up to her mouth to hide her guilt at laughing at her brother’s naivety, but the giggles wouldn't stop. The joke was totally lost on the manager, who stared from one to the other in bewilderment. By now, Dave was wiping the tears from his face, trying not to look anyone in the eye, but if he had caught the manager's eye, he would have been amazed to see that a frown could stretch so far under such a thick beard.

Dave and Jenny must have carried on in this manner for several minutes ; each time one of them gained some measure of self-control, he or she would catch the eye of the other and they would both start again. They were just beginning to calm down when David returned. "What's funny?" he asked, still sporting his multiple layers of outdoor clothing, at which point they started again.

Eventually, the laughter did subside and Dave was able to let out a deep sigh, "Alreet, lass, if tha really wants it, 'ave that 'un tha's picked 'n' I'll pay for 'damage t' t'other."

"No, it's alright," replied Jenny, "we don't want to cause you any more trouble."

"Honestly, Sir, the damage to the coat is only minor. It's not a problem."

"I'll tell thee what, old pal; we'll take coat 'lass 'as chosen, 'n' I'll stick a pony in 'Mountain Rescue tin. 'ow's that sound?" Dave turned to look at Jenny, who shrugged her shoulders and smiled.

"That would be just fine," said the manager, amazed at the unexpected turn for the better.

"And will you be needing the other items?" he added cautiously, nodding at David.

"Oh, aye; we'll not be forgettin' 'Michelin Man, 'n' I need summat 'n' all ; some o' them graters."

"Sorry, sir?"

"Tha knows, fo' keepin' 'mud off."

The manager hesitated for a moment and then smiled, "Certainly Sir, would you like to choose a pair?"

"Can do, Captain. I'll be back in two ticks, tha can start tottin' up. David, take that lot off 'n' gi' 'right sizes t' manager."

Dave walked over to the gaiters and spent several minutes carefully scrutinizing each pair. He eventually chose the most expensive, whilst the manager, the Saturday boy and the counter assistant sorted through David's mountain of clothing and packed one of the correct size of everything into five large carrier bags. Dave added the gaiters to the pile and brought out a huge wad of cash from his jacket pocket, rolled into a bundle and kept in place with an elastic band. At this point he would normally start haggling over the price, but given his accident with the coat and the general chaos they had caused, on this particular occasion he thought better of it and simply grinned and paid up. He wrapped the elastic band back around the role of bank notes, shoved it in his pocket and drew out a slightly dog-eared, silver business card.

"'ere tha goes, old pal. Next time tha's lookin' for a motor, think on. We've 'ad some reet four-be-fours through last couple o' weeks; just reet fo' thee out 'ere."

"Thank you, Sir, I'll bear it in mind."

"Come on then, *tha pair*, we've some reet miles t' cover 'fore it's dark." Dave put down the carrier bags and held out his hand to the manager, who was too confused not to take it. Then he shook hands with the Saturday boy, the counter assistant and even managed to spot the female assistant, who had somewhat naively calculated that the coast must be clear by now and ventured back downstairs. "Nice young lass fo' thee, Davey lad," he laughed, towselling his nephew's hair. David went almost as red as he'd been when he'd come out of the changing rooms and it was impossible to say if he, the girl or Jenny was the most embarrassed.

"Reet then, we're out o' 'ere. Tha's 'ad enough o' ma bundle fo' one day. Twenty-five mile ov'r tops. We'll see thee later," and one hour after their arrival, to everyone's, except Dave's, relief they finally left the shop.

"Tea," said the manager, to no one in particular, "strong, three sugars," as he collapsed in a heap on the counter.

12

As is often the case, the journey back seemed to pass far more quickly, even though Dave insisted on taking the long way round in order to show them Stanage Edge. He pulled the truck over to the side of the road, wound down the window and took a deep breath.

"That up there's where we're meetin' John later," he informed them with great importance, nodding towards the Edge. The children craned their necks and looked up to the forbidding, grey, gritstone cliff face emerging from the white fields below.

"Take a look at that! Tha'll be able t' see thee Mam 'n' Dad if 'weather clears, Davey boy, hee, hee! Mind, tha'll be needin' that new jacket o' thine, Jen," he continued eagerly.

"What a waste of time;" thought Jenny to herself, "drive to a place and look at it, then drive miles away, so you can walk miles back again, to where you've just come from, to admire the view you could have looked at in the first place. Pointless! … Utterly pointless!"

She shivered from the icy blast from Dave's open window. An hour earlier she would have made some caustic comment, but the cabin's warm embrace had been so soothing and she *really* didn't want to risk another fight. The argument in the shop had cleared the air between them for now and, in contrast to the escalating tension of the outward journey, an easy calm permeated the cabin once more. Jenny had no intention of disturbing it and so, keeping her opinions firmly in check, she simply asked, "Can we go now?"

"Ey up, someone's keen - 'as that effect on folks 'first time they see it. Come on then, *tha pair,* sooner we get 'ome, sooner we can get crackin'. Eh, 'n' no lakin' around wi' that computer when tha gets back; up, dressed 'n' out!"

"But we're already 'up'!" wisecracked David.

"Eh, up t' no good. Less on it, Michelin Man!" Dave took one last deep breath, wound up the window and, having checked his passengers had fastened their seatbelts correctly, pulled away.

Jenny sighed with relief and turned to look out of the window once more. She was exhausted and becoming totally pre-occupied with her parents, whose plight was beginning to dominate all other considerations to the point where she no longer even cared who was winning the battle of wills between herself and Dave. As the truck accelerated away from the Edge, Dave turned up the Wilkins Marine 8s and the rolling country music washed gently over her. Jenny closed her eyes and let her head fall against the window. She welcomed the shock of the cold against her skin, but it was no good; the knot in her stomach drew ever tighter and her whole body was beginning to tremble in response. Completely alone, in a desperate attempt to find some respite from the never-ending anxiety about her parents, she forced herself to focus instead on the events of that morning:

It was obvious that she had behaved poorly and needed to make amends, but how was she to go about it? Every time she tried to talk to her uncle it only made things worse, and even though she had responded childishly in the shop and it was never right to lose your self-composure in public, he was still far more to blame for the argument than she was - *he'd* made it happen, not her. But that didn't make the way she'd reacted any more acceptable. For as long as she could remember, her mother had impressed upon her the importance of self-restraint; *If you can't control yourself, you can't control the situation.* So then, she clearly needed to apologise and in doing so, re-establish her ascendancy, proving that she had regained control and making it obvious to this loud, impossible man that she wouldn't normally be provoked by someone so … so … aargh! She checked herself; no - this wasn't fair; she was being snobbish. Jenny's experiences of caring for David since Sally had left had given her a maturity beyond her years and she knew how cutting family slights, intentional or otherwise, could be. What she'd said to her uncle in the shop wasn't fair. This was the same man who had readily opened his home to them in spite of his awareness of the disdain in which their family had held him. He was also the man who had listened to her so patiently last night and, in his own clumsy way, tried so hard to comfort her. Yes … but he was also the man who constantly sought to undermine her and make her feel small at every turn. … And the man who thought buying the best of everything and speaking in that phoney accent impressed people … the man who was always bullying her and David with his pathetic jokes and showing off. Yes, a show off and a bully, *that's* what he was! He should be apologising to her, not the other way round. He could take a running jump! "Oh, this is too complicated," she sighed. She just couldn't be bothered anymore; she'd have to work it out later. On any other day she would have gone over and over what had been said and who was to blame, analysing every word and nuance of the conversation with the keenness of an eagle-eyed lawyer looking for a loop-hole in a contract, but just now lack of sleep and the warmth of the cabin were irresistible. She couldn't think anymore, even if she'd wanted to. So, she let her head bump gently back against the cool glass of the window and gratefully allowed herself to drift off into a dreamless sleep.

She was awakened by the truck pulling to a halt in Highfield. They had driven round the cricket pitch and pulled up outside the post office, which, as the only shop in the village, tried to cater for as many different demands as possible. Jenny was surprised to see that the blue sky had been over-run by low, heavy clouds that threatened more snow and she shivered when Dave opened his door.

"Ay up, Sleeping Beauty's back."

Jenny hated falling asleep in front of other people, especially someone whom she saw as a threat, but before she'd had time to compose a suitably disdainful response, Dave had leapt out of the truck, forgetting to shut the door and was running across the road. "Come on," he shouted over his shoulder, "there's someone I want *tha pair* t' meet, but tha mustn't laugh."

Jenny was too tired to argue, but she guessed that someone else was about to become the victim of his tiresome bullying, and she made a mental note to file away this latest example of her uncle's immaturity in the case for the prosecution. She peered after him scornfully. "He never waits," she grumbled, half-hoping that he might hear, but he was already out of earshot, leaving the children to climb wearily out of the truck and follow him unenthusiastically into the post office.

"'ark at this!" Dave grinned mischievously as he peered round the door. "Alreet, Beryl love!"

"A'ya, my Petal, how are you today?"

"Grand, love. This is me niece 'n' nephew, up from 'Smoke, come t' get some fresh air in them city lungs; Mam 'n' Dad's big shot lawyers. We're off 'ill walkin' so we've come t' stock up on rations."

"Hello my Angels. … What can I get you then, my Flower?"

"Well, when tha's burnin' calories, tha needs high octave replacements."

Jenny rolled her eyes.

"Oh, that sounds a bit complicated for me, my Blossom; I only make the sandwiches."

"That's just what we need; couple o' pork breadcakes; stuffin', apple sauce – the works! Dip 'em in 'drippin' 'n' all if tha's owt left! … Ta Love.

"No way, that's just gross!" said Jenny under her breath.

“It’ll o’ soaked in perfect by ‘time we’re on ‘Edge; we’re off ov’r tops t’ ‘athersage, ‘avin’ a blow - get some fresh air in them city lungs.”

“How many do you want, my Rose-bud?”

Despite the shop assistant’s failure to acknowledge the scale of their adventure, Dave turned to the children, raised his eyebrows and grinned conspiratorially. He was enjoying the joke immensely but the children just looked baffled. “Let’s see now; two each fo’ *tha pair*, three each fo’ John ‘n’ me - ‘ollow legs, that ‘un; ‘n’ I’ll be carryin’ pack, so burning more calories; ‘n’ then one fo’ our Meg. … Best make it a dozen.”

“I’ll just check that we’ve enough bread cakes, my Daisy Chain … back in a second.”

Dave turned back to the children and whispered, “That’s six already, this could be a record.”

“A record what?”

“Names, gormy. Listen t’ ‘ow many names she calls us!”

“Right, my Buttercup, I think we can manage that. Do you need anything else while I’m making these up, Tulip?”

David began to giggle and even Jenny had to turn away to hide a smile. “Parkin!” announced Dave. ‘That’s what we need; curd tarts’ not keep - still me favourite though.”

“If there’s any left you’ll find it underneath the bread, my Strawberry.”

“Reeto,” gasped Dave.

The three of them huddled around the shelves where the bread and cakes were stacked, their shoulders shaking as they pretended to choose some biscuits.

“Stop it!” whispered Jenny, trying to sound cross.

“Sorry, my Blue Bottle,” hissed David, just about finishing his sentence before imploding with laughter.

“That’s enough!” said Jenny censoriously, turning away from the others to avoid eye contact. She walked over to the magazines and bit hard on her lip in an attempt to control herself, but another wave of laughter rose up inside her and in a vain attempt to stifle it, she began to choke.

"Oh, are you alright, my Cherry Blossom?"

Dave, too, began to cough uncontrollably and Jenny doubled up, holding her sides. "I'm fine, thanks," she gasped, "just a touch of stitch. I think I might need some fresh air."

"Off you go then, my Acorn. Come on Dave, open the door for her. … What's he like, Snowdrop?" Jenny rushed for the door, which Dave opened just in time. He winked as she scurried past. "Stop it!" she hissed again. "You're terrible."

Out in the cold air, she began to regain a measure of self-control. She sat down on the bench in front of the shop window and stared out at the cricket pitch that her grandfather had so loved to visit. Five minutes later, Dave and David ran out of the shop and exploded with laughter. "Come on, *tha pair,*" shouted Dave, running to the truck like a naughty boy fleeing the scene of his latest prank, tears running down his face, "let's make a break for it!"

Another five minutes and they were back at the house, The Boys still whooping and laughing and finishing every sentence with an even sillier name than the one before.

"Reet then," said Dave once they were inside, "five minutes t' tog up 'n' we'll be off; don't want t' keep John 'n' Meg waitin', me old Raspberries."

Dave and David disappeared into their rooms to prepare for the expedition but Jenny, having nothing to do other than cut the labels off her new coat, wandered outside to have another look at the house. She had to admit, it *was* a lovely place to live. Although she often adopted the persona of a sophisticated city girl, she had always secretly preferred the quiet of their home in Surrey, away from London's noise and clamour. But here it was *truly* quiet; the road in front of the house was empty and there wasn't another person in sight; the only sounds were the last of the winter wind whistling around the rooftops and the plaintive cry of the curlews on the moor. The wind had chased away the clouds once more and the lemonade sun was trying its hardest to warm her face. It *was* beautiful.

She wandered aimlessly round the side of the house and was amazed by the two things she saw. The first, which she almost walked into, was a colossal satellite dish. "Typical!" she tutted, with a raise of her eyebrows and a slight upward inclination of her head, which made her look like her mother. But before she could muster up the appropriate mixture of disapproval and condescension, her attention was drawn away from her uncle's folly by something far more important; in the field beyond the dry-stone wall were two beautiful chestnut horses, their powerful, athletic outlines at once silhouetted against the glare of the snow. Jenny's heart leapt. She hurried to the wall and beckoned them over. The horses lifted their heads but made no move towards her, so she bent down by the wall and brushed away the snow, revealing what was left of last year's grass, and pulled out a handful and waved it in the direction of the horses. One of them sauntered over and greedily took the grass from Jenny's outstretched hand. She laughed out loud as the horse's lips tickled her palm and then reached out and stroked it between the ears. She nuzzled her face into the horse's cheek, breathing in the aroma of earth and hair. "You're beautiful," she laughed.

"Ta, lass, like t' make 'n effort!"

Jenny's face flushed with anger as she tried to guess how long her uncle had been watching. She turned from the horse, "Don't you know it's rude to listen to other people's conversations?"

"People? I thought at least one o' *tha pair* were 'n 'oss."

"Whatever … anyway, it's probably the only intelligent conversation I'm going to get today!"

"Gi' o'er. Any roads, that 'oss is just a front, I know tha's really gawpin' at 'Raven 2.4."

"What?"

"Satellite dish, old lass."

"Oh yes," mocked Jenny, "very impressive; matches your hat. Come to that, matches your rucksack too. What on earth have you got in there?"

"Aah, wouldn't tha like t' know?"

"Not really. I just can't imagine why anyone would need an eighty-litre rucksack (Exped Expedition (£504.95) - unbelievable!) for a little stroll in the country."

"Little stroll! Tha knows nowt abaht it. Folks *die* up 'ere wi'out 'proper gear."

"Ooooh! Why are we going then?"

"'cos I thought *tha pair* would enjoy it. By look on it, tha could do with a bit o' exercise."

"Thanks, Twiggy. More like you want the chance to show off all your stupid stuff."

Dave had meant that Jenny was looking pale and drawn and, after the previous evening's conversation, he genuinely believed that the fresh air would do her good but he knew she wouldn't believe him, even if he dared express his concern. "Well we're goin' any roads, so tha'd better get summat t' eat, sharpish."

"I don't do breakfast, and while we're at it, I don't do *breadcakes* either – they're called *rolls* and they should never, under any circumstances, be dipped in *dripping*. I'll be fine."

"Tha'll be sorry. Just mark my words! 'n' tha can do that zip up 'n' all while tha's abaht it, *and* tie them laces, or tha'll end up freezin' as well as starvin'. … If owt 'appens t' *tha pair* out there, it'll not be *me* mitherin' Mountain Rescue. Thee Mam left me in charge, so just be said for once."

"For your information, I don't do zips *or* laces, so why don't *you* just be *said* for once!"

Dave was flabbergasted: "Don't do breakfast; don't do laces; don't do as she's said; don't even take no notice of 'er Mam – don't do owt that don't suit, this 'un! Well tha can *suit* theesen! I'm fed-up o' tellin' thee … Little Miss Know All." And with that Dave stalked off to tell his nephew to get a move on.

Jenny waited until he'd gone and then turned back to the horse, "I know; I'm sorry," she said remorsefully, "he just makes me *so* angry." She sighed; every time things started to improve between them, Dave did something to annoy her and she said something she shouldn't. She was trying so hard. A tear of frustration and regret trickled down her cheek … she left it there. She thought again about her parents and was suddenly desperate to speak to them. Why hadn't they called? Or maybe they had! She shuddered as she remembered the look on Dave's face before they'd left the house that morning; why hadn't she gone back in and answered the 'phone? "You don't have to worry about stuff like that do you, boy?" she whispered to the horse, drawing her face up close enough to taste its misty breath, "Just where your next meal's coming from … I know … I'll swap – you go on the walk with Michael Palin and I'll stay here and collect some of this lovely grass for when you come back."

But it wouldn't do; she had promised her mother and David was relying on her, so she'd better make the best of it. After all, it had only taken twenty minutes in the car; how long could it take to walk back to Hathersage? Resolving to remain calm, regardless of the provocation, Jenny took another sigh. It didn't help and so, resigned to her fate, she turned slowly back towards the house.

When she rounded the corner, Dave and David were standing by the steps, staring intently at the map.

"'as tha finished thee intellectual conversation?" goaded Dave.

"Couldn't understand his accent," responded Jenny, trying to deflect the provocation. "Are we off then?" she asked brightly, "it's a bit nippy to be waiting around for *tha pair*."

"Come on then, Davey lad," enthused Dave, as he shouldered the Exped Expedition (£504.95) and attempted to stretch the straps wide enough to fasten around his chest. Without exactly knowing why, he jiggled the huge pack on his shoulders and pulled the waist belt down onto his hips as he'd seen other walkers do. Sucking in his entire torso until Jenny and David thought that he might faint, he clicked the catches triumphantly into place. With a sigh of relief, he fetched his sunglasses out of his pocket and placed them theatrically on his nose before pulling on the straps of his hat and flicking it up onto his head. He went back to his pockets and fished out his Extremities Ice Climbing Gauntlets and began pulling them on. The left one was happy to cooperate, but hampered by its partner, he just couldn't get a grip on the right. After several attempts, he pulled off the left and used his now free hand to pull on the right, but this only reversed the problem. Wrapped up in his Rab Neutrino Endurance and weighed down by the Exped Expedition (£504.95), he was beginning to perspire and becoming increasingly frustrated. He pulled off the right hand gauntlet once more and once more replaced the left, but the right remained as uncooperative as ever. "Come on, what's up wi' thee?" he growled under his breath, "These'll be goin' back, soon as …"

"Need some help Uncle Dave?"

Dave stood searching for a suitably contemptuous response but before it could be found, he looked up along the driveway and a sly grin spread across his face. "Look 'n' learn, lass, look 'n' learn!"

He walked over to the gate and carefully wedged the gauntlet between the hinge and the gatepost. Then he threaded his left hand through the bars of the gate and pushed it back against the gauntlet, which promptly fell to the floor. Ignoring the sniggering behind him, he replaced the loose glove and repeated the manoeuvre, this time with greater care. The gauntlet held and he slowly pushed his hand into it. He sighed with relief and pulled his hand back, but whilst his hand came clear, there was a horrible tearing noise and the gauntlet remained where it had been wedged. He groaned and removed his left gauntlet once again, then using both hands, carefully unhitched the right. He examined the torn glove and sighed in exasperation but, unable to come up with an alternative solution, he could only steel himself and try again. He carefully repositioned the right gauntlet between hinge and post, screwed up his eyes and as gently as possible re-inserted his hand. Jenny couldn't bear to look but, much to everyone's amazement, this time hand and gauntlet came out as one. Turning to his niece and nephew as though he hadn't a care in the world, he announced, "Best not keep Sergeant Major Strives waitin'."

"What about the other one?" Dave stood stock still, stunned by the realisation of his mistake. "Aah well … I were just getting' me bearings like. Allus best to get thee eye in first; Davey lad, thought tha'd o' known that." He pulled off the right gauntlet and with deliberate care re-inserted it into its familiar position before purposefully pulling on the left. "What it is, see, tha can't 'urry things out 'ere – do it reet 'n' tha'll only do it once; first rule o' 'illsman's Code. Make a mess on it out 'ere, 'n' 'tops'll 'ave thee fo' breakfast 'fore tha knows it." Jenny turned to look back at the house, they were five metres away at most. Notwithstanding her disappointment at the mention of breakfast, she couldn't resist grinning at David and raising her eyebrows conspiratorially. David looked away to stifle a cough, prompting Dave to turn and glare suspiciously at them, but in doing so he dislodged the glove from its moorings once again. He stood staring down at the gauntlet, desperately fighting the urge to grind it into the ground under his Scarpa Freney XT GTX silver boot.

"Oh for goodness sake, let me do it!" cried Jenny as she strode over and picked up the glove. Before Dave could object, she grabbed hold of his arm, and with more force than was strictly necessary, thrust the offending item onto his hand. "Happy now?"

Dave's face, already flushed from his exertions, turned a dangerous shade of crimson. "What's tha think tha's doin?"

"I thought you wanted to go walking; it'll be dark before you get those ridiculous gloves on."

"'am speechless."

"Oh well, every cloud …"

Dave was trembling with anger.

"Would you like me to take it off again?"

He paused, quickly re-assessing the situation. "… we've lost enough time already what wi' fettlin' *tha pair*," he eventually snarled. "Can't fathom why thee mam 'uld send thee up 'ere wi'out proper gear in 'first place; she knows what it's like. We can't be 'angin' around 'ere any longer, it'll 'ave t' stay as it is fo'nah - we'll sort it later. Come on Davey lad!" And with that, he strode off purposefully without a backward look, leaving Jenny shaking her head in bewilderment.

"Sir, yes Sir!" shouted David, saluting his uncle as he marched past his sister. Jenny grinned; perhaps her brother wasn't as taken in by her uncle as she'd imagined after all. She fell in behind them as they turned out onto the road and headed down the hill. Just as Jenny closed the gate, inside the house the 'phone rang, but the sound was lost on the wind once more.

13

To Jenny's surprise, they only walked about twenty metres down the hill before turning right through a battered iron kissing-gate onto a path, which actually led them back into the garden at the side of Dave's house.

"Is that it?" asked David.

"Don't be s' daft, Davey, I've told thee I don't know 'ow many times; we're goin' t' 'athersage - tha 'as t' start 'walk from 'start, else it don't count."

Jenny shook her head and tried another sigh. As expected, it didn't work; it was going to be a long walk.

The path led to a stile, which boosted them over an ancient dry-stone wall and out of the garden onto a long stretch of grass. The snow had all drifted to the left of the path, leaving a green ribbon between it and the wall to the right. Without looking back, Dave strode out ahead along the track and David, eager to keep pace, followed suit, but Jenny lagged behind, peering over the wall as she walked, hoping to gain another glimpse of the horses. Not looking where she was going, she stumbled over a half-hidden rock. "Aargh!" she shouted in pain and shock. Dave and David span round to see her stagger forward, regaining her balance just in time to stop herself falling to the ground.

"Enjoy thee trip, lass?" laughed Dave, leaping at the chance to restore the natural order, "*Now* I bet tha wishes tha'd 'ad some boots." Jenny scowled at him as she sat herself down on the next rock to rub her toes. Her uncle turned away and leaned over the wall with a self-satisfied leer on his face. "Proper gear 'save thee no end o' trouble out 'ere."

Jenny ignored him.

"Look at that lad," he went on, pointing up into the clearing sky, "'e allus 'as 'proper gear."

David turned back to where his uncle was pointing and shielded his eyes with his hands. "Cool; what is it?" he asked excitedly.

"It's 'n 'awk," replied Dave knowingly.

"What's it doing?"

Dave shook his head ruefully. " City folks – 'aven't a clue! I'n't it obvious from way 'e's 'ooverin'? - 'e's out 'untin'."

"What does he catch?"

"Owt that ends up injurin' its sen," Dave replied, casting a knowing glance at Jenny.

"Yeah … yeah … yeah … you're so wise about country ways and I'm just a soft, southern city girl. Anyway, you need to watch out he doesn't attack that glove of yours or that'll be another £100 down the drain." Dave, who never forgot the price of anything, stared at his niece in bewilderment – how on earth did *she* know how much they cost?

"Can we please hurry up?" she moaned, the cold and damp rapidly overwhelming her little victory.

"'old up a sec; I thought tha'd be interested in this fella."

"Oh yeah; big wow for the big bird."

"Not *'im,* daft 'ead, *'im."* Dave nodded towards the far corner of the field, where a small clump of hawthorns was casting deep shadows across the snow.

"Who?"

"'im, there! Thought 'e'd be reet up tha's street."

Jenny covered her eyes and looked again. Her gaze widened and she swallowed hard. Walking nonchalantly out of the shadows was a beautiful white pony, which until now had been camouflaged against the snow. Suddenly he began to run, kicking up the snow in front of him and shaking his head. He was perfect; it was like watching a dream. Jenny imagined herself sat on his back, racing across the field; it would be the coolest thing in the world.

Dave watched her and smiled. "Come on then!" he said, feigning impatience, "Jen says she wants t' crack on." He turned away and the children followed, David still watching the kestrel and Jenny, despite her earlier mishap, unable to take her eyes off the pony. They only walked about another two hundred metres before stopping again. Dave turned and looked back up the path towards his house. "There she is; t'old pile. Not s' bad is she?" The children turned and looked back in silence, not sure how they were supposed to respond, but Dave smiled proudly, glad that they were so pleased with it - with him and how well he'd done.

They soon reached another stile, which Dave led the way over in suitably theatrical fashion, stopping at the top to puff out his chest and breath in the fresh, clean air. David followed his hero's example, adding an enthusiastic, "Right grand," as he straddled the top bar, whilst Jenny used the opportunity to take one last look back towards the pony, but he was already hidden from sight. She sighed wistfully and turned back towards the path.

The scenery had changed completely. Up to this point, they had been walking down a gentle slope between two dry-stone walls with open fields stretching out on both sides but now, as the ground fell away more steeply, a dense coniferous wood rose all around them. The sun hadn't penetrated here and the snow still clung to the trees and lay thick on the ground.

"It's Narnia!" shouted David.

"It is!" replied Jenny, temporarily forgetting her mood at the mention of her favourite childhood book. "Where's the lamp post?"

Dave looked round furtively, a frown and a furrowed brow combining to give away his confusion.

"Do you like C.S. Lewis, Uncle Dave?" asked David, anxious that his uncle wouldn't think him childish or soft.

"What's that then, when it's at 'ome then, lad?"

"You know; the Lion, the Witch and the Wardrobe."

"Never 'eard on it."

David looked abashed.

"'old on; is that that one 'bout them posh kids gettin' lost in that daft wardrobe 'n' them meetin' them animals 'n' things 'as can talk? … *Nadia* or summat, i'n't it?"

"That's it; Narnia," replied David enthusiastically, amazing his sister with the subtlety of the correction.

"Oh aye … *Narnia*, that's the one - load o' rubbish! … Tha needs experience 'n 'illcraft out 'ere, not some daft nonsense abaht talkin' badgers. Tha needs t' start growin' up a bit, young 'un, 'n' leave fairy stories t' babbies."

David looked like he was about to burst into tears.

"Well, no … what I mean is … it's alreet fo' little kids 'n' that, but tha's shootin' up now; tha'll be leavin' school 'fore tha knows it."

His nephew's expression didn't change.

"… I think I might o' seen it on 'telly once at thee Na'nan's – she'll watch owt t' fill 'time; sez it's a bit o' company. Any roads, wasn't *that* bad, really. … Nah den, if I think on, some posh woman, who used t' come t' pitch were reet into it. Told me a reet 'un, 'n' all. Listen t' this: 'ang on a sec …". The children watched in bemusement as he rehearsed his lines, "… got it: What does Oslo 'ave fo' breakfast?"

David and Jenny turned to one another and shrugged their shoulders.

"Come on, Jen, lass, I thought tha were meant t' be brains o' outfit."

"I've no idea what you're talking about."

"Course th' 'as. *What does Oslo 'ave fo' breakfast*? – Banadia sandwiches. Heh heh, that's a reet 'un," chuckled Dave, rapidly approaching his most excruciating pitch. "BANADIA SANDWICHES! What's tha think abaht that 'un, Davey lad?"

"I don't get it," said David nervously.

"I think he means *Aslan* and Ba*narnia* sandwiches and it's just not funny."

"Oh," said David, still confused. He decided to laugh anyway, just to make Dave feel better, but Jenny could see he'd been hurt and that their uncle's clumsy attempt to rescue the situation had had little effect. "Hmmm …" she mused as she trudged along behind her him, followed by David, head down, trying to stay out of sight, "… speak in haste, repent at leisure; he always goes too far; just can't help himself." - *Look for patterns* her mother had taught her, well here was one, clear as the back of his hand. Why couldn't he see it? - If he'd only stop showing off in the first place, he wouldn't have to keep tying himself in knots trying to repair the damage.

Unlikely as it might seem, Dave may have been thinking the same thing. Either way, after a moment's hesitation, he set off again in uncharacteristic silence and for the next few minutes nobody spoke, each of them lost in their own private thoughts, as they clambered over styles and sunk ankle-deep into the virgin snow. It was as if they needed to wait for permission before disturbing the stillness of their surroundings, and it not being forthcoming, no one dared break the spell.

By now the snow and ice had found its way through to her soaks and Jenny was feeling increasingly cold and miserable, so when the path led them out of the shadows and alongside a steep grassy bank where the sun had melted away much of the snow, she let out a sigh of relief.

"Best sunbathing in Sheffield that, Davey lad. Not many knows on it, 'n' all," Dave announced eagerly.

"Fat chance of that," moaned Jenny, looking up at the threatening clouds. "How far have we gone?"

"Only just started, lass; two 'ours minimum 'fore we see laddo."

They walked on. Every few hundred metres Dave stopped

and looked at the map. David, whose ability to shrug off disappointment and not hold a grudge never failed to flummox his sister, wandered across and peered over his shoulder. Dave was delighted to see his nephew taking an interest once more and, half-sensing the need to mend a few fences, launched into an explanation of how experienced map readers always knew to use a pencil to plot their progress: "See them pointy trees; them's these 'uns 'ere, 'n' can tha see 'ow I've marked off us progress s' we can keep tags on exactly where we are? So then … we're 'ere, 'n' if tha looks down 'path tha should see another 'un comin' from 'reet …". In spite of herself, Jenny couldn't help looking along the path and, much to her surprise, there actually *was* a path joining from the right.

"'n' why do proper 'illsmens allus use a pencil?"

"So they don't get *lead* down the wrong path. Get in!"

To his sister's secret delight, David began his ridiculous goal-scoring celebration, wiggling his whole body from head to toe as though it were made of plasticene and raising his clenched fists to an imaginary crowd, whilst simultaneously imitating its roar.

"*You'll* be down 'wrong path in a minute! - It's so … is tha listening? (David, oblivious to his uncle's insights, was still basking in the crowd's adulation.) … Will tha gi' 'o'er lakin' abaht fo' one minute, 'n' tha might learn summat useful fo' once. They use a pencil 'cos, fo' one thing, it don't run in 'rain, 'n' for another, tha can rub it out when tha's done."

"Yeah, but for another, can it *run* in the *snow*?" David ran towards his uncle, ready to kick up the large bank of snow just in front of him, but at the last second his nerve failed him and he only feigned the kick. Nevertheless, Dave still cowered and turned away, but immediately realising his mistake, he turned back and growled, "No, but tha better 'ad!" and made a lunge at his nephew. But David was far too quick and leapt easily away, laughing and running rings around his uncle, just out of his reach, not sure if he should be more pleased with his wit or his physical prowess.

Jenny had been enjoying all this immensely, but she also recognised the need to step in before things got out of hand, "Well, when you two *pencil heads* have quite finished, I'm supposed to be having lunch with a dog and her owner, both of whom have more sense than you two put together … so I'm guessing it's this way," and she strode off down the hill. Dave and David turned to one another and grinned. Pleased and, if he were totally honest, somewhat relieved, Dave followed on and after a few minutes of surprisingly strenuous effort was able to re-take his rightful place at the head of proceedings.

They halted at yet another style and Dave studiously marked off their progress on the map. Clambering over, they took a sharp left turn and began to walk alongside a deep gully. Near the bottom was the trunk of a large fallen tree, creating a bridge across the stream below.

"Great place fo' dam building, that, Davey lad. We'll 'ave t' come back in 'summer."

"Can't we go down there now?"

"No chance, lad! Fall in there t'day 'n' tha'll never climb out, then what's thee Mam gonna say?"

Something began to dawn on Jenny: Dave was talking like a tour guide; it was as though he wanted to show them all the things they could do *when they came back.* He actually thought that they would be coming back *again!* She felt the cracks in the ground opening up all around her: What if that were the plan? Her mother had promised her that this would definitely be a 'one–off' and when Jenny had protested she'd assured her that it would only be for the weekend, and that if she'd just go along with it this once, they'd never have to stay here again. But what if Dave had pressurised her mother into a different arrangement? Normally Jane would have sorted someone like Dave out in an instant, but Jenny had never seen her mother so desperate and who knew what she could have agreed to in her hurry to leave for New York. This was awful. She stood stock still, unable to move. One week-end was bearable – just, but no one could possibly be expected to put up with *this* on a regular basis.

"What's wrong, Jenny lass, has t' ice queen turned thee t' stone?" laughed David, looking back over his shoulder.

"Oh shut up! I'm just sorting my shoes out – just leave me alone!" Jenny immediately acknowledged her mistake and bit her lip in frustration. Hoping with all her heart that Dave hadn't overheard, she stared down at her trainers. They were soaked through. The laces hung wet and grey at their sides and her feet felt like ice-blocks, but at least there was no reaction from her uncle. She sighed with relief and sat down on a fallen tree trunk, biting hard on her lip to hold back the tears. Why had her mother had to go to New York? It was so unfair; nobody should be forced to spend the weekend doing *this* - not with *this* man. She knew she was being unreasonable but she couldn't help it. She was lonely, tired, cold and utterly miserable. If it weren't for the desperation in her mother's voice, she would never have agreed to come here in the first place, but now that the reality of Dave's great adventure had begun to bite, things were turning out even worse than she had feared. She rested her chin on her hands and looked into the wood. The bleakness of her surroundings perfectly matched her mood. Perhaps it *was* always winter here. The impenetrable darkness of the wood seemed to close in around her, conspiring with the cloud of despair that hung over her. It was silent and she felt empty and totally alone. She looked around and suddenly realised that she *was* alone; Dave and David were nowhere to be seen! Her self-pity began to give way to apprehension, which quickly turned to fear, which was rapidly overtaken by blind panic. She jumped up and began to run down the hill to where she had last seen David. The path was empty. She stopped and turned through 360 degrees, desperately wanting to shout out but by now too terrified to do so. She was completely alone! She ran on, now at full pelt, but the sun's rays penetrating through the trees acted like a strobe light, making it impossible to see where she was going, causing her to half-stumble and fall against a tree trunk, which loomed large and threatening over her path. She picked herself up and raced on again, almost blinded by the lowering sun, desperately trying to out-pace the unseen terror that seemed to be gaining on her with every stride. Then suddenly the wood cleared and the path curved round to the right, where it met a half-metalled road leading to a bridge over a chuckling stream. Jenny quickly came to a halt and tried to recover her breath.

Dave and David were concentrating on the map and hardly noted her arrival. As her panic began to subside, her anger filled the void. "I could have been lost out there or anything!"

"What's tha moanin' abaht?" asked Dave absent-mindedly, half-lifting his head from the map.

"Out there, on my own. Thanks for waiting!"

"What?" Without waiting for her reply, The Boys returned their attention to the map.

"You're meant to be looking after us!"

Dave looked up quizzically, "What's tha mitherin' abaht?"

"You just… you…. just wandering off, never looking back!" Jenny realised how pathetic she sounded, "Oh, just forget it!"

Dave shrugged his shoulders and returned to the map once more, whilst Jenny nodded angrily at herself, "Stop it! You're fine, don't be such a baby!" She sat down on a wall opposite The Boys; they hadn't even noticed her absence. How irresponsible could they be? She wanted to explode, but to do so would only make her look more foolish. She breathed deeply and pulled her coat tight around her. Unlike her temper, her body was cooling fast and despite her exertions, she could feel the cold tightening its fingers around her chest once more.

"Why don't tha do thee coat up? I never met anyone s' stubborn in all me life."

"I'm fine, thanks," snapped Jenny. "Why don't *you* just make sure we all stay on the right path?" Dave shrugged his shoulders again; he was having far too much fun instructing his new apprentice in basic navigational skills to let his stroppy niece spoil things.

After a seemingly endless, almost entirely one-sided discussion, Dave and David agreed on the way and set off without a backward glance at Jenny, who in search of the sun's solace had quietly shifted her position to sit on the bridge. Her breathing had slowed and, clear of the shadows, she was even beginning to warm up a little. The coniferous planting had given way to native deciduous trees and now that she'd calmed down, the place seemed altogether less threatening. She relaxed a little, closed her eyes and leant back on her arms, opening her face to the sun. She began to laugh gently as she thought of her panic-driven dash down to the bridge. "Very impressive!" she congratulated herself and as if adding to the derision, a dog barked in the distance. For a moment Jenny wondered if it were Meg, but then quickly corrected herself; such an intelligent dog would never consider making so much noise whilst she was working.

Almost simultaneously, the drone of an approaching helicopter made her open her eyes, and as she searched the sky her gaze fixed on three white lines criss-crossing the piercing blue background. It reminded her of her parents and she wondered again what they were doing and how things were going; she had no idea what she would do if they didn't return together. She felt the knot retying itself in her stomach and stood up quickly to look for the others.

"It'll be 'reet, tha knows." It was Dave.

"What will?" asked Jenny distractedly.

"Thee Mam 'n' Dad, they'll be 'reet."

"What makes you say that?"

"I saw thee; watchin' 'viper trails."

“Oh, I was just day-dreaming.” Jenny couldn’t bring herself to correct him.

“Aye, lass, ‘n’ I’m Michael Palin. Any roads, come on, ‘fore ‘wolves ‘ave thee!”

“Wolves?” asked David, trying not to sound concerned as he wandered back up the path.

“It’s just another childish joke,” sighed Jenny, “don’t take any notice.”

“Well, that noise must be comin’ from ‘woods.”

“Why?”

“’cos they’re full o’ bark. FULL O’ BARK! Heh, heh! What’s tha think o’ that ‘un, Davey lad? FULL O’ BARK!”

“Come on *pencil pushers*,” sighed Jenny, “playtime’s over.”

“’old up, lass, map readers at ‘front, if tha don’t mind.”

“Whatever.”

Dave and David set off once more, howling like wolves and Jenny allowed herself a half-smile. Like many teenage girls, she didn’t suffer the failings of her family lightly and her uncle was by far the least bearable of all her relatives, but she could still recognise kindness when she saw it and it *had* been kind of him to come back for her. “Come on,” she said out loud, “every step is a step closer,” and resisting the temptation to try a howl of her own, she followed on.

Continuing down the hill, The Boys high jinks seemed unending. First, they passed under the bough of a giant oak tree. Dave went first and as he drew level with the branch, he jumped up and slapped it with both hands. “This is ‘illsborough!” he shouted wildly, shaking both his fists towards the imaginary crowd as he landed. David followed, “This is Highbury!” he responded, trying to make his high-pitched voice sound as ferocious as his uncle's, but his grasp exceeded his reach and he missed the bough entirely, causing him to over-balance and fall flat on his back. "Ow!" he yelled, rolling over dramatically on the ground.

Dave turned at the noise, "Ay up," he laughed, "they like trips in this family."

Jenny ran to her brother's aid, maternal concern welling up inside her. "Don't move!" she yelled, "Something could be broken."

"My legs, I can't feel my legs," moaned David.

"Lie still!" barked Jenny, leaning over him, "You mustn't move."

"Oooh, Jenny," moaned David, "I didn't know you cared," and he reached up and pushed a handful of snow in her face.

"Aargh!" she yelled, "You're such a child. … Just grow up!"

"Nice one, Davey lad; we'll make a Dee Dah o' thee yet."

"Oh just get lost, both of you!" Jenny brushed the snow from her face and out of the neck of her coat and stormed off down the hill.

"Come on, Davey lad, can't 'ave some stroppy lass out-pacin' us 'illsmens." Dave was having a great time and within a minute he had his next trick in mind: "Wait up, Jen lass, it were nowt but a bit o' fun. 'itch ov'r a sec; map reader allus goes first."

Jenny slowed reluctantly to allow her uncle to pass, sneering at him as he made his way to the front. He pushed his way through the bedraggled undergrowth strewn along the little-used path, accelerating with the increasing steepness of the hill, then his eyes lit up as he saw what he was looking for - another low branch hanging over the way. "Come on, *tha pair*, keep up!" he ordered, looking behind. He turned back, just in time to pretend to bang his head on the bough.

"Aargh!" he screamed, fetching his hands up to his forehead, and turned again to watch for Jenny's reaction. But this was his undoing; immediately after the tree the path fell away even more sharply towards a narrow, fast-flowing rill, flanked by last year's brambles. Dave hadn't seen this and, looking backwards, had no opportunity to adjust his footing before he reached the ramp. The path suddenly disappeared from under his feet and he fell forward, arms flailing as he went. He landed in the middle of the rill a millisecond before the eighty litre Exped Expedition rucksack (£504.95) arrived on top him, pummelling the air out of his lungs.

"And how did you enjoy *your* little trip?" Jenny blurted out before collapsing against the trunk of the nearest tree. Dave could only lay there, gasping like a turtle newly emerged from the ocean and even David couldn't resist bursting into laughter and pointing derisively at his hero.

Dave remained motionless, the water seeping under the waistband of his Rab Neutrino Endurance jacket, whilst the brambles dug their way through his Ron Hill Flex Pants. After a few seconds spent working out what had just happened, he slowly ran his tongue around the inside of his gums and spat out a mixture of dirt and blood. He pulled himself up onto his elbows, looked down at his torn Extremities Ice Climbing Gauntlets and let out a moan, before reaching out for his Stetson El Alamo and, without thinking, placing it on his head. A trickle of freezing water ran down behind his ears and under the collar of his Rab Neutrino, sending a shiver from head to toe down his already aching body. He didn't know what to be depressed about first: the pain, the damage to his gear or the humiliation. He slowly pulled up his knees until he was resting on all fours, but then a quick glance behind him at his niece and nephew leaning against the tree, gripping their sides, instantly turned his self-pity to righteous indignation. "Aah, *tha pair* should laugh 'n' all; I'd love t' see 'ow tha'd manage out 'ere on thee todd if owt 'appened t' me."

"Are you alright?" asked Jenny, in a valiant attempt to sound concerned.

“I’ll be reet as soon as *tha pair* stop lakin’ abaht; it’s not a game this, tha knows; good job fo’ thee I’ve learnt ‘ow t’ fall wi’out injurin’ me sen.”

“Sorry. Are you sure you’re alright?”

“Sorry, Uncle Dave.” The children were just about able to blurt out their apologies before being overwhelmed by another wave of laughter but it was a close-run thing.

“Come on, then,” growled Dave, reaching out for a low hanging branch to aid his standing. But the combined weight of the man and his rucksack was too much for the branch and with a searing ‘crack’, it gave way, leaving Dave grasping helplessly at the air once more before returning to his previous position at the bottom of the rill. David and Jenny stood stock still, staring in disbelief, each aware that their self-control was unequal to the trial. Down in the stream, Dave was equally disbelieving, albeit for completely different reasons.

“Is neither o’ *tha pair* gonna ‘elp or what?” he gasped over his shoulder, “’ere, ‘elp me off wi’ this pack.” David scrambled down the slope and began pulling at his uncle’s rucksack. The immense weight of it took him by surprise, almost as much as Dave’s sudden jerking up and down.

“Gi’ o’er, gi’ o’er! What’s tha doin’?” David lowered his uncle gently back into the rill.

“Uncle Dave, you need to undo the straps!” Jenny had given up trying to stand and had slid down to the ground with her back resting against the tree, “Undo the straps!” By now the tears were pouring down her cheeks.

After several strenuous attempts, Dave managed to roll over onto his back but the Extremities Ice Climbing Gauntlets were still in no mood to cooperate and stubbornly refused to allow him to undo the chest straps. After a prolonged but ultimately futile struggle, he eventually gave up the fight and lay there gasping, staring up through the branches towards the sky, unable to quite take in what was happening.

"'ere, just 'elp me up," he eventually sighed, stretching out his hands. David anchored his feet firmly against the hill and, straining with all his might, pulled uncle and rucksack back to upright.

"Are you okay?" asked David with genuine concern.

"Like tha cares. Just leave all carryin' t' muggins 'ere, 'n' *tha pair* can just look after theesens; that'd be abaht reet."

"That's not fair; you didn't even ask us if we wanted to carry anything."

"Reet there … reet there; I shouldn't 'ave t'ask, not if *tha pair* thought abaht anyone 'cept 'emsens. If it wasn't fo' John, I'd fetch thee 'ome - soon as. I don't know what e'd 'uld say if 'e could see this carry on. … Come on, 'fore I change me mind!!"

The crestfallen 'illsman turned angrily away and shook himself down, hoping desperately not to let the children see how much his body was hurting. He took a deep breath and stepped out, scoring a direct hit on his Oakley Carbon Blade Black Iridium Polarised sunglasses (£348). The crunching sound from beneath his foot stopped him dead in his tracks. He looked directly in front of him, fully aware of what lay below and behind. As the true awfulness of his situation dawned on him, he let out a deep sigh and, shaking his head bitterly at the recurring injustices of life, set off down the hill once more, eyes fixed firmly on the path in front of him. The children followed in silence, willing to risk neither conversation nor eye contact, shoulders quivering with mirth. Jenny thought it was just about the funniest thing she had ever seen. As she reached the half-buried sunglasses, she bent down and carefully pulled the two halves out of the mud. "Thank you," she said playfully. Dave didn't even bother to turn round.

The children, by now growing inured to their uncle's outbursts, carried on in fine form, playfully competing to be the first to say 'thank you' to everything they could think of. They came to an upward turn in the path, where the roots of an ancient hawthorn tree had created a flight of natural steps; "Thank you," each of them chimed as they patted the tree. This only fuelled Dave's anger, but when he flung the map at Jenny and told her that if she were so clever from now on she could lead, she only smiled and added another, "Thank you."

David, for the moment firmly on Jenny's side, showed her where they were on the map and they walked on down the hill together, leaving Dave trailing further behind, limping from a combination of last night's burn, which had suddenly become intensely painful, and the effects of the fall.

"We're not going too fast for you are we, Uncle Dave?" mocked Jenny over her shoulder.

"Tha's pushin' it, lass!" snarled Dave, giving her such a look that she quickly turned back to the path.

Just then, a great tit shot out of the wood from their left and began to scuttle along the path in front of them. "Why thank *you*, Mr Bird," smiled Jenny, "he's showing us the way – it really is Narnia."

David and Jenny carried on in this happy mood for several more minutes, but as they descended, the path slowly became less and less distinct and Jenny began to grow nervous. She stopped and huddled over the map with David, double-checking that Dave, still sulking his way down the hill, was out of earshot.

"Where do you think we are?" she whispered.

"We can't be far from here," responded David, pointing on the map to where the path met a thin yellow line, "so I think if we keep walking downhill, we can't go too far wrong."

Jenny sighed and smiled at her brother with a new-found admiration. "Come on," she said, "how hard can it be?"

14

'Much harder than she thought' was the unwelcome answer. As they set off again, Jenny tried to follow the path as best she could through the decaying undergrowth and half-frozen bogs, but in spite of her best efforts she eventually lost the way altogether. They came to a halt.

"What's up, Little Miss Know It All; not lost in 'dark scary forest, are we?" mocked Dave.

"No!" retorted Jenny. "Just following the map like we were told to." She turned the map round and round, unable to relate it to anything she could see around her. Then she spied some footprints in the mud in front of her. She looked along the direction they were heading and was surprised to see a silver light shining in the distance. "What's that?" she whispered to David.

"I'm not sure." They gazed at the light in silence. As she concentrated, Jenny noticed that it wasn't one light but two. The larger one, hovering at head height, was like a vague glow in the distance, stretching across the horizon, but the lower, much smaller one was clearly defined in the shape of a semi-circle.

"What is it?" she asked again.

"Well," said David in a determined tone, "there's only one way to find out," and he strode out towards the mystery.

After another minute's walking, they stopped again and David pulled the map gently out of Jenny hands, who made no attempt to stop him. Ignoring it for the moment, he circled slowly round through 360 degrees and then turned his attention back to the map. Jenny stood by patiently, hoping against hope that her brother could save them from the onslaught that would inevitably follow should they fail. Deep furrows began to appear on his brow as he stared at the map for what seemed like an age, but then he suddenly lifted his head, looked down the hill one more time and turned to face his sister, as a triumphant smile lit up his face. Jenny had never thought him so handsome.

"I know what it is," he announced gleefully, "look!" He pointed at a blue splodge on the map. "A-g-d-e-n Water;" he read out loud as he traced his finger along the placename, "it's the reservoir!"

Jenny looked at the light again. She narrowed her eyes in concentration until a sly grin slowly spread across her own face. "You could well be smarter than you look, young 'un" she teased her brother, "but what's that semi-circle of light?"

"Well that's the bit that confused me," said David, trying to maintain an air of modesty, "but if you look closely, you can see that the road just cuts across this stream at the edge of the lake, so there must be a bridge; the water underneath it is what's making the semi-circle." He couldn't contain his pleasure any longer and beamed at his sister.

"Tha's brilliant, young Davey lad!" she laughed with delight, and they turned back to the path together, Jenny just about remembering how uncool it would be to link arms with her brother.

Sure of their way, they walked confidently downhill until they arrived at a large gate in a dry-stone wall, beyond which was the road that David had identified when he'd first taken the map. Jenny went to push open the gate, but, to her surprise, it was chained and padlocked. "Oh well," she said cheerily and began to climb.

"What's tha think tha's doin'?" Dave panted. "We're in a reet tangle now."

"Why, we found the road didn't we?"

"Oh aah, proper job! Tha's led us on t' someone's land; we're only *trespassin'*."

"Big deal; let's just climb over."

"Oh, 'n' damage 'gate; that 'uld be reet."

"Why would it damage the gate? We're going to climb over

it, not kick it down."

Dave shook his head, "Typical; city folk comin' out 'ere - no idea! … Look," he lectured, drawing on John's gentle guidance, if not his tone, "if tha climb's ov'r 'ere it puts 'strain on ''inges, 'gate starts t' drag 'n' 'fore tha knows it, it's 'alf 'angin' off 'cos city folk like thee can't read a map. We'll 'ave t' go back."

"No way! You're just sulking because we found the way. Come on David!" Jenny leapt up on to second bar of the gate and performed a faultless gate vault. Landing lightly on the road, she finished with a curtsy aimed unerringly at her uncle. David followed in silence, determined to stick with his sister but still not daring to look back at their deposed leader.

"Reet," stormed Dave, "tha mightn't 'ave any respect fo' 'countryside, but some on us 'ave t' live round 'ere. Wait there, I'll sort this out." He stomped off, intending to retrace their tracks and come back down the proper path. Within a few seconds he had disappeared from sight.

"Now what do we do?" asked David anxiously.

"Wait, I suppose. … You did really well with the map."

"Thanks."

Content in the silence, Jenny looked around her. There was no one to be seen, but looking up at the low, heavy sky, she was suddenly hit by the thought that they could be cut off from Sheffield by the snow and for a moment she began to panic that their parents wouldn't be able to reach them from the airport. Then she smiled. The road in front of her was completely clear; it had been gritted, melting the snow, and beneath the trees had already dried to a bleached white. There'd be no problems getting here. Nevertheless, the reminder of her parents chased away her contentment once more. She was missing them so much that it hurt. The fear of what might be happening was overwhelming, robbing her of reason and movement. She forced it back down, enjoining herself to concentrate on something else. She stared again at the pieces of rock salt on the road beneath the trees, each one a minute island, cut off from the rest of the world by its own tiny reservoir of melted snow. "I wonder if I'll end up like that," she mused, but the bleakness of the idea was too great even for a teenage girl, and she shook herself out of it: she wasn't alone; she had her brother and her parents. It would be all right. Her mother was the smartest woman she knew, she would never let things fall apart. They were a family; they would stay together. She turned to look for David; he was standing a few metres away with his head tipped back and his tongue sticking out, trying to catch the drips as they fell from the trees. She smiled. She guessed that it would be dark by the time they returned to the house, and the day after tomorrow they would all be back together. It would be all right.

But where did Uncle Dave fit in to all this? Was he part of the family? Well, yes, of course, but he was also part of the problem, always trying to make people feel left out. Why did he have to do that? He was so divisive; North against South, city against country, boys against girls. It must be miserable to always think like that; only able to feel better about yourself by making others feel worse. Perhaps he only did it to hide his own loneliness. Perhaps *he* was cut off from the world by his own tiny reservoir. The sudden realisation of her uncle's neediness almost made her feel sorry for him.

"*That* is a really nasty thing t' do."

Jenny turned around and was surprised to see Dave back at the gate. "Where have you been, stuck in traffic?"

"Tha knew I needed 'map, why didn't tha pass it ov'r instead o' lettin' me g' chargin' off on me todd? Probably still got concussion from that 'eavy fall, no wonder I forgot it. 'n' tha thought it 'uld be funny to let me go wandering off and get lost? I'll 'ave t' climb ov'r 'ere now. … We're runnin' even later now, thanks t' this carry on." Jenny turned to David, shrugged her shoulders and smiled. It was another small triumph.

Weighed down by the Exped Expedition (£504.95), Dave

struggled to mount the gate. With one final push, he managed to heave himself onto the top bar and lay there exhausted. At that moment, The Doctors' appeared on the bridge, riding steadily along the road. "Surprised to see *you* abusing someone's property like that, Dave," said the Male Doctor with a wry smile. Dave looked up and tried to give them a casual wave. This altered his balance just enough to pull him over the gate and he landed in a heap on the road. Jenny looked on with a mixture of concern and derision.

"I think I've broke summat," moaned Dave.

"Let me have a look," said the Female Doctor, climbing down from her horse. "Would you mind holding him for a moment?" She smiled kindly at Jenny, who eagerly took the reins and immediately forgot about her uncle and began petting the horse. After quickly checking him over, The Doctor helped Dave into an upright, sitting position and carefully removed the Exped Expedition (£504.95). After another brief examination, she declared him, "Battered and bruised but not broken," and helped him to his feet.

"Reet, well we 'ad better be pressing honwards; hit's a long way to 'athersage hand we mustn't be late for hour appointment," said Dave, surreptitiously flicking at the clumps of mud clinging to his Flex Pants. With a barely noticeable wince, he swung the Exped back over his shoulders, jiggled the frame on his hips, fastened the waist belt and began stretching the straps across his chest. But the Extremities XCRs still hadn't forgiven him and the elasticated straps snapped out of their grasp, striking him spitefully on the chin. David rocked back on his heels, roaring with laughter and pointing at him with the now familiar derision. Everyone else averted their gaze.

"Thank you very much for tha's 'elp, Doctors," said Dave, through gritted teeth whilst glaring at his nephew, "hit's been very thoughtful hof you. Come hon, children, we really must be hon hour way. Perhaps we'll see thee later, halthough we don't hexpect t' be back huntil hafter dark; we're walking hov'r to 'athersage thou knows. Cheerio fo' now."

Dave grabbed Jenny by the elbow. She just managed to pass the horse's reins back to The Doctor before being half-dragged along the road by her furious uncle. "Come on, *tha pair*, what 'ave I just told thee? – We're runnin' late thanks t' thee. John'll not want t' be kept waitin', tha knows, 'e's a very busy man," and they set off, half-walking, half-running down the road, until Dave herded them down a narrow, barely visible path off to the right and the bemused Doctors and their beautiful horses disappeared from view.

14

Dave strode out in front along the narrow path, ignoring his aching limbs, Exped Expedition (£504.95) bouncing up and down as they rapidly descended the steep hill. On one side was a tall wooden fence from behind which a pair of fierce-sounding dogs barked their warnings. On the other was an equally tall dry-stone wall and above them hung the branches of several large trees, standing guard in the garden behind the fence. It was like walking down into an unexplored tunnel and rather intimidating. After fifty or so metres they passed a break in the wall and David looked over to the hills in the distance.

"Is that where we're going?" he asked.

"Nowhere near big enough," replied Dave, with none of his usual mirth.

David and Jenny exchanged concerned looks, but the rasping edge to Dave's voice dissuaded either of them from enquiring further. They continued at the same rapid pace until they reached a flight of steps, which took them further into the wood that had sprung up on both sides of the path. At the bottom of these they turned left and then quickly right to an even longer set of steps. Through the trees Jenny could hear a stream and a few moments later they arrived at a footbridge marking its meeting with the path. Even though the returning clouds had briefly lifted, allowing a few trickles of early spring sunshine to seep back through the bare branches, the wood was dark and gloomy, making them uneasy and discouraging conversation. In silence they followed the path along the stream and finally the wood began to thin, allowing the children a reassuring glimpse of the reds and yellows of a children's play area.

They eventually arrived at a clearing that spanned both sides of the stream, where Jenny was amazed to see a well-tended tennis court on the opposite bank and beyond that a newly built, single-storey stone building. Dave stopped and turned to address his niece and nephew. His anguished expression reflected his inner turmoil: on the one hand, he was desperate to tell them about the new village hall and how they never could have built it without him and how, as a highly respected, permanent resident of the parish, he was entitled to use the refurbished tennis courts whenever he wanted, and how well his game was coming on now that he was having professional coaching. On the other, he wanted to let the children know that their behaviour had been totally unacceptable and how deeply hurt he had been by their ingratitude. His usual strategy when wanting to convey his suffering to the world was to grow silent and withdraw from conversation. He would remain in this self-imposed exile until someone, preferably a woman, expressed her concern for his well-being, at which point he would explain the nature of the injustices against him. But in this instance the only people able to express their concerns were the very ones who had treated him so unfairly in the first place. So he stood, hesitating - audience waiting - civic and wounded pride battling it out on his forehead. "Owt t' say?" he eventually asked, in a tone intended to simultaneously express both his anger and his suffering.

"Do you know anyone with a tennis racquet?" asked David innocently.

A visible shudder of rage passed through Dave and without a word he turned back to the path. "Come on," he snapped as he strode off, "we 'aven't time fo' this."

Jenny and David looked at one another and shrugged: Adults!

The path led them into a car park and, for the second time in as many minutes, Jenny was amazed to look across to her left and see the post office in the distance. She glanced down at her watch. It had taken them forty-five minutes to reach a point which would have taken them fifteen at most walking along the road. This was going to take forever!

Dave's mood was equally bleak. Every landmark they passed added to his frustration. By now they were walking around the far perimeter of the cricket pitch, behind the neat, newly painted pavilion, snuggled in against the bank of yet another chuckling stream. Dave had had a story ready about this, too, and another about how well his batting was coming along now that he was having professional coaching. Now they'd have to miss it all. It just wasn't fair; they really were determined to spoil it for themselves!

He trudged on, burdened as much by self-pity as by the weight of the Exped Expedition (£504.95). The path led them back out of the empty car park to a road junction, where a lonely tree waited forlornly on a small grassy island, before they finally halted at a glass bus shelter, set back from the road against an untidy semi-circle of grass and weeds. Without comment, Dave slowly lowered the pack onto the bus stop's bench. He winced and sighed and stretched his back but the children were too self-absorbed - Jenny wondering if her trainers would ever recover and David increasingly worried about lunch - to acknowledge his suffering on their behalf. He lumped himself down by the Exped Expedition (£504.95), unaware of the small black box falling from the pocket of his Rab Neutrino Endurance as he did so, and gazed disconsolately at his torn and mud-covered Extremities XCRs. He sighed again and carefully began pulling at the fingers of the gauntlets, grimacing at each tug. With his hands free of the gloves he started to slowly clench and unclench his left hand, screwing up his face against the pain. Unbelievably, his niece and nephew seemed more interested in the 'To let' sign outside a house further down the road, which for some childish reason they insisted on reading as 'toilet'. So, Dave turned to his feet, holding his ankle and slowly rotating his foot. Again, the agony was clear for anyone who was interested to see, but, to his dismay, Jenny and David had wandered off up the road to stare at a building site.

"Aya!" gasped Dave, trying to gauge the volume needed to be unintentionally overheard, as he removed the boot with exaggerated care. David turned round and ran down the hill.

"Uncle Dave, Uncle Dave," he shouted as he ran. Dave looked up, eyes alight with anticipation. "Uncle Dave, you can see John's house up there."

"I know, lad," sighed Dave, not sure whether this was part of the act or genuine disappointment at his nephew's failure to respond to his obvious suffering. He began working his fingers and thumb slowly down his foot, feeling for breaks through his socks as gently as he could. "I'll 'ave a butcher's in a minute, pal," he winced. He began pulling off his Sealskinz Waterproof Cold Weather Mid Length Sock, but the pressure from the advanced lacing of his Scarpa Freney XT GTX that had taken him so long to master had welded the sock firmly to the burn left by the cigarette lighter. "AAARGH!" he screamed as the sock tore away from his skin and he began hopping round the bus shelter, foot in hand. "AAARGH!" Now there was no reason to play up the pain; he was in agony. "Ooooh …" he moaned as he slumped back down onto the bench, holding his foot as tightly as he dare, "Ooooh … . It's no good, we'll 'ave t' go back."

"But we've only just started;" protested David, "there's still miles to go on the map."

"Aye lad, but I don't think I can make it ov'r 'tops like this; could end up in serious bother, 'n' where would that leave *tha pair ?*"

"I thought *you* were the tough Northerner," said Jenny harshly. Her uncle leant back against the bus shelter and closed his eyes. He could feel the pain beginning to subside but had no intention of walking another step.

"You can't just let John sit there all day – how bad can it be?"

"It'd stop thee in thee tracks; I'll tell thee that fo' nowt."

"Well we're carrying on - David, where do we go from here?"

David, having been engrossed in the map with all the attention a teenage boy trying to ignore his stomach's protests could muster, had completely missed the latest altercation. He innocently lifted his head, hesitated momentarily and then pointed along the road. "I think we go along this road for about half a mile and then turn off onto another footpath."

"'Think!' 'Abaht!' *Tha pair* not last five minutes out 'ere by theesens wi'out me. There's no way tha's goin' out there on thee todd."

"Well it looks like you're going to Hathersage then."

Dave scowled and closed his eyes to the pain once more. Sat here alone, on his own little island, he contemplated the bus stop sign rattling in the wind and the weeds nodding their disapproval at anyone who would venture out on such a day. What a desolate place this was.

Having seen through Dave's attention-seeking from the first, Jenny had quickly dismissed it with the contempt it deserved, but now that he was genuinely in pain she felt *some* sympathy for him, particularly as his great adventure was not turning out quite as he'd expected. "Have you brought any first-aid equipment with you?" she asked, searching for the right measure of concern.

Dave struggled for a suitably sarcastic response but the ache in his foot and the bleakness of his mood allowed only for a weary, "'ave a look in 'rucksack, lass."

Jenny undid the top of the Exped Expedition (£504.95) and peered in. The first thing she noticed was how full it was. The second was how neatly it was packed. She tried to identify its contents but being so tightly packed, she found it impossible to find anything and so began emptying them onto the bench. First, she pulled out three stainless steel water bottles (far superior to aluminium) and the sandwiches and parkin from the post office, now encased in plastic boxes. Then came three emergency bivvy blankets along with three sleeping bags compressed into inconceivably small sacks. Next she pulled out a high altitude camping stove, a bottle of paraffin and a titanium cooking pot and three matching mugs. Below these were six vacuum-packed 24 hour survival rations, a water filter, a spare map and a miniscule tent. Everything was brand new and many of the items were still in their wrappers. Finally, she came across a first-aid kit in a red case, it too still sporting its cellophane wrapper.

"Here we are," she said breezily and began pulling off the wrapper. Inside the box she found a sachet of burn gel and instructed Dave to remove the rest of his sock. Without hesitation, she tore open the sachet, squeezed some of its contents onto her hand and began rubbing it gently into the small, circular burn on Dave's foot. He sighed with relief. Next she found some gauze and padding and carefully bandaged the area to protect it from the pressure from his boots. Dave was both mollified and impressed. He couldn't maintain his sulk any longer, "Tha's not bad at that, lass, tha should think on abaht bein' a nurse or summat."

"Thanks, but I prefer animals."

"Charmin'," laughed Dave lightly, as he tucked the comment away alongside the others he'd collected along the way. He looked around him with an air of restored contentment. The bus shelter was high enough above the village to give him a view back up to the church and the pylon on the hill by The Doctors' house. "Eh, it's a reet place, this," he muttered to no one in particular. He looked at the solitary tree opposite, standing on its own little island and felt a wave of melancholy break over him. "It would be nice to have someone to share it with," he thought to himself. He turned back to look at his niece and nephew, who were busy reading the bus timetable, hoping to find a route to Hathersage, and felt the loneliness recede. He had to admit that in spite of everything it was nice having them around. "Come on then, *tha pair*," he shouted brightly, "we're gonna be late for John 'n' Meg. 'e'll be catching 'is own snap again if we don't jog on." He reached over and began to repack the contents of the rucksack. "AAARGH," he yelled again, pulling his fingers away from the bench and grasping them with the other hand.

"Now what's wrong?" asked Jenny brusquely.

"Glass! Look at me, now: Jacket's ruined." Dave held his wounded fingers up to show them the blood trickling down onto the sleeve of his Rab Neutrino Endurance, "Wasn't cheap this, tha knows."

Jenny raised her eyebrows. "Just hold still a minute, let me have a look!" She prised Dave's good hand away and stared at the bloody fingers. "Can't see anything like this, hold on a second."

She opened one of the water bottles and poured its contents over Dave's hand to reveal a small, clean cut on his middle finger, then gave him some of the unused cotton wool to press on to it and finally raised his hand above his head.

"Stay like that," she said firmly, "it'll stop the blood flow." Dave looked at her anxiously. "Oh don't be such a baby, it's a *little* cut on *one* finger; this is the easiest way to stop you from bleeding to death."

"Please miss, can I go to the toilet?" mocked David.

"Tha's 'ad it as soon as I'm done 'ere."

After a couple of minutes, the bleeding had subsided and Jenny carefully renewed the cotton wool, added some gauze and then strapped the finger in sticking plaster.

Dave was bravery personified, making no other sound than a few sharp gasps when the pain became unbearable. When she had finished, he inspected Jenny's work and smirked. This was working out perfectly; having such a high pain threshold, the wounds were bearable and now folks would be able to see that neither a deep glass cut nor third-degree burns could keep a true ‘illsman off the tops. Even better, he had the perfect excuse to pass on the cooking for the rest of the week-end. Not that he’d be letting on to David and Jenny just yet, so, screwing up his eyes against the pain, he pliantly held out his hands for Jenny to pull on his war-torn Extremities (£100) and looked round for a new topic of conversation.

“Typical,” he began, “city folks come out ‘ere, can’t afford t’ live ‘ere, can’t afford a car, jealous o’ those on us who can ‘n’ start vandalising ‘place. Chuffin’ ‘eck.”

“Is that who smashed the glass, Uncle Dave?”

“’course it is. Stands t’ reason.”

“Uncle Dave, you are *such* a snob.”

“Me! Tha’s got t’ be kiddin’; I’m just a workin’ class kid who’s done well for ‘issen. Nowt wrong wi’ that.”

“You are. You’re saying that just because some people can’t afford a car or a house in the country, they go round smashing up bus shelters. That makes no sense – they’re the ones who use the bus shelters.”

Dave shook his head and smiled wisely. “Alreet lass, if tha says so … if tha says so. Any roads,” the conversation about snobbery was beginning to make him feel uneasy, “we should be eating tea *‘ere* t’neet.”

“Where?”

“Windy Bank,” replied Dave nodding towards the sign on the opposite side of the road. “Heh, heh. WINDY BANK!! - What abaht that ‘un, Davey lad? WINDY BANK!” David looked across to his sister for an explanation but she simply shrugged her shoulders and began repacking the rucksack for a second time.

“What’s this?” asked David, picking up the black box from under the bench.

“Nah den, young ‘un, wouldn’t tha like t’ know? Any roads, ‘ow’d tha end up wi’ that?”

“What does it do?”

“It’s a compass, gormy (Suunto MB-6 NH, £69). I’ll be needin’ that now we’re ‘eadin’ fo’ tops. ‘ere, pass it ov’r ‘’fore owt ‘appens to it.”

David handed over the compass, but as soon as Dave took it the Extremities resumed their opposition. Sabotaged by their sausage fingers, he fumbled hopelessly with the matchbox-like case, trying to slide out the compass, but he just couldn’t gain the necessary purchase. “Chuffin’ useless things,” he growled under his breath. Smiling nervously, he pressed on, this time gripping the black box between his teeth and desperately trying to pull out the compass with his bulging thumbs. But the compass held firm and in desperation he resorted to shaking the box from side to side in order to free it part way. Finally his frustration got the better of him and with a violent fling, he unintentionally sent the compass flying out of the box and crashing into the bus shelter’s glass screen. Jenny glanced at David and grimaced, unsure how to react. After a moment’s hesitation she bent over and picked up the compass, looked at it forlornly and passed it back to Dave; she really was starting to feel sorry for him. He stared at the dented box in silence and then gently shook it, scattering pieces of its broken mirror across the bench. “Absolute cheap tack! Supposed t’ ‘ave ‘reinforced casin’ these. This’ll be goin’ back - Finland or no Finland. ‘n’ I’ll tell thee summat else; whichever chuff wrecked this bus shelter must o’ used some reet force if it’ll stand up t’ being ‘it by summat as tough as that. Good job I can manage wi’out mirror, else we’d be in a reet tangle.”

“It’s alright, Uncle Dave.”

“What is?”

“Your compass – you won’t need your mirror.”

“Oh, ‘n’ suppose thou knows.”

"Not really, but your make-up's not smudged; you look fine."

"Don't tha ever take anything serious? 't'i'n't a game this, tha knows. 'ow's *tha pair* gonna manage wi' a broken compass if owt 'appens t' me?"

"We could always ask Meg."

"Oh, *reet* pair o' comedians we've got 'ere." Dave didn't know where to begin.

"We're sorry, Uncle Dave, will you show us?"

"Forget it, sooner we meet up wi' John 'n' get this ov'r wi', the better. Cost me a fortune this weekend (£742 in damages to this point) 'n' fo' nowt. Tha's not even enjoyin' it, let alone 'elpin' wi' owt. Complete waste o' time; don't know why I'm botherin'. 'ere do summat useful fo' once 'n' 'elp us off wi' these gloves." Jenny walked over nervously and with the greatest of care pulled off the Extremities. " Shove 'em in 'bag wi' rest o' that lot; more trouble than they're worth – same as *tha pair!* "

Jenny looked over towards her brother, who was once again reeling from his hero's latest onslaught. Poor David; one minute his uncle was laughing and teasing, the next he was doing everything he could to make them miserable - no wonder he was confused. She'd promised her mother she'd look after him, but was at a total loss to know how. She sighed and shook her head in despair, her new-found sympathy for her uncle already exhausted. Unlike her brother, *he* deserved everything he got.

As soon as she'd finished repacking the Exped Expedition (£504.95), Dave shouldered his burden once more, making great show of avoiding further damage to his wounds and then in one heroic last effort to restore his status, he grandly announced, "Any roads, by look o' sky we'll be needin' this," and like a self-satisfied child showing off his magic tricks, he pulled out a mud-stained Ordnance Survey Hydroseal map case (£19.99) from under his jacket. Still taking care to avoid his wounds, he folded the map in two, inserted it into the case, and carefully and precisely ran the thumb and index finger of his good hand along each side of the two track LocTop closure and shut it with the secure fastening. With confidence flooding back, he removed his Stetson El Alamo and ceremoniously hung the map around his neck before triumphantly replacing his hat and turning to face his niece and nephew.

"Uncle Dave … I think the map might be the wrong way up," said David nervously.

"Does tha now? So, what; tha puts 'it in upside down does tha? Now, why would I do that?"

"But when you hold it up to read it, it will be upside down."

"Is that reet?"

"Well, yes, it is, actually," chimed in Jenny, coming to her brother's defence.

"Well, aren't I 'lucky one t' 'ave two experts t' take care o' poor old me. I only live 'ere tha knows!"

Jenny sighed and turned away but not before she caught Dave surreptitiously glancing down at the map. She smiled; one more short-lived victory.

"Perhaps I should just go home 'n' leave *tha pair* o' know-alls to it."

"Sorry, Uncle Dave," said David quietly, "but don't you think we should..."

"What?!"

"Well … don't you think we should clear the glass up?"

Dave was fit to explode: "Come on, we've wasted enough time without this carry on. Council can sort it, that's what we pay 'em fo', not that tha'd notice. … Next stretch is on 'road, so keep an eye out fo' cars, *tha pair*, we don't want any more accidents."

Without looking back to see if the children were following, he set off. Cowed once more into obedience, David fell in behind, but, in one final act of defiance, Jenny remained stock still, looking back up the hill towards Dave's warm, dry house.

She glanced down at her watch; 12:15; her feet were like ice, her stomach was in open rebellion and after the briefest of respites, her uncle was back to his unbearable worst *and* it was still five hours before nightfall. Surely all that was worth a second sigh. It didn't help. It was definitely turning out to be a long walk.

15

The new road ran along the side of a steep valley falling away to their left. At the bottom was another of those busy streams that criss-crossed the landscape, skiddling along on its important business. The water ran dark against the snow overhanging its banks and, out of the wind, Jenny was taken again by the remote beauty of the place. After a few minutes walking in silence, they came to a fork in the road. Jenny hoped they'd turn left, which led further down into the shelter of the valley and over an inviting bridge towards a wood, but Dave chose right, striding out heroically towards the hill in front of them. They passed a road sign telling them that they had only walked three quarters of a mile from Highfield and it was still seven miles to Midhopestones and ten to Penistone, wherever they were. Jenny felt the cold beginning to finger through her clothes once more and her heart sank even lower.

"Must o' been a *reet* match, that," announced Dave, sensing that spirits were lagging and that his outbursts at the bus stop might be partly to blame.

"What?" asked the children in unison.

"*That*; Penistone ten, Midhopestones seven."

"More like *Nohopestone.* Accept it Uncle Dave; you're just not funny."

"Well 'e seems like a nice bloke, any roads," Dave continued unperturbed.

"Who?"

"Dale Dyke."

"What?"

"'im, Dale Dyke?"

"Who's Dale Dyke?"

"'im down there," explained Dave, nodding in the direction of the stream, "- Dale Dyke."

“Come on, boys,” sighed Jenny, “time to go.”

The road ran up and round until they crested the hill and then began a long, gentle descent. At the bottom of this was a random collection of buildings, about which Dave knew several interesting anecdotes, but Jenny was concentrating on something far more important: on the opposite side of the road was a small paddock and in it were two beautiful grey horses, each in its tartan winter coat. She walked over and began petting the one nearest the road.

“’ere we go again; no wonder its takin’ all day! What is it wi’ thee ‘n’ ‘osses?”

Jenny reddened at the idea of having revealed her hopeless obsession in front of her uncle and she rapidly re-joined The Boys on the road. Thankfully, Dave was ready with his next piece of local trivia and she was relieved to hear him let the matter pass, or so she thought – he’d secretly logged one more mental note of where Jenny’s true interests lay.

“Used t’ be a pub, this.”

“Wish it was now!”

“Oh aye, pal, ‘n’ what’s tha know abaht pubs?”

“Well they’re warm and dry,” added Jenny, “which is more than we are.”

“Tha can’t ‘ave a dry pub – tha’d ‘ave no customers. DRY PUB! - What abaht that ‘un, Davy lad? … DRY PUB!! … Proper gear, lass, or least roads do thee coat up!”

Jenny ignored him.

“Nah den, Davey lad, ‘ow can tha tell it used t’ be a pub?”

David looked along the row of low stone buildings. “Don’t know.”

“Tha’s not lookin’ lad, that telly’s done fo’ thee eyes.”

“Just tell him.”

“Steady on lass, it’ll do ‘im good t’ use ‘is brains - ‘e’s been sat on ‘em all weekend.”

“Easy,” piped up David, who been staring intently at the

buildings, " - the sign. Get in!" He pumped his fist by his side and, almost as if he were aware of Jenny's need of encouragement, reproduced his plasticene wiggle. She smiled, and looked along the row until her eyes alighted on an empty metal frame set on top of a large, thick-set wooden post to the left of the final dwelling. This was where the pub sign used to hang and she nodded her head in approval; at least the walk was bringing out the best in one of them.

"Not bad young 'un, not bad."

"Why don't they take it down?"

"Then 'ow would tha know it's an old pub?"

"Why would you want to know that?"

"So tha could remember tha'd sent a southerner t' bar.' Heh heh! SOUTHERNER T' BAR! Heh heh, what abaht that 'un, Davey lad?"

Nothing.

Leaving horses, houses and pub signs behind, the three Strives walked on side by side in silence. The children were still trying to decipher their uncle's latest attempt at wit, whilst he was desperately searching for less challenging material. Suddenly he stopped in his tracks. "Oh no!" he gasped. "I can't go on, it's too 'orrible."

"What is?" asked Jenny wearily.

"That, up there, on ''ill! - It's terrible!" David and Jenny looked up towards the hill looming above them from the south, but couldn't identify anything that would explain their uncle's torment.

"Another stupid joke, I suppose."

"It's no joke, lass, look! Some nutter's painted 'is 'ouse red. ... We can't go on; we've no idea what else's out there?!"

Having not the slightest interest in football, the joke was completely lost on Jenny, but David instantly recognised the reference to his adopted second team, Sheffield United, and, of course, his beloved Arsenal. Like so many young boys before him, football offered him a longed-for route into conversation with the adult males in his life, and following their example, he never failed to respond: "That must be why it's at the top of t' hill - t' blue one must be at t' bottom."

"Tha'll be at 'bottom o' 'ill in a minute. Come 'ere, tha cheeky beggar!" shouted Dave, chasing after his nephew. But David was far too quick, the Exped Expedition (£504.95) increasingly burdensome, and to be honest, Dave's legs were really beginning to ache, so the chase only lasted a few seconds. David laughed loudly, mocking his uncle's attempts to catch him and walked on ahead, singing and chanting as he went. Jenny strode out after him in an attempt to warm up, leaving Dave bringing up the rear, the road leading them through a series of twists and turns, always upwards, until finally they reached a plantation of silver birch spread across both sides of the road.

"'old up a sec'," gasped Dave. The children stopped and turned back, trying not to let their uncle see them grinning at his bedraggled appearance. He staggered to a halt about ten metres behind them. "What 'ave I told thee?" he called ahead, in turn trying not to let them hear how out of breath he was. "If *tha pair* keep rushin' off someone's gonna end up lost 'n' 'fore tha knows it we'll be callin out 'Mountain Rescue, then where will we be?" Jenny raised her eyebrows at her brother but said nothing. "Any roads, there's summat I want t' show thee; see them trees over there; tha never really knew thee Granddad, did tha? Nah den, what's them trees t' do wi' 'im? What's tha reckon?"

Jenny and David looked at one another in bafflement.

"Don't know," said David.

"Well, what kind o' trees are they?"

"Can't you just tell us? It's like being at school."

"Well, if tha'd 'a' listened at that fancy school thee Mam 'n' Dad shellin' out fo' tha might know what I were on abaht."

"Alright," sighed Jenny, in the tone she reserved for expressing boredom of the most irritating kind, "what kind of trees are they, oh wise Uncle Dave? I'm sure you're bursting to tell us."

But it was too late; Dave was already far too engrossed to take the bait, "Nah den, them's silver birch, don't that gi' thee a clue?"

"Nope."

"Well what did they used to use silver birch for round 'ere?"

"Bows and arrows;" chirped David enthusiastically, "Robin Hood."

"Tha can be a reet gorm sometimes, Davey lad. *Robin Hood*! What's tha thinkin' o'?"

"Robin of Loxley."

"Tha's way out, lad. … 'ave I t' tell thee?"

"Please," groaned Jenny.

"Well," began Dave with great authority, gratified that his niece and nephew were taking such a keen interest in the matter, "them woods were planted so that they could use 'twigs in rollin' mills."

"What's a rolling mill?"

"Where they roll 'steel."

"Where to?"

"Not t' anywhere. Turn it into strip; that's what they did in 'mills. Nah den, stop interruptin'."

"You must pay attention, David, there's a test at the end."

Dave studiously ignored his niece. "Back in 'day, they took blocks o' red 'ot steel 'n' run 'em back'uds 'n' for'uds under these massive, great steam 'ammers. Every time ''ammer 'its 'block, it makes it a bit thinner."

"So what are the trees for?"

"Well now, tha sees 'ow twiggy they are? Well that's 'cos

they chuck ‘twigs on ‘blocks as they pass under ‘ammer.”

“And *why* would they do that?”

Dave sighed his teacher’s sigh, “When ‘twigs land on ‘red ‘ot block, they catch fire ‘n’ temperature rises; that burns off all ‘slag in ‘steel. … ‘t i’n’t complicated.”

“… oh.”

It was obvious to Jenny that David still didn’t understand; she wasn’t entirely sure that she did herself. “And that has *what* exactly to do with Granddad?”

Dave sighed again, “‘e used t’ work in ’rollin’ mills, di’n’t ‘e? For all tha knows ‘e could ‘ave been shovellin’ twigs from these trees.”

“Fascinating!”

“Aah, well, at least tha’s learnt summat useful this week-end.”

Dave was genuinely offended that they hadn’t appreciated his story; although he’d done everything in his power to avoid following in his father’s footsteps, he was extremely proud of his working life in Sheffield’s steel mills, and he expected others to respond with the same level of admiration and respect. This pair had better up their game sharpish, particularly as he’d several more important stories to tell them before they reached Hathersage. Still, they’d thank him one day and so he set off purposefully up the hill once more, but before the children had even started to follow, he stopped again.

“Oh great, another History lesson.”

“’ere we are then.”

“What, are we there?”

“Don’t be s’ soft, lad; does this look like ‘athersage t’ thee? Look!” They’d stopped at a large blue sign, telling them that this was Dale Dyke Reservoir. “It’s tha mate again.”

“Who?”

“Dale Dyke! Keep up lad! … Ov’r we go then, come on!”

They climbed the stile of overhanging stones protruding from the wall and made their way into another coniferous wood. This one was more mature than those around Highfield and the higher canopy allowed more light to permeate through. It was actually something of a relief to be out of the wind tunnel created by the road, especially as the huge trees provided an effective umbrella from the rain. After walking about a hundred metres or so, they came to a small headstone engraved with the letters C-L-O-B.

"What does that stand for Uncle Dave?"

"Don't tha know, lad?"

"Can't-let-others-be," muttered Jenny, smiling at her own quick wittedness.

"Come on, must be summat t' do wi' 'flood."

"What flood?"

Dave slowly shook his head and puffed out his cheeks in despair at such wanton ignorance. "Come on, it's 'igh time *tha pair* learnt summat abaht where tha comes from."

"But we're nowhere near Cobham."

Dave couldn't believe his ears: "Cobham … Cobham! Did I 'ear reet? Tha might live in some lah-did-dah, poncy southern village now, but *this* ... *this* is where tha comes from. … Cobham … Cobham! … Tha's got t' be jokin'. I am *speechless."*

Even in the midst of battle Jenny couldn't resist turning to her brother and whispering, "If his voice gets any higher, Meg will be the only one who can hear it!"

Thankfully, Dave had already stormed off and so missed his niece's latest *bon mot.* "Come on," he growled, "let's 'ave a look down 'ere, see if we can rescue owt. … Cobham! … In all my days. … Unbelievable!"

He marched on a few metres and came to an overgrown memorial flowerbed, where a small plaque remembered those who'd lost their lives in the Dale Dyke Reservoir disaster of 1864. He stopped to stare at the plaque, confused as to how he should react; he'd been completely flummoxed by David's response about where he and Jenny came from, but now he was faced with the human tragedy of the Flood, his consternation was rapidly overtaken by an inexplicable sense of grief. He didn't stay long, moving on before the children arrived, eager to rid himself of the unease which had crept up on him. A few metres down the track, he found the matter-of-fact nature of the large noticeboard more to his liking. Although it reminded him of the 244 lives that were lost in the flood, it also pointed out that at the end of the reservoir, they would find a solitary tower known as 'Boot's Folly' and by the time he'd finished reading about it much of his anger had subsided

Jenny walked up and stood beside him in silence, she too was strangely moved by the story of the burst dam and the loss of life that followed. She read on until she reached the story of Boot's Folly, nodding approvingly at its namesake's attempts to keep his men in employment during the lean years of the 1920s. She was developing a keen sense of social justice and this example of caring capitalism fitted well into the perspective on the rights and wrongs of the world gleaned from her mother.

"Biggest natural disaster ever,' announced Dave, warming again to the task. "*This* is what they should teach kids abaht it in school."

"Except it wasn't."

"Wasn't what?"

"The biggest natural disaster."

"Course it were. Look, says so 'ere."

"Yes, but it's not a *natural* disaster. The dam was man-made therefore it wasn't natural. Earthquakes and volcanoes are natural, this is just the result of human error."

Dave was bursting with frustration. He knew Jenny was wrong but he just couldn't find the words to explain why. "It's still watter," he declared.

"Yes, *watter* from a man-made dam."

"Aah, but it's still watter. Any roads, just goes t' show 'ow dangerous it is out 'ere."

"Yeah, like it's going to burst again any minute."

"It's not, is it?" asked David anxiously.

"Course not, lad; Yorkshire built, no problems there."

"What like the last one?"

"Tha can be more respectful, 'n' all!" snapped Dave angrily. "All them people dying fo' nowt; 't'i'n't nowt t' laugh abaht!"

"Sorry," said Jenny meekly.

"Aah, tha should be, 'n' all. Come on, if *tha pair* can't show more sense than that there's no point lakin' around 'ere, leavin' John waitin' on 'is todd." … "Another story ruined," Dave grumbled to himself, "'t i'n't fair."

They walked on into the wood, in silence once more, until they came to a fork in the path. Dave lifted the map case and then quickly let it drop. He hesitated for a moment, as if trying to remember something and then chose down and left, towards the bottom of the valley. They were following a long loop in the path when David suddenly announced that he was 'desperate'.

"Plenty o' trees, lad, 'elp theesen."

"What, wee outside? - What if someone comes?"

"Don't be s' soft. First off, 'ow they gonna see thee in all these trees, 'n' second, 'ow many folks 'ave we passed so far? Come on, I'll 'ave one me sen. Jen, tha's on look-out."

"I thought you said no one would come."

"Gi' o'er! Come on, Davey, I'm fair bustin'!"

The pair of them headed off the path and into the trees, the ground beneath their feet bouncing them along as though they were walking on a giant trampoline. "Cool," shouted David, "zero gravity. This is one small wee for a man, but one giant river for mankind."

"Not so giant by 'look o' things. Come on Lance Armstrong, gi' o'er messin'!" They each found a tree and Jenny turned away in disgust. Looking back up the hill, she could see the path running roughly parallel to the length on which she now stood. She gasped as she saw two red shapes appearing and disappearing behind the trunks of the giant coniferous trees. “Uncle Dave, there’s someone coming!”

“Tha’ll ‘ave t’ do better than that, lass; tha’s way too predictable.”

“Suit yourself,” replied Jenny, a devious grin slowly spreading across her face.

Immensely satisfied by how easily he’d outwitted his niece, Dave began to whistle jauntily. Up on the hill, the Red Coats’ terrier stopped in his tracks, pricked up his ears and, after a moment’s hesitation, bounded down the hill towards Dave.

“Uncle Dave, a dog’s coming!”

“Aah, whatever tha says, lass.”

“Don’t say I didn’t warn you!”

Dave carried on whistling until a small brown face suddenly appeared from behind the tree. “Oh ‘eck! Come on Davey boy, ‘as tha done yet?”

“Buster, here boy! Oh, hi there;” called one of the Red Coats, walking swiftly along the track, “didn’t see you there.”

“Oh, ay up there, pal,” responded Dave nervously as he stepped out from behind his tree. “We was just lookin’ fo’ acorns. We’ll pick some up on ‘way back.”

Jenny looked around her; the path and the ground as far as she could see were strewn with fir cones. She started to laugh, but then sensing her uncle’s annoyance, she set off after him as he scurried down the path.

“Come on, then,” hissed Dave to David, “we’re not letting that sort get n ‘ead on us!” He strode off down the hill, outpacing the others. “Get a move on!” he barked over his shoulder as the bewildered children hurried to catch up.

“What’s wrong, Uncle Dave?” asked David.

“We are *not* bein’ overtaken by a couple o’ cheap tacks like that; probably only out ‘fo’ ‘dog.”

“I don’t understand.”

“Look at ‘gear, lad; cheap tack; no way they’re proper

‘illsmens wi’ that gear. We need t’ show ‘em what’s what.”

“Are you saying that we can’t let those two overtake us because our stuff cost more than theirs?”

“Too right, lass, that’s exactly what I’m sayin’. We’re ‘proper job, wi’ ‘proper gear; we’ve standards t’ keep up.”

“Unbelievable!”

“Aye maybe t’ thee, lass, but I’ve t’ live round ‘ere when *tha pair’s* gone back t’ Smoke. What does tha think John ‘uld say if ‘e knew we’d be ov’rtaken by a pair o’ townies?”

“He probably wouldn’t say anything.”

Dave shook his head at his niece’s ignorance of country ways. “Tha’s a lot t’ learn, lass. Least ways, what tha’ll not find in them fancy schoolbooks thee Mam ‘n’ Dad’s shellin’ out fo’.”

Jenny gave up.

“Any roads, Davey lad, we’ve a job t’ do ‘ere. We’ve t’ take bridge ‘fore ‘enemy detergents blow it.” Without breaking step, he stooped down and scooped up a handful of fir cones. “Ammo ready, lad? We’ve two minutes ‘fore they pull ‘trigger. Come on!”

Dave took off down the hill, making machine gun noises. David looked at Jenny and shrugged but the pull of adventure was too great, so, following in the footsteps of his hero, he gathered his ammunition and ran. The path led down through a series of bends and David was struggling to keep his balance on the gritty path. As he rounded the final sweeping bend, he almost collided with Dave. His uncle was crouched by the side of the road, half hidden by the winter bracken, holding his hand up for silence. David fell in behind him.

“See that bridge, lad, we’ve been ordered t’ clear it ‘fore rebels blows it. If we succeed, ‘war’s all but won.” David stared at the wooden bridge in front of him. He had no idea what his uncle was talking about.

“Reet then, young un, ‘ow are we fo’ ammo?” David opened his hand to reveal a mixture of dirt, twigs and a couple of skinny fir cones.

“That all we’ve left?” asked Dave anxiously.

“Sorry, sir,” replied David, the gist of the game beginning to dawn on him, “but a lack of ammo never stopped a loyal soldier.”

Dave turned to his nephew and looked at him intently. David thought he’d said something wrong and was about to apologise when Dave grabbed him firmly by the shoulders. “Tha’s a good soldier,” he said, staring into his nephew’s eyes, “but more than that, tha’s a good man.” With that he was off again, at first crouching as he ran but as the target approached, he stood tall, dispensing justice with every grenade he hurled and when his grenades were gone, he unleashed his machine gun upon the evil enemy. David followed suit, but overtaken by the excitement of the game, tripped and fell as he reached the lip of the bridge.

“Stay down!” yelled Dave, “I’ll cover thee.”

He dropped to the floor and began to crawl across the bridge towards David. When he reached the brave young corporal, he knelt on one knee, providing covering fire against the rebels, who, for some unknown reason, were attacking the bridge from the middle of a large pond, created by a weir about twenty metres upstream. The insurgents were completely taken aback by the ferocity of Dave’s attack. He was even able to use up the last of David’s grenades. The rebels fell back, searching for any kind of cover, but Dave’s shot was unerring and the river turned red. “Jenny, Jenny, come in,” Dave screamed into his imaginary glove, “man down, good man down. We need back up ‘n’ medevac NOW!! ‘n’ I’m nearly out o’ ammo; bring grenades FAST!!”

Jenny sauntered down to the bridge, unable to keep the smile from her face. Her uncle’s behaviour was so immature, but it still made her laugh. Dave looked at her in consternation. “Where’s ‘ammo? Can’t tha see we’ve a man down?” Jenny rolled her eyes and shook her head, but Dave had more pressing matters. “Listen!” he ordered, “can tha ‘ear that? - Aircraft engine!”

Jenny couldn’t help herself; she narrowed her eyes and concentrated and, much to her amazement, found that she *could* hear the noise of an aircraft’s engine somewhere overhead.

“Ours or theirs?”

Jenny turned away to look at the river but Dave suddenly threw himself across his nephew, knocking the wind out of him. “MIG-25 rakin’ ‘bridge!” Then, abandoning all thought for his own safety, Dave stood and raised his machine gun. As the jetfighter came into sight, he took aim and filled the cockpit full of lead. Smoke began pouring out of the MIG as it span away out of sight. Dave looked down at his nephew and fell back down to his knees. He began beating on his chest. “Don’t leave us, Corporal Davey lad, feet it!” he screamed at his bewildered nephew.

“Can we help?” asked one of the Red Coats, peering over Dave’s shoulder, “I’ve done some first aid.”

“Er … no … no … er … I were just showin’ young ‘uns ‘ropes o’ emergency medical care,” stuttered Dave. Jenny had to hold onto the handrail to stop herself collapsing.

“Oh, okay then, if you’re sure there’s nothing we can do,” said the Red Coat, unable to mask the suspicion in her voice.

“No, we’re fine thanks, Love, aren’t we, Davey lad?” said Dave quickly.

For a split second, it crossed David’s mind to feign unconsciousness but the look of pure terror on his uncle’s face held him back. “Yes, we’re just clearing the bridge of rebels. If we do it, we’ll win the war,” he answered without getting up. Then, as if to make one final check, Buster appeared and began to lick David’s face. He laughed and pulled himself up to his elbows so that he could pet the dog.

“Okay then,” said the first red coat, still not totally convinced, “if you’re sure there’s nothing we can do, we’ll press on. Enjoy the rest of your walk."

Dave watched them as they walked away from the bridge. "I do *not* believe that. 'ow cocky can tha get? Me, *obviously* an experienced 'illsman, needin' 'elp from a couple o' cheap tacks! Did tha see 'gear? - Castle Market or I'm a monkey's uncle. Unbelievable! Any roads, 'old back 'til they've gone, we don't want t' be meetin' up wi' them again."

Whilst Dave was talking, behind his back, David had begun to shuffle around on bent legs, pursing his lips and scratching under his armpits with his hands and to avoid her uncle's gaze, Jenny turned away and stared at the pond above the weir. She couldn't stop grinning; *this* was now the funniest thing she had ever seen. She had never met anyone who could embarrass himself in so many ways; it was hard not to feel sorry for him. On the other hand, it was so funny and he *really* did bring it on himself.

As she gazed upstream, she let out a deep sigh and was suddenly taken by the stillness of the water in the pond and the contrast between that and the stream below, tumbling under the bridge. "Dave and John," she thought to herself; "calm and chaos." It was a clumsy analogy but it pleased her young mind and so she turned back to her uncle and whispered earnestly, "Uncle Dave, we can't stay here, they're bound to send re-enforcements."

"Aah, reet funny lass, tha knows what's wrong wi' everyone, don't tha?" At any other time Jenny might well have been stung into a reaction, but her uncle had provided her with far too much entertainment for his attack to hit home and she simply responded with the most saccharine *Thank you* she could muster.

"'''n' tha can gi' o'er wi' that nonsense 'n' all. Come on let's be 'avin' thee."

16

Over the bridge, now securely back in British hands, the path tracked back upstream, climbing the vertiginous incline created by the dam. It was there that they found the 'jetfighter': in the middle of a complicated looking arrangement of pipes was a steel overflow, almost a metre wide. The torrent of water rushing out of the end of the pipe created the noise that Jenny had mistaken for an aircraft engine. Dave stood back and puffed out his chest with pride.

"Nah den, proper job that; Sheffield steel fo' Yorkshire watter. Good fo' 'n 'undred years, that."

"Unless the rebels decide to blow it!" grinned Jenny.

Unable to generate a sufficiently peppery response, Dave turned away with only a sullen sneer left from his arsenal and wearily began the arduous ascent up the flight of steps cut into the hillside to the left of the overflow. After a couple of minutes of strenuous climbing, they reached a small, flattened area, marking the entrance to the steel pipe, which they crossed without daring to pause. To Jenny's consternation, this led to an even longer and steeper flight. As they climbed, she could hear her heart pounding in her ears and she began to feel feint. She hadn't eaten all day and the consequences of her early morning obduracy were becoming ominously apparent. Obviously, informing Dave was out of the question - there was simply no alternative; she'd just have to press on and do her very best not to let slip that she was nearing the end of her resources. The steps eventually turned into a path that ran alongside the overflow ladder from the reservoir, and with the worst of the climbing over, Jenny was able to distract herself by watching the water rampaging down towards the pipe. One final push and they were at the top. Dave took a minute to straighten himself up and then between breaths read proudly, "'Dale Dyke- a source of

Yorkshire *Watter*,'" from a large blue sign and Jenny found herself staring out across a huge expanse of black water.

"Cool," announced David, seemingly unaffected by the steepness of the climb.

"Tha would be if tha fell in there. Heh heh, what abaht that 'un, Jen lass? FELL IN THERE! … Eh, tha might see some sea 'osses, then tha'd not be only one wi' 'long face! Heh, heh!"

But Jenny was also running low on ammunition; the reservoir looked never-ending and when Dave told them that it was only the first of two they'd have to pass, she began to wonder if she could make it. She checked for signs of tiredness in the others. Dave was still puffing slightly and definitely seemed to be feeling the pace but David, who was busy skimming stones across the water, seemed totally unaffected by their exertions. Disregarding her uncle's provocation, she looked down once more at her trainers, which were covered in mud, the laces hardly distinguishable against the dark grey earth where the snow had melted. The mud had climbed up her jeans as far as her knees and her legs were freezing. "Can we go?" she asked mournfully.

"'s up wi' thee, lass? 't i'n't too much fo' thee is it?"

"No! I just thought we were going hill-walking, not standing around all day."

"Reet then," said Dave, trying to appear more enthusiastic than he actually felt, "let's 'ave them reservoirs."

To Jenny's surprise, they only walked a few hundred metres along the bank of the first reservoir before they climbed a style cut into the wall that ran parallel to the path. They were guided straight up the hill by two decrepit dry-stone walls, both of which must once have been above head height. Above these, another coniferous plantation loomed up on either side of the path, once again giving the whole place a gloomy and somewhat threatening feel. The path was steep and uneven and nobody spoke. Eventually they came to a crossroads with a more significant path, and without referring to the map or looking up,

Dave turned off to the right. The new path ran along the contour of the hill, but the relief at having turned away from the steep climb was quickly eroded by the bitterly cold wind that roared down the tunnel created by the path between the trees. Jenny trudged along behind Dave, her imagination alternating between being back home in the warm, tucking into one of Beryl's increasingly tempting pork dripping *breadcakes* or her and David being happily reunited with their parents.

After a couple of minutes, Dave pulled over to the side of the path and sat down heavily on a large fallen tree trunk. "Let's 'ave a blow," he suggested and despite the cold, nobody argued. He undid the straps of the Exped Expedition (£504.95) and with a sigh of relief let it slip to the ground. Jenny flopped down on a second trunk just beyond and behind Dave's and David sat down next to her. She examined The Boys again; Dave was blowing harder than ever and, in tune with their surroundings, for the first time seemed rather disgruntled with the whole business, whereas *David* still seemed as fresh as ever. Jenny was beginning to see a whole new side to her brother and was buoyed by the growing sense of admiration she felt for him. She took a sly glance at him, too quick to be seen but long enough to take in his spreading shoulders and long, sinewy limbs; he really was becoming quite handsome.

"Come 'ere thee!" Jenny was roused from her reverie by the animal-like growl of the voice. She turned to see a stocky pie-bald terrier hastening back towards a man in a green camouflage jacket. She'd never seen a man like this before. She immediately felt small and frightened. The man wasn't particularly tall, but he was *so* wide. His chest was so broad that he had to lean backwards to stop himself from falling and this made him narrow his eyes and swing his arms out to the sides. His close cropped hair and huge hands made him appear even more threatening. Jenny tried to look away but she couldn't. From her vantage point she could see the man was looking at, or, it almost appeared, through Dave, but when she followed the man's gaze she was amazed to see that her uncle had stood up and was staring back. More amazing still, Dave had grown bigger and deeper and his own head, too, was thrown back at an angle that made him squint. Jenny was terrified; they were going to fight, and, as the gap between them narrowed, she clung to David's arm. It was only because she had been staring at the two men so intently that she saw what happened next: when he was about three metres away, the man made the slightest downward inclination of his head towards Dave. Without altering the steel-like set of his face and jaw, Dave responded with a momentary upward flick of his head, causing his eyebrows to rise ever so slightly. The man narrowed his gait momentarily as he passed Dave, who was stood half way across the path. Once passed, he growled again at his dog and was gone. It was over in a few seconds but its effect on Jenny led her to rapidly reappraise her uncle's persona; for the first time since their arrival in Sheffield, she was genuinely grateful he was there.

"Come on then, *tha pair*, we can't be lakin' round 'ere all day; John 'n' Meg'll be wonderin' what's 'appened t' 'snap!" said Dave light-heartedly. Jenny thought she detected a slight tremor in his voice, but his face was quickly losing the harsh intensity with which he had stared down the man. "They'll not want t' be kept waitin' fo' Beryl's parkin. Any roads, it's too parky t' be 'angin' 'round 'ere. … Eh, 'parky parkin' – what about that 'un, Davy lad?" But for once Dave's voice remained disquietingly monotone. "Any roads, any 'illsman worth 'is salt'll tell thee abaht dangers o' 'ypochondria, so let's crack on!" Jenny smiled benignly at her uncle's latest malaprop and let out a sigh of relief, whilst Dave swung the Exped Expedition (£504.95) briskly up onto his shoulders and, leaving the straps to their own devices, strode out along the path. The children fell in quickly behind, neither of them objecting to the brisk pace he was setting towards the edge of the wood and the open spaces beyond. Nobody spoke and nobody looked back.

As the edge of the wood approached, the darkness began to lift and so did their spirits. They began to relax. They could see the top of a large building framed between the last two trees. It was half-hidden by the hill immediately in front of them, but Jenny could see enough of it to recognise it as Boots' Folly. "Yeah, and this must be Dave's folly." Jenny smiled at her joke, cheered by thought that they were leaving the wood and the man behind and that they couldn't be that far from Hathersage now. They climbed a set of stone steps topped with a wooden style over yet another dry-stone wall and gratefully stepped out into open ground. In reality, the cloud base would remain low for the rest of the day but it seemed as though the heavy skies were lifting, and as their mood followed suit, so conversation gradually returned.

They were walking across an open hillside two hundred metres or so above the southern edge of the reservoir. The blackness of the lake, contrasting with the white hills and grey sky made an impressive sight. By the time they came to the next style, Dave felt confident enough to halt astride the top bar and reconnect the straps on the Exped Expedition (£504.95). Despite their renewed resistance, he filled his lungs and breathed out dramatically. "Big country, this, Jen lass. Tha'll not see a sight better than this anywhere in 'country." It didn't seem right to argue.

Shortly after climbing this latest stile, the path split in two, with no clear sign as to which direction they should take.

"What's tha reckon then, Davey lad?"

David gave an unconcerned shrug of his shoulders. Now they were clear of the plantation, he had far more pressing matters on his mind, "Can't we stop for something to eat?"

"Out 'ere? Tha's got t' be kiddin', Davey lad!" Dave's bravado was clearly back in place, as to Jenny's dismay he rapidly ascended to his customarily excruciating pitch. "Weather could close in any minute, 'n' 'fore tha knows it, we'd be lost in no time. … 'n' it'll not be *me* mitherin' Mountain Rescue."

"But there's a pub or something just over there," replied David, abandoning his accent and pointing out the famous Strines Inn on the far side of the valley.

"Come on, Davey lad, think on! If 'mist comes down, we wouldn't know which way t' turn. Then what would we do – 'ask Meg'?" Even in the heat of battle, Dave took a second to enjoy his little victory. But only a second – with the mutual threat behind them, hostilities between niece and uncle were free to resume.

"Isn't that why we brought a compass?" David asked innocently

"Eh, don't *tha* start gettin' cocky; I've enough on wi' Little Miss Know All 'ere!"

"What have I done? It wasn't me who threw his stupid compass at a bus shelter. Pity it wasn't misty down there – you might have missed!"

"Can't tha just gi' o'er wi' snapin' fo' one minute!" growled Dave, the final few remnants of his conciliatory disposition skiddling away at the recollection of his earlier misadventures. "Just fo' once … *just* fo' once, let's see if we can learn *tha pair* o' cocky so 'n' soes summat useful we can tell thee Mam 'n' Dad. … Look, we need t' sort out these 'ere tracks, so just watch 'n' learn … *watch* 'n' learn!"

Dave crouched down and carefully brushed the thin layer of snow away from the path. "… Interestin', *very* interestin'."

"What is it?" asked David eagerly, hoping his uncle's discovery would lead them in the direction of sustenance.

Dave picked up a small twig and studied it carefully. He held it to his nose and sniffed, pondered for a moment and then dropped it to the floor. He raised his head and peered down the two paths, stroking his chin thoughtfully. Suddenly he jumped up. “This way,” he announced confidently.

“How do you know?” asked David.

Dave nodded wisely, “There’s some things takes a lifetime o’ learnin’, young un.”

“You said we should always use the map,” interrupted Jenny.

Dave smiled serenely, “Sometimes, just sometimes, lass, tha ‘as t’ see beyond ‘map.”

Jenny furrowed her brow suspiciously but Dave only grinned and raised his eyebrows in response and they set off on the higher path, leading them further up the hill, away from the reservoir. After fifty metres or so, David spotted a yellow way-marker on a gatepost beside the lower path and they all scuttled back down the hill to where they should have been walking all along.

“Glad tha spotted that one,” said Dave bashfully, “always good t’ keep young ‘uns on their toes.”

“Well, *there are some things that take a lifetime of learning,*” teased Jenny, failing to keep the smirk off her face.

They trudged on again. Her latest victory could only distract Jenny from the chill of the wind, the ache in her stomach and the torment of her ice-cold feet for so long, but at least every step took them further away from the woods and the nodding man whom she’d found so frightening. After another five minutes walking, Jenny was amazed to see a picnic table. “How could *anyone* ever think of stopping to eat in a such bleak place?” she wondered, little knowing all that would occur here in the years that followed. Today, the invitation to stop seemed completely nonsensical, but within a couple of months the table would offer a welcome break for hot, weary ramblers whilst taking in one of the most enticing views in the county. All it did for Jenny was make her wish she were back home with her parents. But she wasn't, so she'd better make the best of it and, at all costs, not to let her uncle know just how cold, hungry and tired she was.

The three intrepid travellers continued along the rising path above the reservoir for another half mile or so, passing through a series of ancient gateways, each one guarded by a pair of increasingly gnarled and withered gateposts. Eventually, they came to a wall without any gate, but after a couple of minutes searching, David spied the small yellow way-marker, nailed to a stone post on one side of a narrow gap about fifty centimetres wide. The post on the opposite side was leaning away precariously from the gap, allowing walkers a fraction more room to push their bodies through. Nevertheless, as David and Jenny led the way through, they had to twist themselves sideways to avoid the posts' embrace.

"Do you need any help Uncle Dave?" asked Jenny, turning to watch her uncle.

"Don't start, lass. I know I've always been well-covered, but I fit through 'ere same as thee."

"I didn't mean anything."

"I knows exactly what tha meant 'n' tha needs t' show a bit more respect."

Jenny shrugged. Dave *was* overweight, but not massively so and she only thought that the rucksack might be too wide for the gap but, if that's how he wanted to be, he could please himself. She was too cold to care.

Dave strode purposefully up to the gap and pushed his right leg through easily but as his body followed he felt the gap narrowing quickly. He pressed forward, hoping the children wouldn't notice; perhaps with a little encouragement the leaning post might give way and allow him to squeeze through. But this particular post had felt the weight of a thousand walkers and had finally had enough of giving way. This time it held fast and Dave was now trapped in its grip. He tried to reverse but the post refused to release him. He tried lifting himself up but his rucksack scraped painfully on the two pillars until he was wedged even tighter, only able to reach the ground on his tiptoes. He reached behind and tried to twist the rucksack free but in doing so he only managed to trap his hand between it and the unyielding pillar. It was as if he were playing some wild game of Twister. Despite the cold, he started to sweat but the more he twisted and tugged, the tighter the pillars held him in their embrace. He breathed in; nothing shifted, he breathed out; same result. He willed himself thin, he threatened the pillars under his breathe, but nothing could set him free. His overstretched calves were beginning to burn and the sweat was forming little rills of its own inside his Rab Neutrino. It was time for desperate measures. "Davey," he barked, "I'm fed up o' carrying this rucksack. Tha's done *nowt* t'day; it's time tha pulled thee weight. Come up 'ere 'n 'elp us off wi' it!"

David plodded back obediently, vaulted casually over the wall and lifted the Exped Expedition (£504.95) easily from his uncle's shoulders. Freed of his burden, Dave squeezed gratefully through the gap, twisting his head from side to side as if to release the tension from his shoulders. He turned round with a sly grin, expecting to see his nephew suffer the same fate as he had. But David was smarter than his uncle and he twisted the rucksack round on its straps and eased it through the gap sideways before squeezing through himself. He threw the heavy pack up effortlessly onto his shoulders and started off along the path without a backwards thought. Then, in a moment of inspiration, he turned back through 180 degrees, quickly double-checked he was out of his uncle's reach and as he continued walking backwards shouted, "Hey, Uncle Dave, is that t' leaning post o' t' pizza-eaters? Heh, heh, what abaht that one, Jenny lass? T' LEANING POST OF PIZZA EATERS!" before spinning effortlessly back round to run off up the hill. Dave turned to Jenny who had watched the whole episode in gleeful silence.

"'n' tha can wipe 'daft grin off tha face 'n' all."

Finally cresting the ridge, the path now led them down and across a small, steep-sided valley, where a lonely sign told them that they were entering Hoyle's Wood, an ancient woodland. This would not have particularly interested Jenny at any time, but in the cold and the mud, it held no appeal whatsoever. As they crossed the stream at the bottom of the valley, she looked up to see that Boot's Folly had disappeared and she wished that she could do the same.

The far side of the valley had been incorporated into the grassy embankment buttressing the next dam wall and Jenny, who was unaware of this, was surprised to hear the same jet engine noise she had heard whilst Dave had been embarrassing himself in front of the Red Coats. She allowed herself a smile. "Don't bother!" she warned, just as her uncle lifted his hand to his eyes to scan the horizon. Dave frowned and her smile returned - a brief break in the clouds on an increasingly gloomy day.

They walked on in silence, Jenny leading the way along the half-mud, half-ice path and as it rose, so the view over Dale Dyke Reservoir opened up behind them. Jenny could see the Red Coats walking along the bottom of the dam wall. They were heading towards the road on the far side of the reservoir, where a solitary car was waiting. Jenny looked longingly after them. She was feeling severely sorry for herself and, unable to ignore her stomach's protests, she couldn't help trying to calculate again how much further they'd have to walk before they met up with John and could finally placate their grumbling stomachs. Incredibly, she found herself wishing she'd paid more attention to Dave's orientation briefing the previous evening and, shaking her head in disbelief, she allowed herself a sour grimace at the irony of it all.

"Typical!" came Dave's voice from behind. Jenny turned round wearily to see her uncle 'tutting' at the Red Coats. "Not worth botherin'!"

Jenny hadn't the energy to comment.

"Any roads …" he continued to no one in particular, "only 'alf-way 'n' already jacked it in; probably takin' gear back t' Market."

Jenny walked on for a couple more strides and then stopped dead in her tracks. "Did you say 'half-way'?"

"Why, lass, tha's never tired already?"

Jenny looked down at her ruined trainers and sodden jeans. She weighed up the ache creeping up the back of her legs and the growing cramp in her stomach. She was colder, hungrier and more tired than she could ever remember and had seriously had enough. "No," she replied lightly, "I just thought we were doing a long walk, that's all."

With perfect timing, for Jenny was on the verge of tears, David came bounding up, seemingly unaffected by the weight of the Exped Expedition (£504.95). "Uncle Dave, you can see The Doctors' house again." His uncle and sister turned back and stared at the furthest hill beyond the reservoirs. David was right; there was the pylon and just to the left of it was a thin curl of smoke rising from The Doctors' chimney.

Jenny imagined the two of them, sat warming their feet in front of the fire after their ride. Now she'd started, she couldn't stop: the horses would be brushed down and enjoying a well-earned feed, the tack would be cleaned and polished and the Female Doctor would have made a thick, sugary fruitcake to go with their steaming tea, waiting in two elegant bone china cups, whilst the deep, resonant ticking of the grandfather clock conspired with the crimson glow of the fire, encouraging them to rest their eyes. She couldn't help letting out a long, mournful sigh. It didn't help and she quickly recovered herself, unwilling to let her uncle's teasing add to her woes.

But for once, Jenny had mistaken her uncle's intentions. In fact Dave wasn't paying *any* attention to his niece and had only the vaguest inkling of how much she was suffering. Instead, he'd made David kneel down on the frozen ground and was ferreting around in the Exped Expedition (£504.95). "'ere we go," he announced triumphantly, proudly displaying a pair of Viking Peregrine 10 x 42 ED Binoculars (£349.00) - in spite of everything, Jenny couldn't help smiling.

"Nah den, let's 'ave a proper butcher's." Dave removed his El Alamo and with great care and ceremony hung the strap of the binoculars round his neck, before replacing the revered Stetson. He then proceeded to give them a running commentary on everything that was happening on their hill.

Truth be told, nothing much *was* happening; the horses *were* all inside, the kestrel was back on her nest and, much to his frustration, his own house was just out of sight. Even so, he still insisted on giving them a field-by-field report.

"Can I have a look, Uncle Dave?" asked David.

"Eh, this i'n't cheap tack, lad, if tha wants t' use 'em, I'll 'ave t' show thee 'ropes."

Jenny shuddered with the cold. "Oh come on!" she moaned.

"'old thee 'osses, lass. … Where's fire? It'll not take long, 'n' it's good fo' 'lad t' learn summat useful for a change. Nah den, where's 'map, so tha can see what tha's gawpin' at?"

Jenny stomped her feet in an attempt to bring back some feeling, but the ground beneath her was sodden with melting snow and she only succeeded in forcing the pool of muddy water that had surrounded her over the top of her trainers. Her feet were so cold she didn't feel a thing, but the dark stain creeping up her socks perfectly summed up her mood.

Dave and David hadn't noticed. David was using all his powers of self-control not to collapse with laughter, whilst Dave was absorbed in a titanic struggle between himself, the binoculars and the strap of the map case: he had tried to lift the map case over his head but it had become entwined with the straps of the binoculars and, as his uncle tugged and turned, David began to fear that he might strangle himself.

"Do you need some help Uncle Dave?"

"Course not! They just make 'straps on these cases too short."

In exasperation, Dave gave an enormous tug on the map case but instead of lifting it over his head as he intended, there was a loud tearing sound and it flew out of his hand, landing in the puddle next to Jenny. Instinctively, she had followed its flight but out of the corner of her eye, she was still able to catch sight of her uncle wobbling on one leg for what seemed an age, before toppling over face-first into a deep, ice encrusted snowdrift.

For the third time today, Dave ran his tongue around the inside of his mouth and groaned out loud at the unfairness of life. He rolled over, leaving a neat snow angel in the drift, with a small indentation, about the size of a pair of Viking Peregrine ED 10 x 42 binoculars, in the middle. By now, Jenny knew what to expect and so she bit hard on her lip and tried to stop her shoulders from rocking whilst Dave sat forlornly in the snow, slowly unwinding the binoculars from around his neck and placing them carefully on the ground beside him.

"If tha'd done summat useful t'day, 'n' took some responsibility fo' 'map, we'd not keep 'avin' these accidents," he snarled.

Jenny felt another shudder of cold. Her aching body and sense of desolation finally pushed her past the point of caring. She stopped laughing and looked straight at her uncle. "Not this again; you're such a pathetic show-off, always trying to impress us with your fancy gear. We just think you're a sad wannabee, don't we David?"

David looked nervously at the ground but said nothing.

"If you weren't always so desperate to impress us, you wouldn't keep having these *accidents*." She almost spat the word at him. "You took the map off us, remember! Why don't you stop picking on us and sort out your own mess?"

For a moment Dave looked shell-shocked and then the Strives' temper took over: "Tha *ungrateful* little so 'n' soes; I only 'ad *tha pair* as a favour fo' thee mam. This were me first weekend off in ages 'n' I've ended up wastin' it on a couple o' mardy ungrateful so 'n' soes, who've done nowt but look down their stuck up noses at me. 'Showin' off,'! 'Showin' off'!! I'll gi' thee 'Showin' off'. Come on!" With that he jumped to his feet and stormed off up the hill. He'd carried these two for long enough and it was high time he showed them what a true 'illsman could do. 'Showing off'! She was about to find out what *showing off* was!!

David lifted his eyes and looked across at Jenny. She immediately turned away. Before today, she would have met his gaze with an older sister's superiority and told him not to involve himself in things he didn't understand, but right now she couldn't bear to look at him. She was supposed to be taking of him but, ever since he had first taken the map in the woods above Highfield, it had felt the other way round. "Come on," she sighed dejectedly, "it can't be that far now." David paused for a moment, then calmly went over to where Dave had been sitting, picked up the Viking Peregrines and followed on in silence.

The path ran across the hillside now and Jenny was finding it increasingly difficult to keep her footing in the ice and mud.

They crossed another stream and then changed directions, heading directly up the slope. Dave was marching out, eyes fixed to the front and Jenny was struggling to close the gap as David strode up easily alongside her.

"Are you alright?" he asked.

"Don't worry about *me*;" she replied through clenched teeth, "I'm not going to be beaten by *him* today."

"Is it a race, then?"

"Oh yes, that's exactly what it is and there's no way that that ridiculous, overweight bully is going to beat me."

"But he won't leave us behind, will he?" asked David in a concerned voice.

Jenny stopped and fought for breath. "You're right," she smiled, "even he wouldn't be that cruel." She relaxed a little and looked kindly at her brother. Dave might be the world's greatest show off but he was still their uncle; he wasn't about to leave them in the middle of nowhere and anyway, he'd be far too scared of their mother to do anything that would really harm them. "Don't worry," she said, stroking him on the shoulder, "it's just a family row."

"I hate family rows; people always end up leaving."

Jenny swallowed hard and smiled again at her brother, "Really … don't worry; nobody's leaving. Come on, race you to the top."

Up ahead, Dave was also re-evaluating the situation. He'd been badly stung by Jenny's latest outburst and had intended to walk them into the ground as punishment but as he strode away from them, he'd suddenly remembered his father's words; "Just enough," he said out loud, "just enough t' let 'em know." When he reached a turn in the path, he slowed and waited. The children must have been running because when he turned round David was only a few paces behind him and Jenny about the same distance back again. He'd waited in front of a particularly withered gatepost and had his conciliatory joke at the ready – it was his way of showing them they were forgiven. "Nah den, 'ave a look at this old lad; nah 'e shoulda kept 'is coat done up." Jenny didn't stop. She cocked her head to one side, treated him to her most sarcastic smile and strode off up the hill.

"'old up, lass, don't take on, I've summat t' show thee in a minute," shouted Dave, running after her. He caught up with her just as they were passing through the next set of gateposts. "Climb up 'ere 'n' gi' this a *coat* o' lookin' at. Heh, heh! COAT O' LOOKIN' AT! - What abaht that 'un, Davey lad? *COAT* O' LOOKIN' AT!"

The lefthand gatepost was set back into the hill, its base about seventy centimetres higher than the path. "Tha sees that hole; 'ave a butcher's through that, 'n' tha'll see 'best view in Yorkshire."

"This better not be one of your stupid jokes."

"Just 'ave a butcher's 'n' stop mitherin' abaht everythin'!"

Jenny wavered for a moment and then her curiosity won her over. As a child, her maternal grandfather had taken her to a seemingly non-descript gate in an ancient wall in the hills above Rome. Through its keyhole, he'd shown her the most wonderful view of St Peter's far below. Such a secret had been irresistible to someone who loved to know what others didn't; perhaps this was something similar. So, she pulled herself up to the post, wrapped her arms around it and looked through the rectangular hole cut decades before as a rebate for the hinges. She stared hard, and, as her focus adjusted, she was treated to the wildest, most beautiful view of the shoreline around Dale Dyke Reservoir. It was truly magical. But before she could fully appreciate it, a large red mouth appeared over the other side of the rebate and blew a hot, sweaty raspberry into her eye.

"Oh, for goodness sake!! Are you ever going to grow up?"

"Told thee we were comin' out fo' a blow. COMIN'OUT FO' A BLOW!! Heh, heh! ... Aah dear. ... What's tha think o' that then, Davey lad?" gasped Dave, struggling to breathe against the laughter. He let out a deep sigh of contentment. “I knew tha’d be impressed. Even John don’t know that ‘un. Come on then, lass, jump down, we ‘a’n’t got all day.”

Furious, Jenny held on to the gatepost with one hand and carefully slid back down the bank; there was no way she was going to let herself fall. As she hit the ground she felt her feet sink through the melting snow and back into the mud below and the tears began to well up in her eyes once more.

“Come on then, I’m abaht ready fo’ me snap,” said Dave briskly, in an attempt to generate the necessary enthusiasm for the rest of the hill. Without looking back, he set off again, although this time at a more measured pace.

Jenny tried to twist her feet out of the mud but they were stuck fast. She quickly ran out of patience and pulled her left foot sharply upwards. It slipped out of its trainer and she started to topple backwards, but just as she prepared to suffer the same fate that had so farcically befallen her uncle, she felt a strong pair of arms come to her rescue. For one brief moment, she thought it was her father. Of course, it wasn’t but it *was* the next best thing; David’s grinning face appeared over her shoulder and as he eased her back to an upright position, he chuckled, “Now then, t’ old Jen, lass, we can’t have thee sitting down on t’ job,” in his finest Yorkshire.

Jenny span round to check that her uncle wasn’t looking and then laughed out loud. “Right,” she said in mock defiance, “it’s time to show t’ good old Uncle Dave what a proper ‘ills*woman* can do.”

“Well, tha’ll need tha’s shoe first.” David balanced Jenny on one leg, lifted her hand onto his shoulder and leaned over to pull the shoe out of the mud. He brushed off the worst and passed it over.

“Thanks bro.” She pulled it on and set off after Dave.

It only took a few strides for her to remember how tired she was. The melting snow was turning the path into a muddy stream, which was now at its steepest. Jenny was reduced to clambering on her hands and knees, pulling herself up on the tufts of marsh grass breaking through the snow. Her hands were freezing, but in contrast her legs felt as if they were on fire. Even so, there was no way she was stopping. Eventually the path flattened out and although she now had to deal with the added problem of large areas of bog blocking her way, she felt her momentum pick up. Up ahead was a neatly laid dry-stone wall and she was determined to reach it without stopping. She made herself look down at the path and concentrate on where she was stepping. Several times she sank above her ankles but she found that by curling up her freezing toes she could grip her trainers much more firmly and, although her heels lifted out with every step, she didn't lose them again.

After another five minutes of increasingly torturous progress, she finally found herself on firmer ground and, looking up for the first time, was surprised to see the wall just in front of her. Another ten steps and she was there. She was gasping for air and, despite the freezing wind, her back was damp with sweat. She crouched down and took the chance to recover her breath, before turning her back to the wall and sliding down onto her haunches.

The respite from the wind allowed her breathing to slow and as she looked back down the path, she saw the Red Coats' car pulling out onto the road. She could feel her body temperature beginning to fall and in search of greater protection let herself slide further down the wall until she was sat on the icy ground. But now that she was stationary, the cold, hunger and tiredness soon returned, more inimical than ever, and she pulled her legs up tight to her chest and bit hard on her lip. She felt a sob rise up in her chest, but just at that moment David arrived once more and, notwithstanding the burden of the Exped's payload, sat down easily beside her in his usual lackadaisical fashion. Trying not to let him see the tears in her eyes, she sucked in her chest and leant her head on his shoulder.

“Look, you can see Uncle Dave’s from here.”

Jenny looked up; her brother was right again. She stared at the tiny speck on the distant hill. “Half- way!” she said out loud. “That means we’re getting closer with every step.”

Hoping David wasn’t looking, she reached down and slowly wrapped the laces of her trainer around her freezing fingers and pulled them towards her. Grey sludge oozed out as the trainer reluctantly closed. Fighting against the numbness, she carefully tied the sodden laces into a knot and then looping the two ends through her fingers, tied a second, pulling on them as hard as she could. She groaned as the pressure on the laces added their own filthy stream of water to the growing puddle around her. The jets of pain shooting through her fingers made her wince and instinctively she half-cupped her hands and held them up to her lips, blowing on them hard before clenching and unclenching them several times. Then, before the numbness had chance to return, she puffed out her cheeks and set about the other lace as quickly as possible.

“Going somewhere, our sis?” asked David with a grin.

“Aye, lad I’m off to meet t’old man Boot and ‘n’ that big lummox in’t gonna beat *me* t’ top.” Jenny pulled herself resolutely to her feet. Looking up, the path wound up and round the hill above the second reservoir and she could see Dave about two hundred metres in front of her. He was moving slowly and stopping every few strides. “Right then, t’old Uncle Dave,” she said, sticking out her chin, “you’re mine!”

She set off as fast as she could, convinced that she could still catch her uncle. But the going here was harder than ever. It felt as though with every step her feet slipped back to more or less where they’d come from, and to make one metre’s progress she had to walk ten. Meanwhile, the stream of half- frozen mud running down the path turned her fingers blue as she clung desperately to the long, wiry tufts of grass, trying to gain some momentum. ‘Mush’ she named her new adversary - a cross between mud and slush. "Well I don't think *mush* of you!" she responded sourly to its unwelcome contribution to the day's trials.

Her whole world now shrunk to the square metre or so of ground directly in front of her. She hardly noticed the return of the lightly falling snow, or even the roar of the water tumbling down the staircase to her right. She ignored the cold and the damp, the mud and the ice; she dismissed her uncle's bullying out of hand, she even forgot her loneliness and anxiety about their parents. She didn't look back to her brother or forward to her uncle; she looked at the ground in front of her and walked, jumped, climbed, stumbled, fell, rose, pulled, crawled, tugged and slogged her way up the hill.

A few minutes later, she'd caught Dave. He didn't speak and she barely acknowledged him as she passed by, but a momentary lift of her head showed her that Boot's Folly was back in view and the hill was almost done. She pressed on, determined that her uncle wouldn't catch her again. She glared with contempt at the sign inviting her to wander around the site of the Folly, as an 'Area of Outstanding Natural Beauty'. Then, much to her surprise, the ground in front of her suddenly turned green; she was walking on grass. The slope flattened out and she lifted her head. There, about a hundred metres in front of her was Boot's Folly. She accelerated again, terrified that Dave might catch her in the final straight. She was almost running. The wind blasted against her face, cooling her glowing cheeks; her socks and trainers were soddened and her legs were frozen; she couldn't feel her toes or her fingers and her best jeans were probably ruined, but she didn't care. She was at the top and she was first. She walked up to the tower and smiled as she came under its shelter from the wind. She turned and looked back down the hill, David was just stepping onto the grass and Dave was nowhere to be seen.

"… Piece of cake, my Yorkshire Puddings."

17

Looking back, the valley stretched out for seven miles towards Highfield. The cloud-covered sky and snow-covered land seemed to have merged into one, broken only by the slate-black ribbons of the reservoirs, liquorice shoelaces of the roads and pencil lines of the dry-stone walls. The wind howled around Boot's Folly and chased away the snow round about and, for the first time in her young life, Jenny was able to recognise the exhilaration that came from acknowledging something greater than herself. The anxieties that had burdened her for so long tumbled away down the hill after the snow and at that moment she could not have worried about her parents if she had wanted to. The power and beauty of this place assaulted her heart and she willingly surrendered to them both. She breathed in the cold air, puffed out her chest and sent a stream of smoke spiralling across the hill on the wind. Suddenly she felt wild and untamed as though she were reconnecting with some long-hidden, secret part of herself that she had forgotten existed: she was a child again. She turned back to the folly and reached out to drag her glowing finger ends across its rough stone walls and let her head fall back to look up into the snow-filled sky. Allowing her hand to fall away from the wall, but still looking up, she stretched out her arms and began to spin, letting out a squeal of delight.

Without her noticing, David had arrived at her side and stood watching her curiously. "Alright?"

"Fine, *Davey lad,* just fine. Where's t'old Uncle Dave?"

"He stopped for a breather; he's fighting off the pain from his wounds and has to take it steady to stop them opening up. … What's inside?"

They wandered round to the windward side of the Folly and found an unguarded doorway. There was little to see of the original interior other than the remains of a staircase and a few gnawed floor joists, which must once have supported an upper storey. Below these, the thick, pungent mud that covered the floor displayed hundreds of footprints from the livestock that had taken shelter there over the years, and combined with the lack of light, the damp, stagnant atmosphere gave the whole place a gloomy, somewhat defeated air. In fact, the only welcoming feature about the inside of the tower was the respite it offered from the wind. "Oh well," said Jenny lightly, "I'm sure the old Boot meant well!"

They went back outside just in time to meet Dave as he reached the base of the Folly. He was limping and very muddy and, above all, furious with them for reaching the top before him, but he was simply too tired to mount a decisive attack and had to settle for a slightly breathless, "What 'ave I've told *tha pair* abaht chargin' off?" But Jenny and David could see that his heart wasn't in it.

"Which way now then, oh Great Leader?" teased Jenny. "We don't want to keep John and Meg waiting."

"No Sir, Hathersage here we come, Sir!" shouted David enthusiastically, and without looking back, the two younger Strives strode out side by side away from the Folly. Dave desperately needed a rest but couldn't admit to either the children or himself that they were beating him. "Back t' 'path 'n' straight on t' road," he sighed, reluctantly turning away from the protection of Boot's philanthropy.

Eager to keep up their spirits, Jenny and David stretched out towards the path, which quickly led them away from the Folly's flat, open surroundings and breath-taking views back towards the reservoirs, before guiding them down towards a clutch of half-hidden buildings.

Suddenly Jenny halted. "You go on ahead," she said quietly, and somehow sensing his sister's need for solitude, David silently complied. Jenny waited for a few seconds and then turned and looked back towards the folly. It took her a few seconds more to locate the resonance, but then it came to her: here too was loneliness, but of a completely different iteration to her own; not cowed and defeated, but proud and defiant. Here was loneliness - no, not 'loneliness' - *aloneness,* that was it - here was *aloneness,* for whom the remorseless, unpredictable assault of life, here on this barren outcrop had always been its intended destination. The Folly was meant to be here, on its own; exposed to the elements; standing tall - a guide to fellow travellers. No primal element or caprice of nature could shake what had been built *here.* Its *aloneness,* its magnificent, unbending isolation, paid heed to only by the wild forces that continually beset it, made it what it was. It had stood unmoved for a hundred years and would continue to do so for a thousand more. Through it all, it had held fast … and so would she. … It would be alright. "Thank you," she whispered, "more than you'll ever know - I hope we meet again." And with the meekest of smiles she turned again to re-join her brother along the path.

In keeping with that proud tradition of teenage boys across the millennia, David had neither capacity nor inclination for deep reflection, but by some mysterious, undiagnosed intuition he'd gleaned that Jenny would soon be seeking out his company once more, and so had deliberately slow-paced along the path until, within a minute, she was back by his side.

"Are you hungry?" he groaned, proving Professor Maslow's point. "I'm starving. How long do you think it will be before we see John?"

"Not too long now, especially if we keep up the pace and don't let Uncle Dave have any more *accidents*."

David grinned at his sister and his spirts soon brightened further when, after a few hundred metres, he spied the next yellow way-marker leading into what looked like a rather stately, if somewhat neglected, garden. "Here we go," he shouted and headed off towards the sign.

Dave, still some distance behind, didn't follow. "That's never reet!" he shouted across the hillside. "Look at 'tracks; we've t' 'ead ov'r t' 'gate."

"But the sign says this way."

Dave pounced at the opportunity to restore some of his lost authority. "'as tha not listened t' owt I've been sayin'? … *Tha pair* can trust them things if tha wants *or* tha could listen t' someone wi' just a little bit more experience."

To Jenny, the rise and fall of this latest example of her uncle's *hauteur,* along with its deliberate deceleration, proved even more irksome than the pitch of his most excruciating squeal and with Boot's Folly behind her, she simply couldn't let it pass. "And how's that gone up to now?" she mocked. "I'm afraid I've lost count of the number of *accidents* we've had. … Can you remember, David?"

And that was the moment, from the many, many alternatives, when Dave's humiliation at being beaten so badly to the Folly; his genuine sadness at the damage to his newly-treasured possessions; the pain in every extremity of his battered and bruised body and, most of all, the never-ending provocation of his ungrateful niece and nephew finally combined to push him way past the point of caring; he simply couldn't believe his ears. It was time to sort this once and for all and he strode furiously over to his niece, throwing out his chest as he did so. But as he approached, Jenny shrank back at the memory of her uncle's confrontation with the terrifying man from the plantation.

The look on her face stopped him in his tracks. … He'd had absolutely no intention of actually harming her and was instantly shaken to the core by the idea that she might have thought so. He took a step back. "Look, let's all calm down a minute." He held out his hands in supplication. "There's no need for a bull ‘n’ cow, Jen lass. I’m sure this way’s ‘reet ‘un; it’s obvious from ‘tracks that’s ‘way most folks ‘ave been. Least ways, why don’t tha just come ov’r ‘ ‘n’ see fo’ theesens? Not take two tick.”

“*You* go that way if you want - *we’re* following the signs.”

Dave found himself powerless in the face of his niece’s intransigence. He had no idea how things had escalated so quickly and could think of nothing else but how to retreat without receiving or inflicting further injury.

“Well I’m goin’ this way. *Tha pair* can do what tha wants, tha’s clearly not gonna listen t’ owt I’ve got t’ say,” was the best he could manage. And with that he plodded off towards the gate, not daring to look back, hoping against experience that this time he would be proven right and that his niece’s disquiet would soon pass.

In truth, Jenny *had* been alarmed, but only very briefly; she knew her uncle would never think of hurting either of them … not *really*. But she was also cunning enough to realise the advantages of allowing *him* to believe that she thought he might, one of which was a temporary respite from his constant bullying - at least for a little while. So seizing the moment, she marched off back to where she’d just come from, as to her immense satisfaction, David silently fell in behind.

The yellow way-marker directed the children towards a kissing gate, through which Jenny merrily led the way. David eased off the Exped Expedition (£504.95) and passed it over and then squeezed through himself. Jenny was amazed at the reminder of the rucksack’s weight and readily acknowledged the achievement of her young brother in carrying it up the hill to Boot’s Folly. “Wow, this weighs a ton!” she gasped. David smiled bashfully, but couldn’t resist swinging the pack back up onto his shoulders with an extra flourish, before jiggling it on his hips and fastening its straps.

The kissing gate led almost immediately to a stile, which in turn led them to a narrow, laurel-lined path. The shrubs on either side had grown so tall as to almost form a tunnel, allowing the children further respite from the wind. After thirty or so metres, the path took a sudden turn to the left, avoiding a sign inscribed 'Notice. Private Property. Keep Out'.

"Nice and friendly!" said Jenny.

"Why does it say, 'Notice?'" asked David, grinning mischievously. "Is that so we know what it is?"

The path skirted the garden to the right, where the laurel gave way to rhododendron, but on the left the ground was clear. Suddenly a squirrel jumped out in front of them and scurried along the path until it found a suitable tree in which to take refuge. Jenny started and David laughed. They were in fine spirits now.

"There should be a sign saying, 'This is a tree – squirrels keep out!'" scoffed David.

"This is a path," added Jenny.

"This is a fence."

"This is a hedge."

"This is a grumpy uncle."

"Where?"

"Oh no, he's gone the wrong way!"

Jenny and David skiddled and scuffed along their way as only brothers and sisters can, whilst the path turned again, completing a u-shaped detour around the garden. They emerged from the undergrowth onto a long drive leading to an elegant Georgian villa, flanked by its own tennis court. Where the path met the drive, it passed between two small posts, topped off with what looked like First World War German army helmets. "Oh no," cried David in mock horror, "not another attack, now it's the Germans!"

"But this time only very small ones."

"Perhaps they're sending miniature spies to keep an eye on us."

"This is a tiny German spy …"

"… disguised as a garden gnome."

Guided by yet another friendly way-marker, they ambled side by side down the drive away from the villa. David had grabbed a handful of ammunition and was keeping a wary eye out for diminutive German spies masquerading as garden gnomes in the undergrowth, whilst, smiling benignly, Jenny took note of the hundreds of daffodils scattered along the grass verge beginning their own arduous journeys. "I bet this is lovely in springtime," she mused, "I wonder if we'll ever come back," but before she could answer, her daydreaming was cut short by a pair of imposing iron gates marking the end of the drive, flanked by two equally forbidding, ornately carved, gritstone gateposts.

"It's Lord of the Rings!" said David excitedly. "This is Mordor … guarded by tiny German spies."

Having checked again for ambushes, they climbed the small flight of stone steps to the right of the gates and, for the first time in over an hour, found themselves on an asphalt road. They were just in time to see Dave emerging from a field about two hundred metres to their left. His limp was more pronounced than ever. He looked more weary and drawn than ever and for the first time Jenny comprehended that age and staying power were on *their* side. When he eventually caught up with them, he could only grunt and they fell in quietly behind. But their high spirits persisted and when they passed a sheep stood on top of a haystack with a long wisp of hay hanging down from its mouth, David leaned towards his sister and whispered, "This is Gandalf." Jenny stifled a giggle and raised her eyebrows mischievously at her brother and when the road turned to the right, offering them a view back towards the house and its garden, she couldn't resist adding, "And this is the Shire." A few seconds later Boot's Folly reappeared, allowing David to counter with, "And this is the tower, built by tiny German spies, wearing enormous … *boots*!"

On they went, brother and sister, side by side behind their uncle, the two of them gleefully mixing jokes about miniature German spies, Lord of the Rings and *This is ...* in that peculiar way children find irresistible and adults impenetrable. Dave, knowing nothing of Tolkien and the other jokes, and still deeply out of sorts, soon tired of being left out. “Reet then, *tha pair*; if tha could be bothered t’ look at ‘map tha’d see we’ve come t’ crease.”

“What?”

Dave tutted. “The map tha’s been ‘oggin’ since that nonsense back there. No kiddin’, where would *tha pair* be in wi’out me? … I’ll tell thee now, tha’d be in a reet tangle. Look at it then! It’s time t’ turn it ov’r.”

It never occurred to the children to ask how Dave knew this, but when they turned the map case upside down they could see what he meant. Dave squatted down by the side of the road and, for the first time since they’d left Hoyle’s Wood, the sly grin returned to his face; he knew how hard it was to handle such a large map on this windy ridge, in fact his first map had been ruined when he’d tried it the previous Sunday. It would be a welcome distraction to watch his inexperienced niece and nephew struggle with the same challenge before setting them right, and maybe then they’d finally start to appreciate him.

Jenny went to pull the map out of its mud-spattered case (Ordnance Survey Hydroseal [£19.99]), but David put his hand on top of hers and gently slid it out of her grip. “Let me have a try,” he said, taking extra care not to sound bossy. He walked over to the dry-stone wall that ran parallel the road and crouched down out of the wind. Jenny followed. David carefully unzipped the map case, slid out the map and patiently unfolded it. Then, having found the next section of the walk that he and Dave had highlighted the previous evening, he refolded it with equal care. “Could you hold the case for me?” he asked gently and Jenny, following his lead, held the map case as straight and as still as possible as he slid the map safely back into its holder. "I think this is right," David said modestly as he handed the case back to his uncle.

Dave had expected his nephew to fair no better than he had and was left struggling with a mixture of frustration at the ease with which he'd succeeded and pride in his student's developing hillcraft. "Aye, lad, decent effort," he eventually pronounced, checking the map case closely, "but I wouldn't like t' think 'ow tha'd manage out 'ere when there's a blow on." He removed his beloved El Alamo and hung the case around his neck once more, before stealing the most cursory of glances to ensure that this time the map was the right way up.

David shrugged innocently and he and Jenny fell in behind their uncle once more. They continued along the exposed ridge of the road for a few hundred metres and then turned off over another stile. The new path led them away from the road, the reservoirs and the Folly, further still up the never-ending hill. The barren, featureless moorland was more exposed than ever and the wind whipped into their faces, making them bend into every step. They were nearing the top now and on a clear day they would have been able to see for miles but today the stinging sleet forced them to bow their heads once more to the grey earth. Thinking about the walk afterwards, Jenny would have said that this was the most uninspiring part, if it were not for one memorable scene:

Halfway across the moor they had come to a gate surrounded by semi-submerged marsh grass and dark stagnant mud. It was too deep even for Dave's new Scandinavian, 'quality gear' gaiters and Jenny was sure that they would have to turn back.

"Don't be s' daft, lass, all it needs is a bit o' 'illcraft," Dave had responded with inexplicably returning bravado. "Come ov'r 'ere, *tha pair!*" He squatted in front of the mire and expertly eyed the scene. "Now, where's 'mud?"

"Everywhere!" replied Jenny tersely.

"No, smart Alec, where's it 'deepest?"

"Right in front of the gate."

"Correct, young un; reet where 'tractor's been churnin' things up. So, we 've t' go round 'edge, where 'ground's more stable. … Eh, 'old up a sec; famer's field - MORE STABLE! … MORE *STABLE*! - What abaht that 'un, Davey lad? MORE *STABLE*!! … 'ang on; MORE STABLE – *MOOR* STABLE, like Yorkshire moors. Heh, heh! Double bubble, Davey lad! *MOOR* … *STABLE*!!"

Jenny couldn't help wincing as her uncle rediscovered his most excruciating pitch, but spurred on by his triumph, Dave couldn't resist staggering back and forth across the path, stretching out his arm and clutching his wrist. "Aargh!! Aargh!! Quick Jen," he squealed, "fetch 'first aid kit, I think 'ave cut me sen again."

"Oh you're *so* funny, but you won't be laughing if we're late for John (*and lunch*!), so if you've quite finished, how *do* we get through the gate?"

Beaming with self-satisfaction, and only slightly lowering his pitch, Dave resumed the children's hillcraft training. "Come on, use thee brains. On t'other side 'mud's same; deepest reet in front o' 'gate."

"And?"

"*And* that means if we shimmy along 'bottom bar we can reach 'far side 'n' slip through 'gap at 'edge, where 'ground's more firmer. 't i'n't complicated."

David and Jenny looked up at the gate. It appeared that Dave was right; the gate was just open enough for them to squeeze through and the ground did seem firmer either side of the path

"But you said we shouldn't climb over gates."

"Never mind 'you said,'" said Dave sternly, "out 'ere tha listens t' experience or tha ends up in bother … tha's in big country now."

Jenny momentarily considered reopening the debate about 'experience', but recalling Tuesday's English lesson and, more pressingly, still distracted by the fallout from their recent confrontations, she accepted Falstaff's currish dictum and opted for discretion (or, as they say around those parts, she *wound her neck in.*) And anyway, she really didn't relish the idea of giving up their hard won progress across the moors. "Are you *sure* that thing will take our weight?" she asked nervously. "It looks very old."

"What 'ave I just said? I mightn't 'ave a fancy education like thee Mam 'n' Dad but out 'ere it's experience that counts. Now, let's crack on: Jen lass, tha's littlest, so tha 'as first knockings."

"What?"

"Come on, tha's up first; gi' o'er mitherin'! John's never gonna believe 'ow *tha pair's* 'eld us up this mornin'."

"Oh, thanks a lot."

Jenny puffed out her cheeks, simultaneously raising her eyebrows and pulling her head to one side. She let out a deep sigh and began to slowly make her way around the left-hand edge of the bog, carefully stretching out from one clump of marsh grass to the next. Surviving one or two minor mishaps and gripping her trainers with her frozen toes as if her life depended on it, she reached the left-hand gatepost unscathed. "Can't we just climb over the wall?"

"'ow many more times? - That's not 'illsman's way. Don't tell me tha's neshin' it; just take thee time, get both feet on 'bottom rail 'n' as soon as tha's steady, shimmy along t' other side!"

Jenny wrapped her arms around the gatepost and stretched out with her foot for the bottom rail. She felt it wobble, but as she gradually lowered more of her weight onto it, the gate steadied and she carefully placed her other foot beside it. The gate wobbled again, but by continually adjusting her body weight she found she could keep it more or less upright and, taking another deep breath, she began to slide her feet sideways along the bottom rail. A minute later she was at the far end of the gate and easing her way through the narrow gap between it and the right-hand gatepost. The ground on this side was even worse, but with a light skip and a jump she was able to reach the relative safety of a low bank of snow. "Come David, you can do it!" she shouted back.

"But what about the rucksack?"

"Fo' goodness sake, gi' o'er mitherin', 'n' pass it 'ere; I knew who'd end up carryin' it once goin' got tough."

David let the pack fall off his shoulders and passed it over to Dave, who, having forgotten just how heavy it was, let it fall to the ground, where it nestled into the half-frozen mud. Relieved of the Exped Expedition (£504.95)'s considerable heft and with watertight trust in his 'quality gear' boots, David gleefully hopped and skipped his way to the gatepost and slid easily across to the far side of the gate.

"And with one giant leap for mankind, David and his rocket-powered *boots* escape the tiny German gnome-spies once more!" he yelled and then launched himself onto the snowdrift next to Jenny, who was forced to catch him in her arms to stop herself toppling backwards. "Oooh, David," she grinned, planting a wet kiss on his cheek, "I didn't know you cared." Neither of them saw the gate sink further into the mud as she did so.

Back on the other side, Dave shouldered the dripping Exped Expedition (£504.95) and walked unsteadily but determinedly towards the bog. After one last cursory check of the terrain, he too stretched out for a clump of marsh grass, but the weight of the rucksack dragged him off and his foremost foot sank deep into the mud. He stumbled forward and as his back foot came through to check his fall, it too sank, this time knee-deep into the stagnant water. On the other side of the wall, Jenny was suddenly distracted by the plaintive cry of a lone curlew fighting its way across the sky and David knelt down to check his laces, each carefully avoiding the gaze of the other.

With super-human effort, Dave managed to pull both feet out of the mud and wade towards the gatepost. He grabbed it with both hands and immediately began to examine the surface of the stone. "Reet piece o' Yorkshire gritstone, that. 'last 'n 'undred years o' more, will that," he said authoritatively, hoping to divert the children's attention away from his mud-soaked boots and gaiters.

"Uncle Dave," said Jenny hesitantly, "you don't think …"

"No, I don't think - I know. I know what tha's gonna say, 'n' I know what I'm doin', so save thee breath."

"Huh … suit yourself."

Dave took a deep breath and stretched out his right foot onto the bottom rail. The gate wobbled wildly and then settled as Dave cautiously transferred his entire weight from the gatepost. The children stood motionless as he eased himself along the rail. Dave let out a sigh; it was working. He would have made it, too, but was so exhilarated by his success, so comforted by the returning evidence of his superior hillcraft, that he just couldn't help himself:

He stopped halfway and grinned at the children. "Yorkshire craftsmanship, good for 'n 'undred years," he repeated, shaking the top rail with both hands. But this was one trial too many for the long-neglected gate. A low creaking noise to the left wiped the grin from Dave's face as the rusting hinges began to twist on their mountings. The metal pin holding the top hinge of the gate sheared off with a painful screech and the gate began to tip forwards towards the mud. At first, Dave leaned back, trying to hold the gate upright, his hands welded to the rail as he fought to regain his balance. He swayed backwards and forwards and for a few moments managed to stay upright. But he couldn't fight gravity *and* the Exped Expedition (£504.95). A particularly violent wiggle pulled all the weight forward and Dave, the rucksack and the gate descended gracefully into the bog with the stateliness of a newly launched ship slipping into the sea.

Nobody moved. Dave lay motionless in the mud, fists still clinging to the rail. David looked up anxiously at Jenny, who shrugged uncertainly.

"Uncle Dave, do you need any help?"

For the penultimate time that day, Dave's tongue travelled round the inside of his gums and he spat out a foul-tasting gob of stagnant mud.

"What does tha think?" he snarled, spitting again off the end of his tongue. To be honest, the children didn't know what to think; he certainly looked as though he needed some help, but with Uncle Dave you could never be sure.

"I thought better o' thee, Davey boy, leavin' me wi' pack 'n' then fixin' gate t' fall. There's jokes 'n' there's jokes but this in't funny. If I 'a'n't o' known 'ow t' fall proper tha could o' put me in real danger there."

"Hold on, are you saying David did this on purpose?"

"Well, it's never 'appened before."

"Unbelievable! *Why* do you have to judge everyone by your own sad standards? David's not like you; *he* doesn't have to make everyone feel bad about themselves. It would have served you right if he had have done it on purpose."

Looking up from the mud, Dave was speechless; not only had the children risked causing serious injury by playing such a foolish prank, but now, on top of everything else – the sneering, the insults, the leaving him to do the donkey work and then rushing off without a backwards thought, the constant looking down their noses at him – on top of all of that, now they were ganging up on him. It was all so unfair; anyone could see that: he'd taken Friday off from the yard, shelled out a shed load for proper gear and, ever since Jane had called, spent every waking minute planning their adventure. And were they grateful? Were they 'eck! - Couldn't give a monkey's, either of them. All he'd wanted to do was to help his brother and give them a good time. He hated ingratitude more than anything.

"I'm finished with *tha pair*. Do what tha likes."

"Fine by us, come on David!"

But David didn't move. He looked from his uncle to his sister and back again to his uncle, confusion and hurt clouding across his face. Suddenly, he lumped himself down on the snow and began to cry.

"I didn't do it on purpose, I didn't! You're my uncle and Dad always says, 'if you can't take care of your family, you don't deserve to have one.' I didn't break the gate on purpose. I didn't!" He buried his face in his folded arms and sobbed.

At the mention of her father Jenny flinched, the recollection of the promises she had made to her mother stinging her conscience and making her bite hard on her lip. Instinctively, she sat down next to David and pulled him towards her.

"Happy now?" she hissed at her uncle.

Dave glared back from the gate but said nothing. Mention of Danny had stung him too, and he couldn't help but gaze despairingly at the boy who reminded him so much of his brother. The same innate goodness he saw there caused him to drop his gaze to the ground. He sighed, no longer at the mud seeping through his Rab Neutrino jacket and his Stride Flex Pants or the ache in his shoulders from the weight of the ruined Exped Expedition (£504.95), nor even at his ever-growing sense of failure and discomfit at the way the day was turning out: No, truth be told, he was sighing with immense disappointment *with himself*: this had been his chance, his one, long-awaited chance and he'd blown it.

He was inconsolable.

"Sorry David, I shouldn't o' said owt … I were bang out o' order. Sorry …". From out of the mud, he stared forlornly into the distance, slowly shaking his head and then wearily began to look round for a way to extricate himself from it.

It was a precarious exercise, but in spite of everything the bottom hinge had held fast and the gate served as a raft along which he could shuffle crab-like to the far end. On reaching the right-hand gatepost, he pulled himself cautiously to his haunches and then finally back to standing. “Things coulda been worse, Davy lad, I could ‘ave fell …” he was about to say “backwards,” but before he could, the bottom hinge finally gave up the fight and he did. He landed with a mixture of splash and thud, this time arriving a split second after the rucksack but the effect was much the same: the wind was knocked out of him and his teeth clattered painfully against one another.

Forgetting their argument, Jenny immediately ran, or at least waded, towards her uncle. She reached out her hand and tried to heave him up, fighting against the weight of the rapidly filling Exped. She almost over-balanced but Dave helped as best he could and a minute later they were both back on the relative safety of the snowdrift.

Dave’s mishap and the image of him and Jenny staggering through the mud had made David laugh and he was already recovering from his uncle’s comments. “I didn’t do it on purpose, Uncle Dave, I’d never do anything to hurt you,” he said, looking up plaintively.

“Aah, I know lad; I’ve said I’m sorry. Let’s just forget abaht it.”

“Easier said than done,” said Jenny, easing the rucksack off Dave’s aching shoulders. “Give us a hand, David.” Between them, they tipped the Exped upside down and watched in silence as a stream of mush began to stain the snow beneath. “I’m not sure we’ll be having pork sandwiches today, my Flowerpots,” said Jenny with a grim smile.

Dave brushed himself down as best he could but he was still cold and wet and very, very disappointed. He had tried so hard to give the children a good time but it had all turned out so differently from what he'd expected. How had it all gone so wrong? He had no idea. "Come on," he said with a sigh, "it's not far now."

They crossed the top of the moor in silence, each of them head down, trying to avoid the whip of the wind on their faces, all now wishing their journey were at an end. They skirted some scruffy farm buildings and walked down a grassy path towards a main road. The sky had briefly cleared again and from here, if they had lifted their heads, they would have been able to see over to Hollins Cross and Mam Tor on the horizon, peaking out from behind Win Hill and Lose Hill across the valley. Dave knew that they were all looking on, but was no longer in the mood for telling stories, so they trudged on in silence. Finally, after three hours of walking, in which they'd seen no one other than the Red Coats and the man in the woods, they reached the A57 and a sign that informed them that they had reached the boundary of the City of Sheffield, 'home of stainless steel'.

18

"How on earth did you do that?"

Jane smiled, but modesty, which always came easily to her when she knew she'd done well, prevented her from answering directly. "Do what?"

"Bring them round."

She threaded her arm through Dan's and rested her head on his shoulder, reflecting in silence on her amazing day. They'd decided to walk back from City Hall and had stopped to gaze up again at the greying façade of the Woolworth Building.

"Five and Dime team … inspired," mused Dan on Jane's earlier comment. "Did you know that he never owed a cent on the place?" Jane looked up in surprise, not at F.W.s financial probity, which was common knowledge round and about, but at Dan's sudden familiarity with New York folklore.

"Oh yes," he continued in best guidebook, "there's even a relief of him paying for the *Cathedral of Commerce* in five and ten cent pieces in the horse-shoe shaped lobby of what was briefly the world's tallest building."

Jane's eyebrows arched even higher. It was one more surprise in a day full of wonderful surprises. "Well, it will have to be in The Walk now."

"Couldn't not be."

Jane smiled again.

They'd already done The Walk that morning but now they were repeating it in a lap of honour. They strolled triumphantly along Broadway, stopping to buy coffee in solidarity with a dispirited looking coffee-cart vendor and stood drinking it over an air vent, grinning mischievously at one another, warming themselves in contented silence. Impervious now to the city's never-ending clamour for attention, they wandered on, arm in arm against the cold, until halting again to stare at the Charging Bull on the Bowling Green.

"Arguably the world's best ever real estate deal was done right here on this spot," announced Dan, returning to guidebook mode, "when, in 1626, Peter Minuit, director of the Dutch West India Company, paid the equivalent of $24 worth of beads, trinkets, a jar of Mayonnaise, two pair of wooden clogs, a loaf of wonder bread and a carton of Quaker oats to the Canarsees tribe for the title deeds to the island."

"Yes," countered Jane, trying to sound unimpressed, "but did *you* know they actually bought it from the wrong tribe?"

"Should have hired a better lawyer."

Jane pulled him towards her in mock annoyance. Dusk was falling and the wind was whistling in from the waterfront, sending the litter spiralling into the air along the deserted Downtown canyons. Yet the evening seemed so much warmer and the empty streets far more benign than when they'd walked this way earlier in the day:

Six hours ago, the morning was still surfacing begrudgingly from its slumbers and in the February half-light the whole place had appeared sullen and grey. Jane had hoped that a brisk mid-morning walk would revive her, but the ice-cold wind and threatening skies had only served to confirm her fears, whilst the lingering mounds of greying snow still littering the sidewalk perfectly summarised the demise of her New York adventure; for some unfathomable reason her beloved City had turned against her, and she'd felt as if she were being mocked. It was cruel and it hurt her deeply.

They had walked on in silence through Battery Park, lost in their individual thoughts before stopping to stare out at the islands, desperately seeking inspiration. Jane had huddled in close against the spray but Dan had stood resolute and unbending, deep in deliberation as he gazed across the bullying waters towards Ellis Island.

"Land of opportunity," he'd eventually said, nodding towards the island. "Some people gave up everything just for the chance to give it a go here."

Jane hadn't replied.

"So, what are we going to do about *our* opportunity?"

"We've had ours … it's over." said Jane quietly. "I've decided; it's time to go home."

"Well maybe *we* should undecide."

"Don't do this," said Jane to herself, "I love you for it, but don't make me think about this anymore." Even after the hours of turmoil that had preceded her decision, finally convincing her once and for all that it was over, she was still terrified at the hope she felt rising within her.

Dan didn't speak again for a long time. Eventually, he sighed and turned to look her full in the face. "I see what this place does to you. You love it here; it brings you to life."

"But we tried and it didn't work. I'm not prepared to jeopardise your happiness and the children's future just for some crazy idea. I was wrong and that's an end to it. … We need to go home."

"But maybe this isn't just about *you* and what *you* think; maybe it's about me and Jenny and David too. Maybe *we* don't want to be the reason you never achieve your ambitions. Maybe what *we* want is the Jane who comes back from New York so full of life and fun."

"But we *can't* do it."

"Says who?"

"You, me, them. Everyone!"

"But I think we can."

"How?"

"Look; you need to be here, not me. This is your thing, so this is what I think: you could work here for the first part of the week and then come home for the rest. I can find some more help for the London office and that way we'll still cover all the bases. Then I can come out every few weeks and help you out if you need it. It would work, I know it would."

Jane's heart was soaring but she refused to let it go. She had greater responsibilities in her life than *dreams*; if nothing else, New York had taught her that." And what about the children and you and us? You know how difficult things have been."

"I'll be fine, we'll be fine and, if they get their old mum back, they'll be fine too."

The guy ropes were slipping their moorings one by one, but still Jane refused to let go. "And who's going to look after them when we're both out here? My mother isn't about to step up and I can't really see us leaving them with Karen, can you?"

Dan hesitated for the first time. "Well … if things work out, Dave might help again and I'm sure my mum would help out."

Jane's heart landed with a thump. "She'll never buy it."

"Who?"

"Jenny; I used up all my emotional blackmail to get her up there once, she'll never go for it a second time."

"Look," replied Dan, recovering his resolve, "I'll do you a deal; if you can sort out the mess I've made of the business, I'll sort things out with the children."

"And how, exactly, do you intend to do that? I promised her; this was definitely a 'one-off.' And anyway, how come you're suddenly prepared to ask your brother for favours?"

"Maybe I'm just prepared to do whatever it takes to make you happy," responded Dan, sounding harsher than he'd intended. He paused, "Look … if I can trust you to rescue the deal, can't you trust me with the rest? This isn't about money or prestige or any of that, it's about me wanting my wife to be happy. I don't want to be the reason you never fulfil your dreams."

Jane's mind was close to overload. She knew now just how hard it would be for Dan to ask Dave for help but he was still prepared to do it. She should have responded more positively to his suggestion. But then why should she be the cause of so much trouble and pain for everyone else, just so she could have her own way? - She wasn't a child! And anyway, who was to say Dave would agree and, more to the point, what on earth would Jenny say? And even if all that could be worked out, there was no guarantee that she could rescue the deal; although she had hidden her surprise well, she was shocked to see just how far behind schedule things had fallen. She had thought that Dan had been exaggerating, but now she'd had chance to look over the paperwork more closely it was perfectly clear that he wasn't.

Yet in spite of all of this, she could feel her heart straining against the anchors and in possibly the most irrational and impulsive moment of her well-ordered life, to her own eternal surprise, she decided to let go. "Alright …" she began slowly, "suppose all that could be worked out, there's still no guarantee that we'll even have the contract by the end of the day."

"Well, I guess that's why you're here."

Having made their decision, they rapidly abandoned The Walk and hurried back to the hotel. Now that Jane had taken charge, Dan lay on the bed, watching in bewilderment as she had rifled through every detail of the various contracts. She'd worked like a whirlwind, moving from laptop to voice recorder to notepad - pencil rattling between her teeth as she made constant notes. Every few minutes she would ask him for clarification on some point or to check over her notes, but Dan found it more and more difficult to stay awake and in the end Jane let him sleep, smiling fondly as his mouth fell open and he began to snore.

She woke him around one with coffee, already showered and changed and ready for the meeting. Within thirty minutes they were on their way. Being Saturday, the financial district was almost empty and twenty minutes later they were sitting nervously in The Client's outer office under the glare of a very unhappy P.A.

"I hope her boss is in a better mood," whispered Dan, hoping to lighten the mood.

"She's just ticked off because we've dragged her in on a Saturday."

"Do you blame her?"

"Depends how much she's being paid."

"Not enough by the look of it."

Jane smiled, pleased to feel some relief from the tension. She knew that things must be bad if they'd agreed to a Saturday afternoon meeting, but at least she felt fully aware of the situation now, and she was sure that, given the chance, she could bring things round. The tricky bit was convincing *them* that they were up to the job.

The Client and his advisers had appeared just after two, polished and smiling tightly. He politely offered them coffee, which the standoffish P.A. had studiously avoided doing. She was obviously hoping for a short meeting; perhaps she knew something Jane didn't. The P.A. had smiled condescendingly when they'd refused and then let the smile slide into a smirk as she handed The Client a large leather-bound folder. "Homework," said Jane to herself, "- bad sign." She turned to Dan for encouragement but he looked as nervous as she felt. "Suits on a Saturday," Jane noted, turning back to The Client, "– going downhill fast." The Client and his two advisers led them along the corridor and into the boardroom; "Formal setting – yep, we're sunk!" So, after the usual banalities, Jane had let out a deep sigh and suggested that they have a look at how things were going.

"Well …" began The Client, "to be perfectly honest, we've got some major concerns about bringing this deal in on time. We've got a lot of investors' money tied up here and some of them are getting pretty nervous. It's not that we don't appreciate what you've done - far from it," he continued cautiously, "… but maybe a New York firm would be better placed to help us over the line."

Jane reached into her briefcase and pulled out a notepad. "Could you be more specific?" she asked modestly.

Without referring to the leather-bound folder that now lay exactly square to the table 's edge about six inches in front of him, the balder of the two advisers broke in and fired off a list of a dozen areas where they weren't keeping to schedule. Jane scribbled in silence. The adviser finished with a look of pity and smiled sympathetically, gently shaking his head. Dan wanted to knock it off his shoulders.

"That's very interesting," said Jane, aiming her comments exclusively at The Client. "May I show you this?" She reached into her briefcase and brought out an identical notepad, folded over the first few pages and handed it to him. He stared at it for what seemed an age, a look of growing surprise spreading across his face, before handing the pad to the senior adviser, whose own face soon took on the same expression.

"How did you do that?" The Client asked.

Ignoring him momentarily, Jane reached down for a third notepad. "I suppose I'm a little surprised that you didn't think to mention these," she said firmly, looking the adviser straight between the eyes, before offering him a smile of her own. The adviser took the pad and started to read. His brow furrowed and he began to rub his forehead with his finger ends. Avoiding eye contact, he offered the new pad to The Client, who read it in silence.

"That's fantastic!" enthused the second adviser, who'd been busying himself skimming through Jane's first list. "You should have your own stage show!" he exclaimed, before being drilled back into his chair by a glare from his manager.

For the next few minutes there was an uncomfortable silence, whilst the two advisers read through Jane's notes, one trying to remember as much as possible for The Guys, the other desperately looking for something to criticise. The Client stared out of the window, pursing his lips behind his hands, rhythmically tapping his upstretched fingers one against the other. Out of sight, beneath the deeply polished table, Jane gently rubbed her foot up against Dan's, but both of them looked straight ahead, neither daring to even begin to consider the consequences of what was unfolding in front of them. Jane wondered if she would faint.

Suddenly The Client spoke; "Well, Jane …" he began thoughtfully, "… you really do seem to know this deal better than anybody."

Feeling the relief surge through her body, Jane was instantly able to regain her composure. "And here are the responses to those concerns," she purred. "May I?" She reached over the table and slid the third notepad out of the senior adviser's hand, turned a few more pages and handed it back to The Client. "Most of it is Dan's work; I just pull it all together. The *Five and Dime* team, that's us; keep on top of the small change and before you know where you are …"

The Client lifted his eyes from the notepad and smiled a completely different smile, this time allowing his eyes to join in. "But there's one thing I've just got to know," Dan felt Jane's shoulders tense again, "who's the *five* and who's the *dime*?"

Jane laughed out loud, "Dan's the dime and the diamond. There'd be no *Whynn* without *Strives*."

"… and you say that *you'll* be heading up the New York end from now on, Jane?"

"That's what Dan says, and after everything he's done to get us this far, I'm not going to argue."

“Well Dan, if you can spare your wife for the next few months, I think we’ll be quite happy to keep the law firm we have - *Strive and Whynn*; what a great name.” He smiled again. “Jane, you should bring the family over next time. You do have children, don’t you? They’d love it here.”

“Yes, we do. We’ll have to see. … Dan’s got some exciting plans for them while the deal’s going through.” She turned to her husband, eyes sparkling and raised her eyebrows conspiratorially, before presenting him with a once in lifetime ‘I’ve done my bit …’ smile. Dan smiled back, never more thankful in his life that she was there.

Now they could relax, Dan and Jane had accepted the coffee, although Jane hesitated momentarily when she thought of what the P.A. might have done to it. For the next forty-five minutes she’d talked The Client through each next step of the deal, taking careful note of any new concerns and by four p.m. everyone was satisfied and eager to rescue what was left of the day, apart from the balding adviser and the P.A.

Dan and Jane left the office with more smiles and handshakes and headed back to the lifts. As they turned a corner, hiding them from the PA’s icy glare, Dan let out a huge whoop of delight and began to leap and skip along the corridor. Amazing herself, Jane had joined in and found herself racing Dan to the lifts.

“Last one to the foyer buys the champagne!” shouted Dan as he easily outpaced her. As he passed the elevators, he pressed the ‘Up’ arrow for each one and then bolted for the stairs. “Seventeen stories,” he laughed, “piece o’ cake.”

Jane arrived soon after. In spite of the excruciating effect of running in stiletto heels, she was grinning slyly at Dan’s mistake; the building was almost deserted, so pressing the 'Up' button was a waste of time! Even so, she waited impatiently as the display showed the elevator rising unhurriedly to her floor, determined not to be shaken out of its Saturday afternoon lethargy. As soon as it arrived, she dived in and pressed the foyer button, but before the doors could close an unseen voice barked, "Hold, please!" Jane put her hand over the door but immediately wished she hadn't as the disgruntled P.A. appeared round the corner, coat and bag thrown hastily over her arm. Treating Jane to her most sanctimonious smile, without a word of thanks, she stepped in.

"Foyer?" asked Jane plaintively.

"Where else?" replied the P.A.

They rode in silence, each staring straight ahead. Jane decided to give it one last shot; "I hope we haven't spoilt your week-end." There was no reply. Jane wasn't sure what to do; she was convinced that the P.A. had heard, but she'd continued to stare straight ahead as though the elevator were otherwise unoccupied. Jane considered repeating herself, but then thought, "Why should I? If she doesn't like working Saturday's, she knows what to do." She was far too excited to let one put-out secretary spoil her day.

After an age, the lift doors opened and the P.A. stepped out smartly, straight past Dan, without the slightest acknowledgement. Jane followed, relieved to see her husband's grinning face.

"Nice chat?" he panted, eyes twinkling.

"Oh, I suppose you think your funny!" replied Jane linking arms. "You don't deserve champagne."

"Well, we'd better make it somewhere warm after you've spent five minutes in the lift with the ice queen."

Jane smiled. What an amazing day.

They hadn't been able to find anywhere open nearby, so after waiting five minutes for a cab, they'd decided to walk uptown, picking up some shopping along the way and then take the subway back to the hotel. In the end they had walked the whole way, giving them another chance to gaze at the Woolworth building and Dan the opportunity to show off his new-found knowledge.

Too exhilarated to stay still for long, after toasting their success with more coffee, they'd completed their lap of honour by processing triumphantly back down Broadway to the Bowling Green for a second time. Then, when it became clear that the ticker tape wouldn't be arriving anytime soon, they finally acknowledged the weariness that had been irresistibly gaining ground ever since they'd left the meeting and headed back up Broadway to the hotel.

Now that the contract had been rescued and she felt that she fully understood what was needed, Jane was finally able to put the business to the back of her mind and her thoughts began to turn towards a far more pressing problem; how were they going to contact the children? She quickly calculated that if she waited until six p.m. EST they were bound to be at Dave's, so their pace quickened noticeably as the hotel came into sight. Dan called in at reception to check for messages and was about to hurry after Jane when he was caught gently by the arm.

"Hi again, Mr Strives, I'm sorry to disturb you on Saturday evening." It was Detective Short from the mugging. "I called this afternoon but you weren't picking up."

"Yeah, busy day," replied Dan, hoping to communicate his reluctance to continue the conversation.

"Look," said Short, scratching his head, "you look like you're pretty much done for the day; I'll try to make this as short as possible, okay? Is Mrs Strives … sorry Ms Whynn, available?"

"Come on up," sighed Dan, "she's gone on ahead to 'phone the children."

"You got kids?" asked Short as they walked across the foyer. "You must miss them."

"You're not wrong there; I've not seen them for three months."

"Okay, you've got more important things to do than talk about those no-good pieces of …". His voice tailed off, unsure as to what the appropriate term should be. "Let's keep this as brief as possible." He flicked open his notepad and, before the lift doors had closed he was already writing down Dan's account of the attack. By the time they'd reached their suite, Short was halfway through his questions and ten minutes later he had everything he needed from Dan.

Jane had tried hard to hide her annoyance at seeing the detective. It wasn't his fault that Dave still wasn't answering his 'phone and, even more to the point, if they could sort this out tonight, it might not delay their return to England. When her turn came, she gave her statement in as much detail as possible, and was relieved almost to the point of tears when Short told her that they could come down to the precinct station house in the morning to sign their official statements. Given that they were to be regular visitors to New York over the next few months, there was no need for them to alter their plans for returning home.

Jane knew that they had a lot to do tomorrow, but if everything went to plan they would still have time to call in on their way to the airport. She recognised this was as good as she could hope for and despite her disappointment at not being able to speak to the children, she surprised Dan with her philosophical response to the intrusion. "After all," she said quietly, after the detective had gone, "when you think what could have happened …".

Dan pulled her close and reached for his drink. He hadn't had time to think about the attack, but now he did he felt the rage rising within him once more. Jane felt it too and reached out and pulled his chin towards her. "Thank you for rescuing me …" she whispered, "… twice."

She kissed him tenderly on the lips, but before he could respond she jumped up from the sofa, walked over to the table and lifted her laptop out of her bag.

"You can't have anything else to do tonight," moaned Dan, "surely it can wait."

"I won't be long; you get some sleep." Dan gave her his most sorry look but when she only frowned in response, he gave up and went to bed, chuntering about only wanting him when she needed something.

Sunday morning room service woke them before it was light. Jane had ordered before turning in, knowing an early start to be the best way of ensuring that they beat off the jetlag. In spite of everything that had happened, they had both slept deeply and she had to force herself to throw off the bedsheets. She struggled to the door and brought in the breakfast trolley, only remembering to rifle through Dan's wallet for a tip after a polite cough from the doorway. Dan opened one eye and grimaced. "What's going on?" he groaned.

"Breakfast," replied Jane trying to sound enthusiastic.

"Why?"

"Because there's something I need to show you."

"Sounds interesting."

"Drink your coffee and get dressed. We've got a busy day."

"I'll see you later."

Dan rolled over and pulled the covers close round his shoulders but by now Jane's excitement at what she had planned the previous evening had overcome her tiredness and his lack of enthusiasm was beginning to annoy her. She poured out his coffee and took it over to the bed, but just as he reached out for it she pulled it away and placed it on the table in the centre of the room.

"That's grounds for divorce."

"Get dressed, we haven't got all day."

"Why, where are we going?"

"If you don't get up, you'll never know."

Dan didn't really care; he'd had enough excitement for one weekend, but he did as he was told and thirty minutes later was sat in a cab heading uptown. He was surprised to see Central Park slipping by the window and as they left it behind his curiosity got the better of him. "Where on earth are you taking us?" he asked, staring at the unfamiliar tenements.

"Nearly there."

"'you Strivers then?"

"Yes. … What?" replied Dan, confused by the cab-driver's question. "… What's he talking about?"

"Just ignore him;" said Jane light-heartedly to the driver, "he's from Downtown."

"More and more of you folks moving up here."

"Is that a problem?" asked Jane, a slight trace of concern lacing her question.

"Not to me, lady – more Downtown folk come Uptown, more they need to go back Downtown." Jane smiled.

Dan gave up and looked out of the window. "Frederick Douglass Boulevard," he read to himself. "Are we in Harlem?"

"Sure are, best kept secret in Manhattan until ten years ago, then the money began to arrive. … Here we are."

Jane paid the cabdriver, adding a generous tip for his early start (and, if she were honest, to ease her sense of guilt both at rousing Dan so early from his bed and, more deeply, for using their wealth to lever their way into a community in which she was far from certain they had any right to be.) They were left standing at the end of a perfect row of brown-brick terraced houses. “1-3-9 … 139th Street,” read Dan sleepily, “what on earth are we doing here?”

“Ah well, do you know where ‘here’ is?”

“A long way from bed.”

“Daniel Strives, welcome to Striver’s Row.”

“What?”

“That’s where we are; Striver’s Row; named in your honour, I’m sure.”

Dan still didn’t understand, but as he looked along the row of neat symmetrical houses and ran his hand along the frosty wrought iron handrail guarding the first house, the greying dawn gave way to true daylight and the wind whistled through the bare branches of the trees, welcoming him to Harlem.

“If I’m going to be away from the rest of the Strives, then at least I can be with the Strivers.”

Dan’s brow furrowed even deeper.

“On account of the aspirations of their previous occupants, this elegant row of townhouses has always been known as ‘Striver’s Row,’” explained Jane, borrowing Dan’s guidebook voice from the previous afternoon, “so what better place for us to set up base?”

“It’s miles from the City,” said Dan unconvincingly, “and, anyway, how do you know there are any to let?”

“There aren’t. Someone bagged the last one last night,” said Jane triumphantly.

“And I wonder who that was,” said Dan, with a knowing grin.

“One, two, three, four, five, six,” counted Jane, walking slowly along the street. She stopped and turned to face the house. “This is it, amazing: recently renovated, long lease, great investment, perfect home-from-home. Even comes with its own parking – how’s *that* for Manhattan? We can’t go in but the pictures are fabulous.”

She turned to register Dan’s delight but he wasn’t there. Surprised and slightly annoyed, she looked around but there was no sign of him. She marched back to the end of the street and found him gazing at the gates guarding the courtyard between theirs and the next row of houses. She shuffled up to him and punched him hard on the arm. "You weren't listening, were you?"

"Hmmm?"

Jane allowed her gaze to follow Dan's. He wasn't actually looking at the gates, but at the gateposts or, to be even more precise, their inscription: "'GATE NUMBER SIX,'" Jane read out loud, "'PRIVATE ROAD. WALK YOUR HORSES.', … *fascinating.*"

"Eh, it's more than 'fascinating' t'old lass - it's brilliant is that!"

They stayed in Harlem for second breakfast. Jane was ravenous and the food hot and spicy enough to chase away the late-winter chill. By one o'clock, they were back at the hotel and by three, Jane having checked through her notes one last time and rushed off the final few e-mails, they were ready to leave. It seemed as though the entire foyer staff had turned out to see them off. They were treated to a second round of applause, and the concierge re-iterated their admiration of their courage of the previous day and his hope that their earlier misunderstanding was now behind them. Jane fixed him sternly, but couldn't keep up the pretence. A smile curled up the corners of her mouth and she hoped that they would visit again soon.

At the police station, Detective Short was equally accommodating and kept them waiting no longer than was necessary to read, confirm and sign their statements. Within half an hour they were finished and after another round of handshakes and pats on the back, they were on their way, armed with more good wishes than they'd known since their wedding day. Jane smiled smugly as their cab pulled up at La Guardia fifteen minutes ahead of schedule. There was one thing left to do; she must 'phone Jenny.

19

Not long after crossing the A57, the three adventurers' solitude finally came to an end. Leaving the road to its onward journey towards Ladybower Reservoir and the infamous Snake Pass, their own path rose steadily along a rocky, steep-sided gully, worn deep by eager rock climbers and the incessant harrying of rain and snow. In some places the mud between the rocks reached up to their knees, and as they slowly slogged their way up they were surprised to be caught by a young man pushing a bike.

"Hi, do you know if the path is this rocky all the way to the top? I was hoping to do more cycling." The three Strives looked up from under the rain at the fresh-faced young man, his American accent only adding to their surprise. He smiled brightly. "Wow, when they told me about the precipitation on the Pennines, they weren't kidding."

"Pennines?" responded Dave, his pitch rising proportionately to the young man's error. "'Pennines' – 'as tha' 'eard 'im, Davey lad! Never 'eard owt like it! … 'Pennines'! Tha's way out, young 'un. This i'n't *'Pennines* – op'n 'eyes - tha's smack in middle o' 'Peak District."

The student flinched momentarily before directing a knowing but not unkind glance towards Jenny, who offered the faintest of smiles in return. "So where are you folks headin'? You look like locals to me," he asked, gently steering the conversation away from geography.

"'athersage, lad. Started in 'ighfield ov'r three 'our ago 'n' come straight ov'r 'tops wi'out a break," said Dave impressively. "Walkin' – only way t' get abaht up 'ere," he added superciliously, smirking at the young man's bike.

The student smiled again. "Well maybe I could *walk* with you a while until the path flattens out … if that's okay?"

“Yes, fine,” said Jenny quickly, arguing that the company of an intelligent young adult would outweigh any further potential embarrassment from her uncle. She could see Dave wasn’t happy. “Cramping your style, Uncle?” she asked mischievously under her breath as they walked along.

“I’ve allus fancied Australia …” said Dave suddenly. Nobody was quite sure to whom he was talking. “Oh aye, them places need business magnums like me - if they want things doin’ proper like. … See, what it is, young ‘un, I’ve got so many folks relying on me wi’ business ‘n’ that, else I’d be off in a flash. I’ve allus fancied Ontario me sen.”

“Uncle Dave,” hissed Jenny, already fearing she’d miscalculated, “Ontario is in Canada and he’s *American*, not Australian.”

“American? ‘tha sure abaht that, lad?”

“Yes sir, New York State born and bred.”

“Ah … reet … ah … I’d ‘a’ reckoned New York me sen - tha can tell wi’ accent, Davey. … Tha’s not in ‘Mafia then?”

Jenny shook her head in disbelief.

“No sir, my father’s NYPD, so that wouldn’t look too good.”

“Reet,” said Dave, nodding his head knowingly. “Looks like ‘bike could do wi’ a bit o’ fettlin’.”

‘Fettlin’?”

“Ah, tha knows; proper clean ‘n’ service ‘n’ that; tha don’t want t’ get caught out out ‘ere tha knows. Tha’s in big country now, young un.”

“Oh right. Okay, well, I’ll make sure I give everything a good *fettlin’* this evening. - Never let me down yet and I’ve ridden her all over England.”

“Are you a professional?” asked David innocently.

“No, just a humble geography student.”

Dave stifled a laugh; fancy a geography student not knowing the difference between the Pennines and the Peak District. Still his gear looked good.

“’these ‘proper job then, these Ca…non…dale?”

“Yes sir, Connecticut’s finest; used by professionals (and geography students) the world over. Yes sir; like I said; never once let me down.”

“… Reet then,” said Dave thoughtfully. Having gained this valuable piece of information he couldn’t see any further reason for the lad not to be on his way. He let the conversation fall silent and, recognising that it was time to part company and that the path was beginning to flatten off, the young geographer mounted up and wished them well.

“’fore I forget, young ‘un, when tha’s ready t’ trade up t’ four wheels, gi’ us a ring ‘n’ I’ll see what I can do; sat nav ‘uld come in ‘andy, if nowt else. I’ve no cards on me at ‘minute – couldn’t risk extra weight - but me name’s Dave Strives. I’m in ‘phone book or else look out for me on ‘telly.” Dave grasped the American’s hand firmly and gave it a proper Yorkshire rattle.

“It was a pleasure Mr Strives. I’m James Short; Jim to my friends,” replied the student clenching and unclenching his hand.

“Ah, well take it easy, Jim lad, ‘n’ don’t be getting’ theesen in bother on them *Pennines;* Mountain Rescue ‘as enough t’ do wi’out chasin’ after lost geography students. ‘n’ fetch theesen a map next time - our Davey’ll fold it fo’ thee.” Dave winked at his nephew.

The young New Yorker smiled patiently, “Okay, enjoy the rest of your walk. Take care now.”

“Bye,” called David and Jenny in unison as he pedalled away.

Waiting until he was out of earshot, Dave let out a loud guffaw. “Cheek on it; it’s ‘im who needs t’ *take care*! Can’t even recognise an experienced ‘illsman when ‘e sees one – *Pennines,* who’s ‘e kiddin’? Someone needs t’ ‘ave a word wi’ ‘is teacher. … ‘Geography student’- ‘as th’ ‘eard ‘im?”

“I thought he was nice,” said Jenny.

“Ay up Davey lad, someone’s feeling a bit warmer.”

“Oh, get lost.”

The detective's son made his way steadily up the rock strewn path towards Stanage Edge, but Jenny saw little of his progress. Hunching up her shoulders against the bullying rain and staring down at the path, she was concentrating all her efforts on avoiding the worst of the water-logged ground. As a result, she also failed to see this same path opening up to the moors and the beginning of the gritstone debris from the Edge.

Dave, on the other hand, knowing the route well, made sure they didn't miss the seemingly inconsequential left fork that took them away from the main trail. The new path continued to rise steadily, whereas the one to the right fell sharply away. As a result, they were soon walking along a grey escarpment about ten metres above the moor.

This was the beginning of Stanage Edge proper and as the cliff face pushed through the boulders around it, Jenny allowed herself a glance to the right and immediately came to a halt. The sky was low and threatening and visibility was poor, but, even so, she felt herself irresistibly drawn into the view across the valley.

She lifted her head and looked around. This was a wild and desolate place, but instead of feeling threatened, she felt alive and free. Here there were no cares and responsibilities to restrain the youthful exuberance pulsating inside her. That same wild energy that had burst out of her at Boot's Folly was about to erupt again. She couldn't have stopped it if she'd wanted to. She didn't try; she had played the adult for too long; it was time to be a child. "Don't step on the grass!" she yelled to David. "There's a law against it."

"Says who?"

"Says Gandalf, the tiny German spies and … ME!" she screeched, charging at her brother, and pushing him backwards off a bare patch of rock, onto the dark, peaty earth. "Come on then, *Davey lad,* last one to John and Meg eats the soggy sandwiches!"

With a whoop of delight, she leapt gracefully onto the next rock and, like thousands of children before them, they began to scurry along the top of the Edge, skipping from one gritstone outcrop to another. As they bounded along with ever more daring leaps, the warmth returned to their arms and legs and their chests heaved in the cold, damp air, drawing out all their youthful energy and filling them with a sense of well-being.

Jenny skipped from rock to rock with the light-footed elegance of a dancer or a deer, straining every muscle and sinew to stay ahead of her brother, but she had no answer to David's natural strength and he soon surged ahead, leaving her far behind.

Panting heavily, she stopped again and turned head on to face the squall racing up from the seemingly endless moor stretching out below her. She opened her arms wide and let out what could only be described as a 'primal scream'. As the wind carried away the last of her cares, she leant out as far as she dare over the Edge; in that moment she could almost believe she could fly. Without warning, she was suddenly a girl again and as she surrendered once more to the wild beauty that engulfed her, the tears poured untouched down her cheeks. Laughing and crying, she shouted, "What an amazing day!" without the slightest sense of irony. And then, just when she'd decided it couldn't be any better, she remembered that very soon they would see John and Meg; as she turned back and began to skip again across the huge slabs of gritstone littering the path, she felt her heart would burst.

Stanage Edge is over five kilometres long and Jenny's pace eventually slowed. She began to walk, still keeping her feet on the gritstone but now with the time to look around more carefully. A lone female walker ("Proper gear, obviously experienced,") passed by in the opposite direction but other than that there wasn't another soul in sight. Jenny was amazed when they came back in the summer to see the cliff-face swarming with spidery climbers spinning their threads across the rocks, but today she had the place pretty much to herself and she wandered on, blissfully alone, David shrinking into the distance in front and Dave dragging up the rear. She meandered on past Goliath's Groove singing absent-mindedly to herself, but by the time she'd reached High Neb she had cooled down again and she began to scan the horizon in earnest for John and Meg.

She spotted them not long after passing the old Roman road that leads down off the Edge towards Hathersage. John was seated beside a huge boulder, staring straight ahead, Meg curled up by his side. They sat so still that David, intent on his footfalls, hadn't noticed them. Jenny was about to call him back when she hesitated. She stood perfectly still and gazed at the two friends. His right arm draped across Meg's body, John stared straight into the distance, completely at ease with the wind and the rain. There was a sad and faraway look in his eyes. "What are you thinking about?" Jenny asked out loud.

She walked on, trying to take in as much detail as possible, hoping for some further clue about this wonderful, mysterious man. He wore an old cloth cap and a wax jacket that must have once been green. His battered trousers gave no hint of their original colour and his boots were scuffed and worn. Sitting there so still, it was hard to tell where the rock, the coat and the man started or ended; they all seemed to have been hewn from the same source. She'd never seen a man in such harmony with his surroundings and she thought it would make her cry.

It was Meg who roused her from her thoughts. As she lifted her head, John turned to see Jenny and waved. With the slightest motion of his hand, Meg was off, bounding up to Jenny. She knelt down and petted the dog, who seemed to be wagging her whole body. "Hello girl, can I have some of that energy?"

“Tired?” asked John, who’d wandered over.

“A bit; it’s a long way, and I didn’t have any breakfast.”

“Don’t worry, lass, I’m sure your uncle will have sorted that out. Where are the others?”

David had turned to see the three of them and was now wandering back along the Edge, still carefully avoiding the ground and Dave was slowly approaching from behind. Two minutes later and they were all together again.

“Trouble?” asked John, raising his eyebrows at Dave’s sodden and bedraggled appearance.

“Bits ‘n’ bobs, lad, nowt special. Any roads, let’s find a bit o’ shelter ‘n’ ‘ave some snap. Young uns ‘ll be starvin’. … This’ll do …”. They followed Dave into a steep, tight gully, spanned by a huge slab of gritstone. They all crouched down out of the wind and Dave opened the Exped Expedition (£504.95). His face fell as he stared inside. Its precious cargo was covered with a film of dark, pungent mud. His falls had broken several of the items and the lids had sprung off the sandwich boxes. As a result, the white paper bags containing the sandwiches had disintegrated and congealed with the soggy, grey bread.

“Anyone for a sandwich?” asked Dave dejectedly, holding one by its corner to let the muddy water drain off. He threw it back in the bag with a scowl. “Reet tangle, this,” he moaned, wincing with the shame of his inadequacies.

“I hope you don’t mind, Dave, I brought the Land Rover up and there’s a few bits in there, if it’s any use.”

Dave smiled quietly. Sometimes the ease with which John strolled through life drove him to distraction, but on days like today he was just grateful. “Come on then,” he sighed, shouldering the Exped, “we can get down this road can’t we John?”

“You lead, Dave; we’re parked down the quiet end.”

The gully was steep and slippery and Dave led the way slowly and cautiously, never taking his eyes off the treacherous rocks.

It was bad enough to have been embarrassed in front of the children, but the humiliation of failing in front of John would be unbearable. He needn't have worried and once down the gully, the path through the winter bracken was relatively straightforward. Jenny's only surprise was to see the numerous large millstones scattered around the hillside. "I see they like icing on their doughnuts up here," she quipped, dragging her fingers through the thin covering of snow on one of them. On another day it would have been a good joke, but with Dave pre-occupied with the disappointments of the day and David still in shock over the fate of the sandwiches, today only John raised a smile.

The Land Rover was parked by the edge of a long ribbon road running parallel to the Edge. They clambered in and slammed the doors on the weather. For a few moments they sat in silence, listening to the retuning rain hammering on the roof and the wind whistling around the solid walls of the ancient vehicle. The windows were already half-steamed up and Jenny was beginning to shiver. John took off his cap and wiped his brow. He turned to Jenny and asked her to pass over a large, grey canvas bag. "Now then, anyone for a drop o' broth?" He pulled out a green, stainless steel flask, as ancient and battered as the Land Rover, along with four pitted enamel mugs and placed them carefully on the dashboard.

"Me, please!" shouted David, who'd never heard of 'broth', but as it sounded like food was overjoyed. John carefully poured out the first mugful and passed it over. He did so three more times and the silence returned as each of them hugged his or her mug, allowing the steam to rise over them, bringing the delicious aroma to their nostrils.

"Any more?" asked David hopefully.

"'fraid not," laughed John, "but there's some sandwiches."

"Great," said David, reaching out and taking two doorsteps from the biscuit tin John was proffering.

"I should fill thee boots quick, lass," laughed Dave.

"What's in them?" Jenny asked nervously.

"Wet feet. Heh heh! WET FEET!! - What abaht that 'un, 'ollow legs?

"Just cheese and pickle, lass," sighed John.

"Oh, yes please."

John handed over the sandwiches and they all munched on. Like Mary Poppins, he continued to bring out marvellous and mysterious objects from the canvas bag. The sandwiches were followed by a pork pie and then, tea, with four more mugs and a little glass bottle for the milk, another for sugar and even a spoon and, finally, best of all, a huge slab of John's secret recipe parkin, which he cut up with his pen-knife.

"Anything else?" asked David, peering between the two front seats.

"Well, I've some jelly you can try."

"Any ice-cream?"

"'ere lad," laughed John, breaking off a square of raw raspberry jelly. "Full of energy; keep you goin' for hours."

Dave nodded sagely. David took the jelly apprehensively, sniffed it and then popped it in his mouth.

"That'll keep thee quiet, lad," laughed Dave.

"All that's left now is a bag of apples," John announced.

"Uumurgh," moaned David.

"Crackin'," said Dave, "we'll take 'em wi' us."

"Take them where?"

"Rest o' walk, lass; we're not finished yet."

"You're joking, right?"

"I'm not jokin', lass. 'illsmens don't start walks 'n' then not finish 'em."

"You never get it, do you? We've all had enough, let's just go home and not spoil it."

"Spoil it! If it won't fo' me tha'd o' been lakin' abaht 'ouse all day, mitherin' abaht thee mam 'n' dad. I spent all week plannin' this. … Come on, we're finishin' it."

Dave opened the door of the Land Rover as if to climb out and Jenny was just about to reply in kind when John gently touched him on the arm and said, "I've got a suggestion; why don't I drive down to North Lees and we can all meet there. If it's going okay, we can walk down together, if not then the Land Rover's nice and handy. … Your uncle has put a lot of work into this, Jenny, and it would be quite an achievement to finish such a long walk."

"How far is that then?" asked Jenny.

"'bout a mile, lass, all down 'ill. Come on, Davey lad, 'a'n't tha finished 'jelly yet?"

Dave jumped out of the Land Rover and began a series of rigorous warming up exercises. "Restores 'blood navigation 'n' prevents injury," he shouted through the open door. "Come on then, *tha pair*, let's be 'avin' thee!"

Jenny sighed and put her hand on the door handle but before she could open the door, John leaned over once more. "I thought these might come in handy," he said gently, passing a second equally battered canvas bag over to Jenny. She smiled and looked inside. There was a pair of thick, warm-looking socks, some gloves and a woolly hat.

"Thanks," she replied, smiling again, "but my shoes are soaked."

"See if any of these fit you," said John passing over yet another bag. Jenny gratefully took the bag, knowing already that she would find what she was looking for, and pulled out several pairs of boots, one of which looked about her size. "Where did you get all these?"

"Oh, 'ere 'n' there, lass."

She didn't want to touch her old laces with her warm, dry hands but she forced herself to untie them and slowly pulled off the sopping shoes and socks. John handed her a towel and she dried her half-frozen feet. The towel felt rough and angry against her rosy skin but the thick, soft, green socks were worth the effort. She sighed as she pulled them on. Pulling the bootlaces tight added to the sense of warmth and comfort and by the time she'd dried her hair, pulled the hat down tight over her ears and wriggled her glowing hands into the gloves, she was actually beginning to warm to the idea of finishing the walk.

"Can you manage your zip with them on?" asked John gently.

"I'll be fine, thanks." she replied, furtively brushing yet another tear from her cheek, and then quickly moving her hands down to fasten the zip of her jacket. "Thanks for everything."

John smiled a faraway smile. In five minutes of kindness he'd achieved what seven hours of Dave's bluster could not. Full and warm, she jumped out of the Land Rover, bracing herself against her uncle's sarcasm and the unremitting weather. As it turned out, it was neither raining nor snowing and, to her amazement, Dave only smiled.

The Land Rover pulled away, leaving the three travellers alone once more. David had asked if Meg could stay, but John had responded that as they couldn't be sure what they might meet, it was probably better that she went with him. However, he did promise that they would both walk up to meet them as soon as they'd found somewhere to park.

"Come on then, *tha pair*, it's down 'ill from 'ere," Dave repeated, taking up the half-emptied Exped Expedition (£504.95). He jiggled it on his shoulders, pulled it down onto his hips and, doing his best to ignore the consequences of John's feast, sucked in his chest and clipped the straps firmly into place for what he hoped would be the final time.

Without looking back, he set off along the road and within two minutes they'd reached a fast-flowing stream, littered with large boulders. Dave turned off and began to follow the stream downhill, but recalling his 'illsman's duties, he soon came to a halt. He stepped out onto a suitably sturdy boulder, carefully crouched down and looked back towards the point where the stream emerged from beneath the road. "More great dam-building 'ere, Davey lad, there's even a tunnel tha can crawl through if tha's not gonna nesh it. … Goes reet through t' other side." David bobbed down and stared expectantly into the narrow opening, but in the gathering gloom there was little to see. "Don't fret, lad, we'll come back in 'summer," said Dave and, for the second time that day, Jenny, who'd been observing The Boys from the safety of the bank, found herself warming to the idea of returning to this wonderful place.

They walked on through the bracken, eventually meeting up with a grassy path, which led them still further away from the Edge and out of the wind, until they reached a settlement of half a dozen immaculately restored farmhouses and converted outbuildings. Jenny thought them idyllic, but Dave instantly dismissed both houses and owners with a contemptuous, "… playin' at it!"

Without consulting the map, Dave led the way through the settlement to a large metal gate, supported on its outer stile by a small rusty wheel, which squealed in protest at being pulled along the curved strip of concrete beneath its arc.

"Hey, Uncle Dave, sounds like someone needs to put t' fettle t' metal!" chirped David.

"They *wheely* do," laughed Jenny.

"Eh, any more carry on 'n' *tha pair'll* be barred!"

Jenny turned to David and shrugged.

"Tha knows … five-bar gate. BAR – *BARRED*; five-BAR

gate. What's tha think o' that 'un then, Davey lad?"

"*Bar, barred, bar*?! We're a bit old for nursery rhymes, Uncle Dave."

"Gi' o'er! Any roads, I need t' show thee summat. Come ov'r 'ere!"

Quickly moving on, but still taking time to demonstrate the correct technique, Dave led the way as they sidled one by one along the edge of yet another muddy track, hemmed in by two low dry-stone walls. As they crabbed their way nervously along, as per Dave's instructions, they clung to the coping on top of the wall, each exercising far more caution than earlier in the day; now that they were dry and relatively warm, no one relished another soaking. More importantly, there had already been too many fall-outs following *accidents* involving mud. And in light of this and the harmonious mood that had prevailed since leaving John and Meg, Jenny again chose to ignore Dave's blatant disregard for both *''illsman's Code'* and the farmer's property.

Having more or less avoided the worst of the mud, after fifty or so metres their travails were cut short by a turn to the right through another tight stile. Dave coyly invited the children through first and then pointed them in the direction of a lightly wooded area diagonally opposite. He waited for them to move on and then, imitating David's technique with the Exped Expedition (£504.95), he furtively slid through the stile, quickly reshouldered the rucksack and hurried on to resume his place as trip leader, just in time to lead them into the wood.

Three months later the whole area would be awash with bluebells but today the wood felt rather bare and neglected and Jenny was glad when they re-crossed the busy stream and the wood petered out. Climbing yet another stile (Jenny had lost count), they finally arrived at the last, and soon to be legendary, field of the day.

"Now tha'll be glad tha came, David Attenburger," announced Dave, standing astride the stone stile. "Look, even

Meg's come t' 'ave a butcher's." The children looked up and there on the other side of the field was the border collie's laughing face peering over the top of the wall, unseen tail wagging excitedly.

"Come on ov'r," shouted Dave.

"We'd better not," John shouted back, "'farmer mightn't be too happy."

"Suit theesen; we'll be ov'r in a mo. … Reet then, Jen lass, now tha'll see summat. … Where's them lemurs?"

Jenny furrowed her brow, trying to work out what on earth her uncle was talking about. She looked to David for an explanation but he could only offer the usual shrug of his shoulders.

"I know what'll fetch 'em out." Stretching himself and its straps to the limits, Dave reached over his shoulder, unclipped the top pocket of the Exped Expedition (£504.95) and brought out one of John's apples. "They'll not resist these."

Jenny looked anxiously at David. "Uncle Dave, you're not really supposed to …". Her voice trailed away, not so much shrinking under her uncle's intimidating stare as from finding herself at a complete loss to explain exactly what it was he wasn't supposed to be doing.

"Gi' o'er, I'm not feedin' 'em, I'm just showin' 'em who's alphabet male."

Jenny creased up her eyes into a wince.

"Don't tell me tha don't know abaht alphabet males. 'thought *tha* were 'animal lover."

At that moment, the sheep-like head of an alpaca appeared round the doorway of a small shed-come-stable in the corner of the field. "Oh …" said Jenny, "… are you *sure* this is a good idea?"

"Watch 'n' learn, lass, watch 'n' learn; alphabet male allus 'as first dabs on 'snap. When they see me wi' apples, they'll know who's top banana 'n' fall in behind. Eh, TOP BANANA

… TOP BANANA … APPLES – BANANAS. Heh, heh! What abaht that un, Davey lad?"

Jenny raised her eyebrows apprehensively. "Er, perhaps we'll see better from here."

"Suit theesen, lass, it 'll be tha who's missin' out."

Dave strode purposefully out into the field, taking a huge bite out of the apple as he went. The alpaca lifted his head and sauntered out of the stall, heading towards Dave. "What did I tell thee?" shouted Dave. "Alphabet male." The alpaca lengthened its stride and was soon followed by three others, nodding their way comically across the field.

"See, nowt t' worry abaht, just come for a chat … reet friendly us Northerners, tha knows. … Thought even a southern frosty would want t' come and say ''ello' t' these fellas. Watch 'n' learn, lass, watch *and* learn!" strutted Dave. "… Come on thee, fall in!"

He turned away and walked on; the leading alpaca followed, steadily narrowing the gap between them. "Just enough," he whispered with just the slightest trace of uncertainty, "just enough to let 'em know." He turned back to the children. "Piece o' cake, well, piece o' apple, any roads … PIECE O' APPLE! Another un! Nah den, what's tha think o' that, Davey lad?" squealed Dave, his voice rising to a pitch that could halt a small herd of alpacas.

To this day it remains unclear whether Dave was trying to impress the children, intimidate the alpacas or ramp up the tension for his wider audience, but whatever his intentions, the gap between the two continued to narrow, presenting him with a first glimpse of the alpha male's flaring nostrils and jutting teeth. The rest of the herd followed their leader, closing in quickly on their unexpected windfall, and now the confidence flickered on Dave's face and he quickened his pace … so did the alpha male. Dave broke into a trot … the herd followed suit. He threw the apple over his shoulder and made a run for it … so did everyone else. As he bounced across the field, apples sprung out of the Exped Expedition (£504.95), drawing his pursuers on. Dave was now at full tilt but the alpha male was gaining quickly.

"Run, Uncle Dave!" shouted the children with a mixture of terror and hilarity. "Run!"

Dave was nearly there, but the alpaca was still gaining.

"Jump for it!" shouted David.

"Go Dave! Go Dave!" cheered Jenny, convinced that the danger was almost over. But Dave wasn't so confident, and to make absolutely sure he took a giant leap over the wall, scattering John and Meg for cover.

For the last time that day, he felt the wind being forced out of his chest from the impact of the Exped Expedition (£504.95) pinning him to the ground. "Oooh," he groaned, his tongue following its familiar path, "Aaargh!" He tried to roll onto his back but the Exped prevented him and he could only hold out a hand to John, who pulled him gently to his knees, trying his best not to laugh, whilst Meg growled protectively over the wall. Dave fell back onto the snow-covered grass, and looked up despairingly at the sky and then across to his friend. "Fetch 'Land Rover, will tha lad; I've 'ad enough."

20

Jenny sat in the back of the Land Rover in a state of contented exhaustion. She had to admit that she felt slightly cheated at not finishing the walk, but all things being considered, she was happy and relieved to be going home. It had been a very long day and the jolt of every bump and twist of the road through the ancient Land Rover's unforgiving suspension reminded her just how much her body was aching. She was looking forward to having a long bath, cooking something easy (Dave having already explained how his injuries might limit his culinary contributions) and then turning in – she couldn't remember being more physically spent. But none of this could dimmish the glow of victory warming her from the inside out: she'd made it - admittedly with a little help from John and David, but then wasn't that what old friends and younger brothers were for?! She'd walked further and harder than ever before in her young life; twenty miles (or so she thought) from Highfield to the bottom of Stanage Edge, uphill and down dale, through wind, rain and storm, covered in mud and frozen to the core, under the constant barrage of her uncle's ridiculous attempts at humour and put-down. She'd been more tired than she could have imagined possible, hungry enough to faint and, at times, desperate to give up. But she hadn't. And she'd survived. And she'd walked – the whole way!! She was a … walker, an *experienced* walker. … She was a … n *'illswoman!* … Definitely - an *'illswoman!* Who'd have thought it. … She allowed herself a grin. As David would say, "Cool!"

She looked across at her brother idly drawing comically mis-shaped animals and writing *Uncle Dave is a piggy* in large wobbly letters in the condensation covering the Land Rover's roof, and letting her head fall against the side panel, she closed her eyes and smiled a smile of self-satisfied contentment. For the next few miles she drifted in and out of the blissful sleep of a young woman who had proven her qualities to herself and to the world. Her mum was going to be so proud.

It was only now, when she remembered her parents, that her sense of well-being was disturbed. She hadn't thought about them since they'd left Stanage Edge but in an instant the tide turned and the anxiety inexorably began to overwhelm her once more. … Why hadn't her mother 'phoned? She wouldn't have forgotten; it could only mean that things were going badly. Her heart sank. She closed her eyes again, knowing full well that sleep was now beyond her, but at least it would allow her to avoid conversation.

With only John not having to fight off the tiredness of the day or pre-occupied with matters elsewhere, they travelled on in silence for the rest of the journey, and it wasn't until they passed the cricket pitch that Dave finally roused himself. "Pull ov'r a sec! I'll fetch 'meat from Reg 'n' a couple o' buns t' tide us ov'r 'til tea." He climbed clumsily out of the Land Rover and headed towards a small white trailer tucked in the driveway leading to the village hall. "Nah den, 's up wi' thee?" he bellowed, as he swaggered across the road.

This was all Jenny caught of the exchange; she was far too tired and pre-occupied, and even if so inclined, she simply couldn't concentrate for long enough to marshal the disdain that her uncle's return to form undoubtedly deserved. Five minutes later he re-opened the door and deposited three large carrier bags full of meat into the passenger side foot well. "Now *that's* what I call a deal!" he exclaimed. "Back in a tick," and he disappeared into the Post Office. He soon re-appeared, grinning and carrying two paper bags stuffed to the brim with all manner of delicious smelling cakes. "That's all she's got left; they'll just 'ave t' do fo' now. Onwards, me old Gooseberry!"

John, who for the children's sake had left the engine running, pulled away and the Land Rover dragged itself up its own final hill of the day. As they drew up outside the house, the three Strives shook themselves wearily and began to gather up their belongings. They climbed slowly out of the back of the Land Rover and wandered up the drive, none of them tempted by the invitation to vault the gate. Six hours and forty-seven minutes after setting off on their great adventure, they were finally home.

The children dutifully removed their muddy boots on the doorstep, fighting off the shivers as Dave tunnelled through the Exped Expedition (£504.95) in search of the door key amongst the crush of hastily repacked, mostly unused, mud-encrusted outdoor equipment. Once inside the house, the warmth enveloped the three of them like a blanket and they raced against the rising tide of exhaustion to remove the remainder of their outdoor gear, before flopping down onto the furniture. Nobody could find the energy to speak until David spied The Chair. He suddenly leapt up and ran over to it, sliding gracefully into the deep, welcoming leather. "Awesome, let's go!" he shouted.

Jenny smiled at his amazing recovery and stood up wearily. "Cup of tea?"

"I'll get it," said Dave, not moving.

"It's alright. What's the plan for dinner?"

Dave raised a quizzical eyebrow. "We've 'ad it; John sorted it. Tha's not forgot already?"

Jenny looked confused. "What, we're going there again?"

"Where?"

"John's, for dinner." Jenny paused. "It's not stew again is it?"

Dave shook his head and smiled magnanimously. "This i'n't dinner, this is tea. Tha's in Yorkshire now, lass; look out 'window! … Must be 'fratigue, even if it were only a short 'un. Any roads, no need t' fret theesen - I've got it covered."

Jenny smiled knowingly at the provocation, "What like last night?" She made sure that Dave detected the lightness in her voice. It *was* meant as a joke and she didn't want him to be offended.

"Don't mither theesen, old lass! - It's me secret ingredient t'neet, can't g' wrong."

Too *fratigued* to enquire further, Jenny wandered into the kitchen and busied herself with the drinks, grinning to herself at her uncle's unique grasp of the English language. She looked over at the range and frowned. When she tested it with her hand it was stone cold; the arrival of The Doctors that morning had driven the need to bank it up completely out of Dave's head. "Er, Uncle Dave …"

"I know, lass – what 'ave I've told thee ? … Don't fret!"

Jenny shook her head. "Doesn't learn, does he?" she sighed under her breath. By the time she'd returned with the tea, Dave was asleep. She put the mug down quietly and crept back into the kitchen, peeked into one of the cake bags and pulled out a half-squashed vanilla slice. Tea in one hand, cake in the other and smiling mischievously, she tiptoed past The Chair and over to the stairs … she was going in the bath!

Forty-five minutes later, she was woken by the lukewarm water. "Uurgh," she shuddered and sat up wearily, every inch of her body aching from her achievements. Downstairs, Dave had dozed for about half an hour and then started from his dream with a jump, just before being eaten alive by an alpaca in a red jacket. He instinctively reached for his tea. "Uurgh," he spluttered, "what do I 'ave t' do t' get a decent brew round 'ere?" He looked blearily down at his watch; nearly seven; time to start tea.

Notwithstanding the complaints coming from her legs and back, Jenny felt relaxed and warm in her bedroom. She treated herself to not getting dressed and lay on her bed in her dressing gown, allowing her mind to wander wherever it wanted. She read for a while but was too relaxed to concentrate and soon dozed off again, waking only in response to Dave's gentle knock on the door. "Jen lass, tea'll be ready soon."

"Yeah, okay," she mumbled, "I'll be down in a minute."

She dressed in a daze and sauntered unsteadily down the stairs. As she reached the bottom step, there was a loud knock at the door. She hurried over and opened it to a familiar face; it was the delivery boy from the supermarket. She blushed and tucked her hair behind her ear.

"Supper's here!" announced the boy with a smile, holding up several handfuls of carrier bags crammed full of takeaway meals. Jenny instinctively reached out for the bags but then suddenly pulled her hand away. "Oh, er, could you just leave them on the step? I'll just fetch some money. … Uncle Dave," she called, retreating into the living room, "the delivery boy's here."

"Well, tell 'im t' come in then!" he shouted back from the kitchen.

Jenny went back to the door in a state of growing confusion. "Er, you're to come in," she said nervously. The boy carefully picked up the bags and stepped inside and she shut the door behind him. He looked at her quizzically. Not knowing what to do, she went to consult Dave. "He's in," she said, walking into the kitchen.

"Well tell 'im t' shift 'issen 'n' fetch 'food in 'ere. 'n' 'e'd better take 'is coat off 'n' all if 'e's stoppin'," replied Dave, who was busy counting out paper plates. She walked back through the living room and passed on Dave's instructions.

"Thanks," he responded, "er, Cathy's here as well."

"That's good," replied Jenny, more confused than ever.

The boy placed the carrier bags carefully on the floor, took off his coat and hung it on one of the pegs. He looked as confused as Jenny. "I'll just take these through. You do know Cathy's here don't you?"

"Er … yeah …"

"Nah den, young 'un, tha's not been chuckin' my 'grub down 'drive again 'as tha? Where's tha lass 'n' tha kid?"

"Hello, Mr Strives. Cathy's outside and Tom will be along in a minute, he's just come in from work."

Jenny was starting to grow uncomfortable, "Whereabouts outside?" she asked nervously.

"Er … on the doorstep probably, she was just parking." This time Jenny *wanted* the cracks to appear and swallow her up. She ran back to the door and flung it open. There in the cold was a young woman in her late teens, her breath sparkling in the glow of the mariner's lamp

"I'm so sorry," stuttered Jenny, "I'd just woken up and didn't know … I really am sorry."

The girl smiled thinly. "Don't worry about it!" she responded, in a tone that indicated she should. Jenny ushered her in, still apologising and turned to give Dave her fiercest stare. He had no idea what he was supposed to have done and simply carried on as if everyone knew everyone else and why each of them was there.

"Come on then, tha lot, it'll be cold 'fore we've even started. Fill thee boots, but don't be forgettin' t' leave some fo' tha Tommy; workin' lad needs 'is fill – still growin' that 'un. 'tha listenin', young 'un?"

Ensconced in The Chair and its headphones, David, at whom this last comment had been aimed, was steadfastly maintaining the proud tradition and so hadn't heard a word. Nevertheless he soon found himself being torn between the final five minutes of the most intense Sheffield derby for a generation and the delicious aroma emanating from the kitchen. He wavered momentarily and then, finally forsaking the esteemed Professor, returned to his game.

Dave ushered the others into the kitchen and began to ceremoniously peel off the lids from the takeaway boxes, sniffing the air theatrically as he did so. “There tha goes, Jen lass; secret ingredient!” he laughed, waving his ‘phone triumphantly, before standing it precariously on its end in front of the redundant microwave, which to Jenny’s surprise had been restored to its place of honour.

Jenny was delighted to see the food, knowing now that she wouldn’t have to cook, but she was completely bewildered by the presence of the boy and Cathy. “Er, how do you know Uncle Dave?” she asked the boy.

“We don’t really. He just called in last week and asked us if we’d like to come for tea tonight. It was a bit of a surprise when he asked us to drive into town to pick up a takeaway. Still, ‘fair exchange is no robbery’.” Just then, there was another knock on the door. “That’ll be Tom, shall I get it?”

“No, it’s okay,” said Jenny, smiling sweetly, “I’ll go.”

She walked back through the living room and opened the door to another surprise; this time it was the boy on the bike. She blushed again and welcomed him in, before looking round the door to make sure he was on his own.

“Hi again,” smiled Tom.

“Er, hi. … Is your bike okay?”

“Yeah it’s cool - James is the man for fixing things.”

“James?”

“Over there,” Tom nodded at the delivery boy. “- Big brother and that’s Cathy, his girl-friend. They’re getting engaged next year when they come back from Kenya, but don’t tell anyone though - it’s top secret.”

“Great,” said Jenny, trying not to sound disappointed. Tom looked at her intensely, as if trying to come to some sort of judgement and then shook his head as the thought slipped away.

“Awesome!” he exclaimed on seeing The Chair, and wandered over to watch David completing the Blades’ greatest ever Deby Day comeback.

Jenny felt the relief wash over her; was she really that obvious? She waited until she was sure that the game had Tom’s full attention, and then returned to the kitchen to find James and Cathy each holding a paper plate of Indian food and looking very uncomfortable. Eager to redeem herself, she spotted the problem immediately.

“Uncle Dave, where’s the cutlery?”

“Ah … er … ‘ave a butcher’s in ‘drawers ‘n’ see what’s there.”

Jenny already knew what was there and was sure that Dave knew too, but was leaving the embarrassment of the moment to her. She scooped up the few sorry looking forks and spoons and lay them on the table before sorting out two reasonably straight forks and handing them to Cathy and James, making sure their hands didn’t meet. “We’ll have to make do with these, I’m afraid.”

“That’s fine,” replied James kindly.

Jenny felt herself blush again. “So, you don’t really know Uncle Dave very well then?” she asked, anxious to avoid any silences.

“No, I don’t think he goes to church and we’ve only ever seen him ‘round the village. Oh, er … our dad’s the vicar at St Mark’s.”

“Cool!” exclaimed Jenny, having no idea whether being a vicar’s son was cool or not. “And I hear your going to Kenya … that would be *so* cool.”

“Yeah,” replied James, somewhat taken aback, “we’re going out to the school Dad started.” Jenny nodded enthusiastically, hoping to convey her approval, whilst simultaneously trying to ignore the growing sense that she’d somehow managed to offended her guests for a second time.

"Any left?" shouted a voice from the door. It was John. Jenny sighed. "Sorry, more guests," she explained and hurriedly removed herself from the conversation. Without waiting, John had already hung up his coat and wandered into the living room. He seemed surprised to see Cathy and the boys and quickly made his way into the kitchen. Not knowing what else to do, but painfully aware that their gaze hadn't left her, Jenny sat back down on the enormous settee next to James and Cathy, wanting to be the good host but still confused as to why they were here and desperate not to make an even greater fool of herself. She stole an unseen glance at Cathy, envying her thick, straight, jet black hair and then suddenly realised where she had seen her before.

Cathy, recognising the game was up, spoke first, "I'm sorry about the shop; I only work there on Saturdays."

Jenny couldn't help smiling. "I wish I could have followed you. Does he come in often?"

"Pretty often," replied Cathy with a wince and a mischievous grin.

"Is either of you going to tell me what you're talking about?" asked James, feigning offence.

"Oh nothing," replied Cathy airily.

James' experiences in Africa had produced in him a wisdom beyond his years and he had already concluded that in such a situation girls are best left alone, so excusing himself he wandered over to join Tom and David at The Chair.

"I'm sorry if I was bit off before," said Cathy, "I knew it was you and was really embarrassed about running away."

"Oh, forget it; I tried it too but got caught. … Just make sure *you* lock *us* out if we ever come back again." She stole another look at Cathy and the two of them burst out laughing.

The rest of the evening was one of the best ever. Despite her disappointment over James being taken, Jenny couldn't help but warm to Cathy. She'd always been drawn to the company of older girls and Cathy seemed kind and caring but with a wicked sense of humour that Jenny found irresistible. She was already upbraiding herself for her earlier attitude. Cathy explained how Dave, totally out of the blue, had invited them over the previous Thursday to meet his niece and nephew and how they hadn't known how to refuse. James had said it would be okay and, anyway, they'd wanted to see inside Dave's house for ages. *"No cheap tack 'ere lass!"* she'd added, causing Jenny to spit her drink back into her glass.

The boys had moved here three years ago, when they'd returned with their father from Africa, but Cathy was Highfield born and bred. All her family were farmers and she'd spent her entire life amongst animals. "Amazing," said Jenny breathlessly, as they went on to discuss her favourite topic; it turned out that Cathy had learnt to ride as soon as she could reach the stirrups and she invited Jenny over to see her horses the following afternoon. Jenny beamed with delight.

"Eh, 'as tha pair 'ad owt yet?" shouted Dave across the room. There was no response from The Chair. "Oi, daft 'ead," he continued, crossing the living room and clipping David round the ear, "go 'n' get some snap 'fore it's all gone. … 'ere, Jamey lad, tha set this rodeo game up 'n' I'll sort *Chuckle Brothers* out." Dave grabbed the back of his nephew's neck in a pincer of his thumb and forefinger and lifted him out of The Chair.

"Aargh!" screamed David. "Thou's a right football hooligan."

"Come on, glory boy!" ordered Dave. "Snap!" And pincer still in place, he marched his nephew into the kitchen, followed by Tom.

"Cool microwave," whistled Tom spying the DCS 24. He brushed the stainless steel door with his hand. "Can we warm our food up?" he asked, pressing the door release button. The door sprang open and he jumped back, just in time to see it hit Dave's 'phone full force and send it spinning into the sink.

"Looks like you'll need a new secret ingredient," laughed Jenny, who'd wandered back through to replenish her and Cathy's drinks.

Dave fished the 'phone out of the sink and held it above his head. "'be reet; watterproof case must o' done its job," he announced, staring up into the connections. He gave it a shake and a stream of water trickled out onto his face. Everyone except Dave and Tom fell about laughing.

"I'm really sorry, Mr Strives … I'll pay for a new one … I didn't mean to … I'm really sorry …" spluttered Tom.

"Too reet tha will!" snarled Dave, wiping his chin with a tea towel. He glowered around the room, looking from face to face, daring anyone to find it funny. "Wasn't cheap tack, neither."

Jenny caught Cathy's eye and, the two of them burst out laughing again. "Oh come on, Uncle Dave," Jenny said, recovering at least some of her poise, "you did it last night and it *was* a daft place to leave the 'phone."

Dave pondered for a moment and then let out a sigh of acceptance. "Aah, well maybe tha's got a point. Any roads, I can allus pick another 'un up off one o' me business contracts. … One o' me mates is into these, 'e'll sort me out wi' summat - probably time fo' an update any roads." Then, relishing the opportunity to show off his magnanimity, he looked slowly around the sea of enquiring faces once more, before adding, "Don't worry theesen, Tommy lad. … Tell thee what; tha can do a few jobs fo' me 'round 'place 'n' we'll call it quits."

"Thanks Mr Strives," said Tom sheepishly. "It was an accident, honest," he pleaded once more, before scurrying back to the safety of The Chair.

David piled up two plates full of food and hurried after him, but they'd forgotten that James was loading Wild West Rodeo and when they realised that Dave intended to play, they slunk back into the kitchen, where Tom declared himself the South Yorkshire relish eating champion and David challenged him to a lime pickle-eating contest.

The remaining hours sped by in a happy haze. Jenny and Cathy talked for an age, their fledgling friendship growing with every story and joke. The boys, having each beaten Dave's best ever score on Wild West Rodeo, remained huddled around The Chair whilst Dave, displaying unexpected restraint in the face of his latest disappointment, retreated to the kitchen with an air of unconcern to chat with John for the rest of the evening. The whole house hummed with a sense of well-being.

John had left first, claiming to everyone's surprise and concern to be feeling under the weather. The others followed around eleven, having first helped Jenny to tidy up. Jenny and David saw them to the door.

"See you tomorrow," said Jenny brightly, following their new friends out into the cold night air.

"Bye," shouted Cathy and James over their shoulders.

"Bow war," grinned Tom and David to one another.

Jenny watched them for a moment and then turned to her brother. "What's all that about?" she asked suspiciously.

"Pucka artin compotisha."

Jenny tried half-heartedly to mask a smile. They stood side by side in silence watching the lights of their new friends' car disappear into the night. "Thanks for helping me today, bro, I don't think I could have made it without you." David turned to look up into the clear night sky, following his breath in the light of the mariner's lamp as it gradually faded from sight. "It's okay. … Do you like it here?"

"I think I do."

Just then the 'phone rang. Jenny froze.

"Do you think that's Mum and Dad?"

"'not sure. Anyway, Dave's inside."

"It's *Uncle Dave* to thou, me t'old lass."

Jenny smiled and punched her brother playfully on the arm just as the 'phone fell silent. "We'd better go in." She turned to push the door but to her horror it didn't move. She pushed again but there was still no response. "Here; you have a go!"

David pushed his shoulder hard into the door. "I think it's locked."

Jenny brushed her brother aside and began banging with her fists on the solid oak panels of the enormous door. "Uncle Dave! Uncle Dave!" she shouted, "Uncle Dave!" There was no response. She suddenly felt very cold and began to shiver. "Come on David, you're hands are bigger than mine." David began thumping the door with his fists as the two of them hollered for their uncle to respond, their voices echoing across the empty moor.

"What are we going to do now ?" asked Jenny on the verge of tears. She slumped down on the steps and David sat down quietly beside her.

"Do you think we could break in?" he whispered excitedly, staring up at the outside of the house.

"Don't be ridiculous!"

"Well you suggest something."

"Let's try again." They began banging on the door together, yelling at the top of their voices, but there was still no response.

"What's wrong with him? Do you think something's happened?"

"I've no idea, but we can't stay here - we'll freeze."

"What are we going to do?"

Neither of them having an answer, they sat back down in silence. Jenny was just about to suggest walking down to the village when she was disturbed by a wet nose brushing across her face. It was Meg. Her heart soared.

"It's a bit cold for camping out."

"John!" the children exclaimed together.

"What are you two up to, sat out here? Thought you'd be ready for an early night after walking all that way."

"We're locked out and Uncle Dave can't hear us."

"What is it with them Strives? No wonder he leaves a key at mine."

"Can we go and fetch it?"

"No need, lad … here." John smiled kindly and passed the key to David, who carefully opened the door, and for some unknown reason the three of them crept as quietly as possible into the living room. They found Dave fast asleep on the settee, head lolling backwards, mouth open.

"Alphabet male … alphabet male," he mumbled hoarsely.

"Dave …" whispered John, shaking him gently by the arm, "… Dave!"

Dave half-opened his eyes, "Get 'em away … get 'em away!"

"Get what away?"

"Apples, sling 'em some apples!"

"Uncle Dave!!"

Dave sat bolt upright and stared round the room. "Oh … think I must been power nappin'; ex-SAS youth showed me 'ow – *sleep's a weapon* - if tha knows 'ow t' use it, like. Oh, ay up, John, what's tha doin' 'ere?"

"Oh, I was just passin'."

"What time is it?"

"Half past eleven. Uncle Dave, who was on the 'phone?"

Dunno, lass. 'as it been ringin'?"

Jenny paused, a thousand conflicting responses rushing round her head. She was certain it was her mother who had 'phoned and she could easily have given way to the anger she felt rising up inside at her uncle's shortcomings. On the other hand, the events of the evening had restored a measure of equilibrium which she was loathe to disturb; maybe it would be better to leave it until the morning. In the end, it didn't really make much difference one way or the other; nothing she could say or do now could alter their decision. It was out of her hands, and it didn't take long for her newly-discovered pragmatism to overcome the attractions of the moral high ground. "Don't worry;" she said softly, "if it *was* Mum, I'm sure she'll try again in the morning. There's nothing we can do about it tonight. Come on David, it's time for bed."

"Okah, ah'll jaus geh a drah o' wattah."

"Bed! And clean your teeth!"

21

Sunday brought out the very best in Jenny. She'd been woken around nine by John's gentle knock on the door. He'd called round earlier, but finding no signs of life had walked on with Meg, and now, on his return, he'd guessed Jenny would want to be up.

"Feeling better this morning?" she asked blearily, as he piled up the wood in the range.

"Hmm? Oh … much better thank you; good night's sleep sorts everything," he replied unconvincingly. John was as straight as a dye and even a half-lie sat uneasily with him.

Jenny knew instinctively that something wasn't quite right, but she was far from certain what to do about it. "Did you enjoy last night?" she fished.

"Aye, it were grand. Long day, lass, that's all. … Now, let's get this range going."

His busyness made it clear that he'd said enough, and Jenny cared for him far too much to risk making him feel uncomfortable. She couldn't bring to mind a single individual she respected more than John, other than perhaps Sally, and although it upset her immensely to think of him struggling alone with some problem or other, for now she let it drop; it was up to him, and he must have his reasons.

John didn't stay long, leaving Jenny with the place to herself once more. Dave had set his alarm for eight; "no lie-ins fo' country folk; 'place not run itssen!" His 'phone had gurgled and spluttered for half an hour before giving up for good, having elicited nothing more than a groan from its owner. Next door, it would be another two hours before his nephew woke to tea, the smell of frying bacon and the driest mouth he could ever remember. So, seeing there was no reason to hurry, Jenny decided to treat herself to another bath, whilst the range warmed up.

She came back down feeling much better prepared to face the day, still relishing the respite from the boys. Knowing what they were like, she wasn't expecting much help and she sighed a grown woman's sigh as she tried to make sense of the muddle of last night's leftovers and today's ingredients in the exceedingly generous fridge (Sub-Zero PRO 4850 Refrigerator/Freezer - £14 484 - "That can say what tha likes, *I'll* not be takin' chances, amount o' 'ospitalisin' I do. Any roads, got 'em t' throw in 'drawer dividers [£ 192 each] fo' nowt. 'n' it'll last 'n 'undred years 'n' all, that. No cheap in cheap, tha knows.")

Jenny had never cooked on a range before and she only had one old frying pan to work with. Even so, after two eggs she'd mastered the hot plate and soon worked out how to control the cooking time. Feeling more confident, she decided breakfast could wait half an hour and made a start on the vegetables for lunch. She stood at the sink, gazing out of the window at the snow flecked fields and the white hills beyond. In the distance she could see the field where The Doctors kept their horses and she smiled as she thought again of her trip to Cathy's. She daydreamed her way through a small mountain of potatoes, carrots, parsnips and swede before finally beginning to feel hungry and deciding it was time for breakfast. She made tea and took it up to the boys. Dave groaned and pulled the covers over his aching shoulders. David grabbed the cup out of her hand and downed the tea in one before asking if there was anymore. "Only if you come down and get it - I've started breakfast now."

David emerged first, wandering over to the fridge and filling a glass with milk. "Don't drink all of that!" Jenny chided. "I'll need some for lunch." David didn't reply. He dropped the glass in the sink and sauntered over to The Chair. Twenty minutes later, just as breakfast was reaching critical point, Dave appeared carrying a mug of cold, stewed tea.

"Alreet if I put 'kettle on?" he asked.

"Tea's made," replied Jenny primly. "It's on the table. Sit down and I'll bring your breakfast over."

Dave did as he was told and was soon rewarded by an enormous plate of bacon, sausage, black pudding (Jenny's first – *propa northern*) mushrooms, eggs, tomatoes and beans. "Smashin' lass," he enthused. "I'd 'ave done it me sen, but what wi' me 'and 'n' that, I'd only be in' road."

Jenny smiled to herself; she really was getting the measure of him now. "Don't worry Uncle Dave, I'll sort out the meals today," she replied brightly. This suited her down to the ground. She could be in control for a while and it would give her something else to think about until her trip to Cathy's. "It's fine; I enjoy cooking. Mum let Sally teach me when I was young."

"Great," said Dave, losing interest fast. "Any toast?"

Breakfast was long and filling. They surprised themselves at how much they managed to eat, especially given the amount of Indian food Dave had ordered the night before. "Must be all 'fresh air," mused Dave, before quickly adding, "… fo' *tha pair*, any roads, seein' 'ow tha's not used to it 'n' that."

They drank tea and nibbled on toast until they were more than full and then Jenny turned her attention to lunch. She'd realised last night that there were nowhere near enough saucepans and utensils and had asked John that morning if he'd bring some up. They arrived, along with crockery and cutlery, shortly after twelve and soon after that John and Dave disappeared *t' see a man abaht a dog,* causing an anxious exchange of glances between the children and bringing a sly grin to Dave's face. David, too, was soon back in The Chair and out of the way, giving Jenny full rein in her new domain.

Dinner was a triumph. Everything was perfect - even the Yorkshires, and John, who seemed back to his old self, declared it the best he'd ever tasted.

"Good as thee Na'nan's but don't *tha pair* be sayin' owt!" was Dave's verdict, whilst David simply recorded his appreciation by eating everything in sight, including the last three slices of apple pie, before licking his plate clean enough to go straight back in the cupboard. John persuaded Dave that they should wash up the rest of the dishes and Jenny, in the best form of her life, beat David four-two on Soccer Pro, leaving him as speechless as the night before.

Cathy arrived just after three. To Jenny's surprise and slight disappointment, James and Tom were with her, but she soon recovered as the five of them piled into Cathy's father's Land Rover and headed off up the hill, theirs the only tracks in the latest dusting of snow. Cathy drove and Jenny sat beside her. The boys were relegated to the back benches.

The girls carried on from where they'd left off the night before: Cathy's parents' farm was just over the hill, at about the same height as The Doctors'. The family had farmed there for four generations and Cathy had hoped that she'd be the fifth. After James arrived, those hopes were put on hold but she still felt the pull of the hills whenever she was away for any length of time. Having never travelled far from the valley, she was actually quite nervous about their upcoming trip to Kenya, but she had implicit trust in James' judgement and he had promised it would be fine. After that, they'd have to see.

Bumping along in the Land Rover, Jenny was taken aback at just how much Cathy was prepared to share about herself. Her own revelations seemed miserly in comparison and she vowed to make amends at the first opportunity. The only problem was she didn't quite know what to tell her; until her mother 'phoned, she had no idea about how things with her family really were. Still no contact. It was so unlike her. She must be waiting to give her the bad news face to face. Jenny didn't even know if her father was coming back. How could things have gone so wrong?

"Tha's a whaa Cahy laa," shouted Tom across the Land Rover.

Jenny came round from her musings, "What did you say?" she shouted over the rumble of the engine.

"He shaa, 'tha's a whaa Cahy laa'," yelled David in her ear. "Daa yaa narh u'erstaa Pickaa?" Tom fell about laughing, only stopping when he banged his head on the window, which in turn led David to collapse uncontrollably.

"What?" shouted Jenny in exasperation.

"Pickaa, daa yaa narh u'erstaa Pickaa?" gasped David, who by now was almost crying.

"You're an idiot."

"Yaa." Tom and David fell back into further fits of hysterical laughter, accompanied by increasingly vigorous arm punching and some excruciating finger bending that only added to the streams of tears running down their cheeks. Jenny frowned and shook her head.

"They're talking 'Pickle'," shouted James over her shoulder. "It's how you talk after eating six mouthfuls of lime pickle. … that's what happens when you're landed with a brother who's fourteen-going-on-seven!"

"Oh, don't I know it; I've got one who's twelve-going-on-three!" replied Jenny, fighting to keep a straight face. She would have lost but was saved by a left turn into Cathy's farm.

This was the leeward side of the hill and less snow had settled here. Nevertheless, as Jenny stepped out of the Land Rover, she felt the ice crunch beneath her feet. She had secretly dared to hope that Cathy would take her out riding, but now realised that this was impossible. And anyway, now that she was actually here, with the farm being where it was, the sun was already disappearing behind the hill and it was obviously far too late in the day. And then, to her surprise and delight, this latest disappointment almost immediately melted away under the glow of the heart-warming conviction that there would be another time.

Cathy linked arms with her and led her over to the stable. “You lot can go and see if there’s any food left the four Lumps haven’t already scoffed their way through!” she shouted dismissively over her shoulder to the boys, as they walked across the yard and into the warmth of the stable. Inside were two horses; a beautiful chestnut hunter, which Cathy’s mother rode out, and a perfect grey pony with a flowing silver mane. This was Jess. “Hello girl,” whispered Cathy, stroking the pony’s flanks, “I’ve brought someone to meet you.”

“She’s beautiful,” said Jenny, laughing as Jess nuzzled into her coat. “Your own pony, that’s so cool.”

`“You’ll have to come again in the summer and ride her out.”

“Really?”

“‘course. I’ll take Sam,” Cathy smiled fondly at the handsome chestnut. “And you can see what my beautiful girl can do,” she smooched, kissing Jess between the eyes.

Cathy had deliberately left the horses’ grooming and feed so that Jenny could help. It was a typically generous act and one that Jenny appreciated deeply. She loved being around animals and no animals came close to horses. For Cathy’s part, she could see Jenny’s natural affinity to the animals and her instinctive understanding of their needs. It was such a relief to have someone to share her enthusiasm with. The girls worked around one another as if they’d been partners for years. Once or twice Jenny, feeling unsure of herself and much to her own amazement, found herself asking for help without a moment’s hesitation; not unlike James, for such a young person, she had a very clear understanding of her own qualities and defects and, reflecting on this sudden willingness to be led by someone more or less her own age, Jenny decided that country life must be bringing out the best in her.

Twenty minutes later they were finished and Jenny leaned

back on the whitewashed wall and looked around properly for the first time. She was struck by how neat and ordered everything was; the paint was fresh and the wooden stalls were newly varnished; outside the stalls the flagstones were even and freshly swept and along the walls the highly polished tack hung in neat rows.

"Are these stables new?" she asked.

"No, don't think so," replied Cathy airily. "I think my grandfather built them. Come on, let's go and see if they've missed any cake."

Jenny smiled to herself. "Neat, tidy, warm and cared for; just like stables should be."

The farmhouse matched the stables perfectly: warm and welcoming and everything equally neat and well-ordered. "It's like John living in Dave's house," Jenny mused, rather impressed by her own insight.

When she met Cathy's parents, her theory received further corroboration. Cathy's mother was a tall, striking woman, toughened by life on a high Yorkshire hill-farm with a laconic sheep farmer and their four boisterous sons, yet still retaining the gentleness of spirit to chide her boys for failing to acknowledge Jenny's presence and shooing them off the settee to offer her the best place by the fire.

Cathy's father was remarkable for his huge hands, hardened to gritstone by years out on the tops, one of which he held out in the most formal manner to Jenny. Yet he, too, welcomed her with an open smile and a twinkle in his eye, cementing his place as a 'True Yorkshire Gent' by cuffing away a pair of ginormous feet that were too slow to move out of her way.

"Perfect," thought Jenny: the contrast between the light and life and nurturing warmth of this house and her own troubled and increasingly cheerless home back in Surrey was becoming increasingly apparent and she already knew that this was destined to become one of her favourite places (although, to be fair, this *was* before she'd met The Lumps.)

Cathy's parents quickly excused themselves to set about their afternoon chores, leaving the young people to their own devices. The Lumps were something quite different: their huge frames seemed to fill the whole room and they appeared to interpret the arrival of James, and particularly Tom and David, as an invitation to engage in various trials of strength that only served to further reduce the available space, whilst their clamour rose inexorably until they had to shriek to be heard.

They continually sparred off one another, making up for in volume what they lacked in wit. Cathy, although the oldest, appeared to be a particularly favourite target for their teasing. Jenny shrank down in her seat, hoping to remain unnoticed. "Large, loud losers," was how Cathy described them, but then years of prods, pokes and pointless provocations had probably clouded her opinion. Jenny didn't know what to think; she found the noise and general boisterousness of the whole occasion quite overwhelming and let out a sigh of relief when Cathy, with a flash in her dark eyes, rounded on one of her brothers and told him that they weren't about to waste their afternoon listening to the 'Seven Intellectual Dwarves' showing away, even if they paid them. Puffed up with their victory, the girls beat a hasty retreat to Cathy's room, leaving the boys to their roughhousing and increasingly unlikely tales of eating exploits to rival any pickle eating competition.

"- Pathetic."

The next hour or so was spent in blissful conversation about horses and boys and growing up in different places, but Jenny couldn't keep ignoring the ever-tightening knot in her stomach and so, with a deep breath, took the plunge and told Cathy about her parents. No sooner had she started than she collapsed in a flood of tears. Cathy put her arm round her and hugged her shoulders. She said nothing, which, Jenny reflected later, was the best thing she could have said. Jenny cried for a long time, Cathy never loosening her hold and then she suddenly looked up and declared, "That's enough self-pity for one day, let's have another look at those photos."

She dried her eyes on her sleeve and they leafed through the album of Cathy and Jess's show-jumping exploits for a third time. By the time they'd finished Jenny said she felt sufficiently recovered to face the boys. Cathy's mother immediately recognised that something was wrong and shooed the nonplussed Lumps off to their evening chores much earlier than usual, whilst James, Tom and David reluctantly pulled themselves out of the furniture and said their good-byes. The visitors thanked Cathy's mother for her hospitality and the five friends stepped out into the cold early evening air. Letting the boys go on ahead, Cathy pulled Jenny to one side and gave her another long hug, before whispering, "Try not to worry; if your parents are anything like you and David, I'm sure they'll work it out. … *No cheap tack in tha's family, tha knows*!" Kindness reaped its intended harvest and, letting out an enormous sigh, Jenny smiled back at her friend and then started to giggle. She eventually gathered herself and quickly wiped her eyes. "Thanks," she replied, as they climbed back into the Land Rover, "for everything."

"We're back," shouted David. There was no reply. They found their uncle fast asleep in The Chair, snoring contently, a mug of cold tea hanging precariously from his fingers. Jenny smiled affectionately, but David only stared in disbelief at his uncle's name, sitting proudly at the top of the leader board on Wild West Rodeo once more.

"Come on," said Jenny, falling into maternal mode, "let's make some sandwiches and you can tell me what lessons you're missing tomorrow." Mollified by the thought of another day off school, David shuffled into the kitchen behind her and leaned lazily against the sink, perfectly positioned to be most in the way. "Do you like it here?" he asked again absent-mindedly.

"Yeah, it's fine, why?"

"I think it's cool. Do you think we'll come again?"

"Maybe, depends on Mum and Dad."

"Suppose so."

In-depth analysis over, David returned to stare at the plasma screen and wait for his uncle to resurface. He did so about fifteen minutes later, promptly spilling cold tea down his Wrangler PRCA jeans. "Uurgh!" he exclaimed. "Not again!" But his annoyance didn't last. The spillage had instantly brought to mind his latest acquisition and he quickly brushed himself off, puffed out his chest and walked solemnly over to the enormous oak table. He paused and then ceremoniously reached out for a rectangular blue box. He paused again to allow his audience the opportunity to fully savour the moment and then triumphantly lifted out a Blackberry 8700G mobile 'phone. "Another Strives' master stroke, I think tha'll find. Now *that's* what I call a deal!" he chuckled, standing his new trophy carefully on the sideboard and grinning at himself in the mirror. "What's tha reckon t' colour screen then? … 'can send them g-messages 'n' everythin'! … Gonna take some *reet* fettlin' this bad boy. *And* I'll need a new cover; this 'un's much bigger. … Oh aah, proper job this fella, don't' worry theesens abaht that - t'other load o' rubbish went in straight in 'bin, no messin'. … Eh, tha mate's got one these, tha knows, Davey."

"Who?"

"That Noel Armstrong; no cheap tack 'ere tha …" he paused

for a moment and then smiled and let out an amused sigh. "… Any roads, I reckon thee Mam'll 'phone fo' definite t'neet. … Be reet though; she'll be best off using 'ouse 'phone – what wi' not being up t' speed wi' this 'un."

""I suppose so," Jenny replied with a shudder as she returned from the kitchen with the sandwiches. "I think I'll just go and have another bath, if that's alright," she added quietly.

"Not 'avin' owt?"

"No thanks. I'm still feeling a bit tired from yesterday."

"Suit theesen, lass; more fo' me 'n' Davey lad. … Fill thee space boots, young 'un! … FILL THEE SPACE BOOTS! Heh heh! What abht that 'un, Davey lad? FILL THEE SPACE BOOTS!!" roared Dave gleefully rubbing his hands together.

The truth was Jenny wanted to be on her own. She still felt incredibly nervous about her parents 'phoning, but talking to Cathy had released a lot of the tension. She felt drained and just wanted to curl up and go to sleep. After several minutes 'umming and ahing', she eventually decided against another bath and, so without undressing, pulled her dressing gown tight around her and crawled up the bed and under the quilt. She fell asleep listening to the wind whistling in off the tops. She woke at eleven, just before the 'phone rang.

22

The house 'phone rang three times before Dave lifted the receiver. Jenny bolted out of her room and then immediately stopped dead in her tracks. She could feel the colour draining from her face and was trembling from head to toe. She reached out for the banister to steady herself and leant over, straining to hear Dave's voice: "Ay up Jane lass … champion. … Good as gold … no, not really … well, nowt t' speak o' any roads; they've 'ad a crackin' time …". To the uninitiated Dave sounded like a man who had never had a moment's self-doubt in his life, but Jenny's trained ear detected a hitherto unheard thinness in his voice that made her fear the worst. She stood stock still, unable to move.

"Does tha want a word? 'reckon she's nodded off but I know she were dead keen t' speak t' thee. … Oh, okay, put 'im on," Dave's voice stretched a little tighter. "Ay up, our kid, what's up?" Well at least Dad was there but why did he need to speak to Dave? Jenny felt her knees go weak and reached out for the banister with her free hand. "Oh, okay," said Dave, sounding taken aback. "… Reet …. Reet … Reet … Aha … Reet … Reet, Reet … Reet. … Aah, I reckon I can manage that." Jenny could hear the relief in his voice. There was something else, too; he sounded gratified and reassured. What on earth were they talking about?

"Reet then, I'll go 'n' see if she's still awake; big day on 'ills yesterday, pair on 'em's shattered."

Jenny ran back into her bedroom, turned off the light and dived under the covers. "Jenny," called Dave softly, abandoning his customary patois, "Jenny are you awake? It's your Dad." He knocked and peered round the door. Jenny sat up in bed and stared round. Dave turned on the light and held out the 'phone, he was grinning his *I know something you don't* grin, which screwed up the knot in Jenny's stomach until she thought she would faint. She took the 'phone and lifted it slowly to her ear.

"Hello."

"Hello, darling, are you okay?"

Jenny's eyes began to fill with tears. "I'm fine. Is Mum with you?"

"Yes, she's here, we're both fine. We can't wait to see you. How's David?

Jenny's heart was beating so fast it felt as though it would punch a hole through her chest. She had a thousand questions and she was terrified of every answer. She didn't know where to start. "Oh, he's fine," she said limply, "same as usual." There was an uncertain pause and then Jenny, unable to bear the uncertainty any longer, blurted out, "Are things okay between you and Mum?"

Dan laughed. "They are, they really are. We've had a long talk and come to some big decisions. It'll mean some changes and there's some things you and David will need to help with, but if it all works out, we'll all be fine."

"You are still together, aren't you?"

"Of course we are. Whatever gave you that idea? We're not going anywhere, well not in that way at least. Look, Mum's desperate to talk to you. We'll see you tomorrow."

"Okay. … Dad?"

"Yeah?"

"It *is* alright isn't it?"

"Well, it all depends on you and David really but I reckon we're going to be fine. … Here, talk to your Mum."

"Hi, Jenny, how are you?"

"Fine, thanks. When will you be back?"

"Well, our flight lands around ten and Dave said he'd come over and pick us up, so hopefully before twelve."

"Was your trip okay, Mum?"

"It was fine," it was Jane's turn to take a deep breath, "but there is something I need to ask you and David."

"What?" Jenny asked almost before Jane had finished speaking.

"Well, wouldn't you rather wait until we're there?"

"Please Mum," said Jenny in desperation, "what is it?"

"Well ..." there was a momentary pause, then in perfect synchronisation each of them brought her thumb and forefinger to her mouth and bit hard on her bottom lip, "Dad and I, well I, I mean, me, well, I would like to keep the New York business going."

"Yeah?"

"But Dad thinks, and I agree," she added quickly, "that it would be better for the business if I spent more time out here."

"Oh," said Jenny flatly.

"But don't worry," Jane knew she was in too far to stop now. "I'll be home most of the time and ... " she hesitated again; she was about to play her trump card; if it didn't win the trick, the game was over, "it does mean that Dad will be staying at home - for most of the time anyway."

There was no response.

"Jenny, are you alright? ... Jenny?"

"T'old lass is a bit upset - nowt t' worry abaht." Dave was stroking Jenny's hair, her face hidden in her pillow. She was sobbing as though her heart were about to break.

"Can she talk?"

"I'll ask."

With her head still half buried in the pillow, Jenny nodded, wiped the back of her hand across her face and sucked in as much air as she could before carefully taking the 'phone from Dave.

"Jenny, I'm so sorry, it was a stupid idea. I'll tell them that the deal's off and that'll be an end to it. ... I'm coming home."

Jenny sniffed and shivered, breathing deeply before speaking. "No, don't do that."

"But I can't put you through this, it's not fair, it was a stupid idea."

Jenny sniffed and laughed in the same breath, letting out another long shudder. "It's not that. I thought you and Dad were going to split up."

"Oh Jenny, *that's* not going to happen," said Jane, willing herself to sound convincing. "There's so much to tell you, I don't know where to start. But Dad and I are fine, honestly."

"Really?"

"Really. Better than ever in fact, you wait and see. Look, you need to get back to bed. Please don't worry; everything's fine. We'll tell you all about it when we get back. Is David there?"

"I think he's asleep."

Dave nodded.

"Okay, well we'll be home before you know it. Take care and please don't worry, we love you very much."

"Bye. Love you, darling," shouted Dan over her shoulder.

"Bye Mum."

"Bye." Jane hung up and turned quickly to hide her face in Dan's shoulder.

You okay?" he asked tenderly.

"Fine," she replied, running her fingers under her eyes.

"You didn't tell her about staying at Dave's," Dan said in the same gentle tone.

"I couldn't, she was too upset."

"What about?"

"I think she thought you weren't coming back."

"Well at least she still doesn't know better than us about *everything* yet."

Jane smiled bravely and snuggled back into his shoulder. "Close run thing, though," she thought to herself.

In Highfield, Dave wasn't quite sure what to do, so when Jenny asked him to 'give her a minute', he was glad to oblige. He looked in on David and then went downstairs to put the kettle on. He mashed two mugs of sweet, milky tea and was just thinking about taking them up when Jenny appeared in the doorway. "Alright?" he asked gently.

"Yeah. Thanks."

Dave twitched and turned away to remove the tea bags from the mugs. He turned back and held one out to Jenny. "What did they say?" he asked.

"Not much really."

Jenny began to cry again. Dave reached over and took the mug from her. He placed it on the work surface and pulled her towards him. She was sobbing uncontrollably and almost collapsed into his arms. He held her tight, patting her rhythmically on her back, stopping only to quickly run his thumb under his own eyes. They stood like that until their tea was cold and then Jenny lifted her head and smiled. "Do you ever get a hot cup of tea?"

"Not wi' *tha pair* around!" Dave replied, carefully pitching his voice to ensure Jenny knew he wasn't being serious. He was responding to some half-formed sense that it was down to him to lift her spirits, and although he'd been quite taken aback by how painful it was to see her upset, he'd quickly recovered and now found himself warming to the familiar task, "Nah den, what's my kid brother 'n' 'is missis been up to? I should never 'ave let *them pair* anywhere near a set o' spanners."

Jenny, had no idea what he was talking about but smiled gently and refilled the kettle. The familiarity of the action seemed to calm her nerves.

"I thought they were going to split up;" she said quietly, "I thought Dad was going to stay in New York."

"'e's not is 'e?"

"No." In spite of everything, Jenny laughed lightly. "They're both coming home tomorrow and Mum’s going to take over the New York side of the business.”

“’n’ what’s tha think o’ that?”

“Alright, really.”

“So what’s tha roarin’ for?”

“Roaring?”

“Aah, tha knows, cryin’, like.”

Jenny laughed again, “I don’t know, just … everything.” She let out a deep sigh. “I’ll be fine now.” She stood up and began to make some fresh tea but just then the ‘phone rang again.

“Nah den, who’s that past midnight?” Dave asked, walking back into the living room. He picked up the ‘phone and was surprised to hear Jane’s voice again.

“Hi Dave, sorry to ring again so late.”

“Don’t worry theesen, lass,” he replied, bravado firmly back in place, “what can I do thee fo’?”

“Oh, our flight’s been delayed, we won’t get in until twelve now.”

“No worries, Jane. Mind, I’ll be strugglin’ t’ pick *tha pair* up *and* do t’other thing.” He cast a glance across to Jenny. “I’ll tell thee what; I bet John’ d do it. Don’t fret theesen, I’ll sort it.”

“Er … thanks,” said Jane with genuine warmth in her voice. “We want to get back as soon as possible. … Is Jenny alright?”

“She’s ‘ere t’old lass, brewin’ up. Does tha want another word?”

“Please, if it’s okay.”

“Jen, it’s thee Mam again,” he called into the kitchen.

“Hi Mum, sorry about before. Is everything alright?”

“Oh, yeah, we’ve just been delayed that’s all. Are you alright? You sounded so upset.”

“I’m fine now; just a bit tired that’s all.” There was a moment’s silence.

“… Jenny?”

“Yes?” Jenny felt the knot tightening its grip again.

“You know for our plan to work …”

“Y-e-a-h …”

“Well, there’s something I should have asked you before; it would mean Dad and I would have to come to New York together sometimes.”

“Y-e-a-h …”

“Well, we were wondering … how would you and David feel about spending a few more week-ends with Uncle Dave?” Jane winced as she finished the question.

Jenny looked up from the ‘phone. Dave was over by the door, already wearing his favourite fringed jacket and pulling on his cowboy boots. He reached up and took his beloved El Alamo from the peg. “Nippin’ down t’ John’s”’ he mouthed with a sideways nod of his head, imitating a pair of revolvers with his thumbs and forefingers.

“Okay,” she mouthed back, waving with her fingers.

Dave blew down both barrels of his Colt single action ‘Peacemakers’, span them around his fingers and holstered them in his Tennessee genuine handmade rattlesnake skin belt ($299.98), and closed the door behind him.

Jenny smiled, “That’ll be fine Mum.”

“Oh … are you sure?”

Jenny looked around the sitting room and sighed. “Yeah, I’m sure; don’t worry about it, it’ll be reet.”

“What?”

“Nothing. Honestly, Mum, it’s fine. See you tomorrow. Oh, are you at the airport yet?”

“Yes, why?”

“Have you got time to do some shopping? I’ll pay you back …”

An hour later Dave crept back into the house, removed his hat and coat, shook off the rain and wandered into the kitchen. He spied his tea on the side, but then remembering how long it had been waiting stopped himself mid-reach. He glanced momentarily at the kettle before turning away and walking back to the front door. Not making a sound, he opened it and stepped half out, making sure that one foot remained wedged against the door frame He looked up into the cloud covered sky and let out a sigh of anticipation; tomorrow was going to be a busy day.

23

Even as she slept, Jenny could sense the fatigue of the previous days' exertions accumulating in her limbs. Yet she still woke well before the alarm, anxiety and excitement already hard at work and the threat of a headache beginning to cloud her mood before she'd even had time to get out of bed. It was no surprise, therefore, to hear the annoyance in her voice on coming downstairs to be greeted by a note from Dave. It simply told her that he was *nippin' out t' do a bit o' business* and that John would come round at ten to take them to the airport.

"Couldn't it wait?" she asked out loud. Last night he'd seemed so caring and kind, but within just a few hours he was back to his habitual, unthinking self. He hadn't even bothered to say where he was going or when he would be back, let alone explain the arrangements for the rest of the day. "What a surprise," she sighed sanctimoniously, "but then what else did you expect? Surely you know what he's like by now."

Unable (or possibly *unwilling*) to acknowledge the change in her own mood, she homed in on this latest example of her uncle's selfishness with all the intent of a falcon swopping down on her prey; "He just doesn't get it!" she persisted. "What is this obsession with making money? How can he just abandon us with everything else going on? *Surely* he must know how important today is: ridiculous – just ridiculous!"

Insensible to the deflection, she eagerly re-listed her uncle's shortcomings; his ridiculous way of speaking, the showing off and pathetic jokes at everyone else's expense; the total lack of self-awareness. Ever since they'd arrived, it had just been one put down after another - even David had eventually seen through him. And now, when she *actually* needed him, he was nowhere to be seen. Searching for vindication, she glared at the note again, scrutinising every word, and then, as the condemnation finally pushed her way past caring, she furiously screwed it into a ball, tore it to pieces and threw them towards the fire. "What a *ridiculous* man! Aargh!!"

As she finally vented her frustration, she felt the thrill of release course through her body and let out a deep sigh in response. Her shoulders slumped and catching her reflection beneath the two enormous cow horns, she slowly shook her head and smiled a rueful smile. Was it aimed at the mirror, her uncle or herself? - She didn't know. Either way, it helped, and she settled. For now. … But there was still a huge amount to do before her parents arrived and with no one around to help she simply couldn't afford to be distracted by her uncle's inadequacies. So setting aside her reverie with a second sigh, which proved no more effective than any of its predecessors, she trudged back upstairs to wake David and then busied herself getting washed and dressed, changing her mind repeatedly over what she should wear. She finally settled on her everyday clothes and her favourite denim jacket – 'just another normal day'. Except it wasn't; it was the most important and terrifying day of her young life.

As she dressed, she couldn't help going over the conversations of the previous evening; common sense told her that things were okay now between her parents and coming to Dave's every few weeks was a small price to pay if it meant they would be happy and they would all stay together, but none of this stopped her stomach doing somersaults or her heart racing uncontrollably. She'd been wrong about so many things recently; what if they *weren't* alright? What if her parents were just repeating the same mistakes? After all, it hadn't worked with Dad going to New York, why should it be any different if Mum went? Perhaps she should have tried harder. She sat back down on the bed, overwhelmed by the enormity of what she had just realised: her parents weren't happy together after all, they were simply putting on a brave face and trying to make the best of it for her and David. They couldn't stand to be together and so had just reversed the situation. No wonder her mother had sounded so tense last night. This was the worst possible outcome; she couldn't bear it. If only she could see them, she would know. But did she want to know?

Desperately searching for any sort of distraction, she went back to check on David, snapping at him for making everyone late and berating him for his selfishness. He eventually rolled out of bed just as John arrived, providing Jenny with another opportunity to chastise him.

"There's plenty of time, Jen. … Why don't you 'ave a bit o' breakfast, David? We'll not be back much above one," said John patiently. For once, his calm, considered outlook only seemed to fuel Jenny's irritability. "Hurry up," she snarled, "don't you dare be late for Mum and Dad."

David wandered into the kitchen and lazily fetched down a box of cereals. He leant back on the work surface, plunged in his hand and shovelled a handful into his mouth. As he stood there casually chomping away, staring absentmindedly out of the window, it was clear to Jenny that he was totally oblivious to the catastrophe that was threatening to engulf them. He eventually sensed his sister's eyes burning into the back of his head and turned to take in her mood. Throwing in another handful, he nonchalantly enquired, "What's t' hurry?" through a cloud of cereal dust.

"For goodness sake - just drink this!" barked Jenny, shoving a glass of milk in his hand whilst simultaneously grabbing him by the arm and ushering him towards the door. Walking and drinking, David almost choked, "Wa, sumwah gah art o' de wong si o' be' thi' mornah."

Jenny shook her head in disbelief, "Doesn't anyone in this family understand what's happening here? Hurry up, get your coat on!"

"Ah dah wa' a caa."

"Just do it, will you? You're going to be late." David and John looked up together.

"Are you not coming?" John asked gently.

"Er … no; Uncle Dave's just gone off without telling us *anything* and someone needs to stay here and tidy up *and* someone needs to make a start on lunch." Her voice tailed away to almost nothing. John cast a cursory glance around the room; hardly a thing was out of place. He looked back at Jenny.

"There's the beds to strip, as well," she added quickly, avoiding his gaze.

"Alright, lass, if that's what you want; you know best."

Jenny smiled apologetically. "I think it is. Anyway, Mum and Dad haven't had a chance to speak to David yet, it will give them some time with him."

"Great, does this mean I get to sit in the front?"

"Only on the way there," said Jenny sternly, trying to recover some of her authority, "and just do as John says!"

John nodded and, with an imperceptible motion of his hand, sent Meg bounding out towards the Land Rover. David followed quickly behind, leaving Jenny and John alone on the doorstep.

"Try not to worry," said John, "your Uncle Dave came down late last night and explained what'd gone off. Your Mum and Dad aren't going to do anything to hurt you; they love you both far too much. You're lucky to have them."

"I know," sighed Jenny. Her own emotions were resting on a knife edge but she was still completely taken aback by the intensity of the sadness that briefly cast its shadow over John's gentle face. She put all the love she could muster into the smile she offered in reply to this wonderful, mysterious man. "Thanks, for everything. See you later," she almost whispered. John smiled back and then suddenly, without replying, turned away to follow Meg and David to the Land Rover.

Jenny watched until they'd disappeared from sight. She hadn't felt so alone and discouraged since Friday night's long wait on the railway platform, which already seemed like an age ago. She stood forlornly in the doorway, letting the cold breeze brush against her skin, watching the goosebumps spread along her arms until she began to shiver. She could still hear the rumble of the Land Rover's engine and considered waiting to see if she could catch a glimpse of it across the valley, but it was too cold and she went back in and closed the door quietly behind her.

Curiously, the emptiness of the house seemed to calm her fears and after a quick glance towards the 'phone, she gathered herself and began to tidy up after The Boys. Grateful for the activity, she soon lost herself in her work, 'tutting' at the abandoned mug of tea on the dining table and shaking her head reproachfully at the discovery of a small mountain of sweet papers dug into the cushions of The Chair. As she poured the tea down the sink, she smiled wistfully and stopped for a moment to watch the pony, who was back nuzzling his way across the field. She was beginning to relax. A little.

Continuing her round of chores, but fearing the ensuing lack of activity, Jenny was careful not to work too quickly. For a second time, she washed and wiped everything in the kitchen, swept the floors and then emptied the bin. She stripped her and David's bed and put the bed linen in the washing machine. She even made a move towards Dave's room but, hand on door handle, her courage failed and she settled for moving enough clothes out of the way with her foot to be able to close the door. She vacuumed the stairs, tidied the kitchen drawers (didn't take long!) and re-arranged the coats by the front door. Then, suddenly, there was nothing left to do. She could feel the panic beginning to set in and in an attempt to escape pulled on her new black jacket and wandered outside. She looked over the dry-stone wall at the side of the house and called to the white pony, but now with a fresh bale of hay to keep him busy there was little hope of him coming across. For a moment she thought she saw Dave's hat (Stetson El Alamo premium 500X fur felt – *'only the best will do'*) hovering above the wall on the far side of the field but when she looked again it had gone. "He really has got to you, hasn't he?" she laughed out loud, grateful for the momentary respite and, unable to think of anything else to do but feeling a little calmer, she went in and made herself a cup of tea. She suddenly remembered the cakes that she'd squirrelled away from The Boys on Saturday and, unable to resist, she treated herself to a slightly dry but still deliciously over-sized slice of Bakewell tart. Armed with tea and cake, she wandered absentmindedly to the living room and spied the magazine still in situ on the sideboard. She grinned mischievously, sat down and began to re-read the article about the house. Within minutes she was asleep, exhausted by the combination of the weekend's exertions and the never-ending fight to keep the anxiety at bay, and didn't wake until disturbed by the now familiar rumble of an ancient Land Rover dragging its chassis back up the hill. She stood up with a jerk and in her half-awake state kicked over the remains of her tea. Ignoring it, she ran to the door, raised her hand to the latch and then suddenly froze. She stood stock still, unable to move, the tiny cracks all around her rapidly widening into bottomless crevasses. "Come on, girl, you've got this: you can do it; you've got to."

She forced herself to open the door, just in time to see the Land Rover pull up outside the gate. Jenny wasn't sure what to do, but as the passenger door opened and her mother stepped down instinct took over and she ran to greet her. For the first time since Sally had left there was no hesitation in their movement towards one another. Jenny almost leapt at Jane and the two off them fell back as one toward the Land Rover. Still leaning against its mud-spattered door, Jane hugged her daughter with all of her strength, rocking her from side to side. Jenny, who seemed to have grown whilst they'd been apart, buried her head in her mother's shoulder and sobbed. Her father appeared and wrapped his arms round them both, kissing each head in turn, whilst David, appalled by the whole scenario, unloaded their luggage and Meg danced around in circles.

They stood like that for an age, until Jane gently pushed Jenny away in order to see her face. "Hey, come on," she said, gently brushing Jenny's hair away and tucking it behind her ears, "what's all this about?" Jenny tried to speak but couldn't. Dan took Jane's place and Jenny squeezed him as hard as she could. "I thought you'd be pleased to see us," he joked.

"I am," Jenny sniffed, "I am."

He held her for several more minutes before finally shifting her round until his arm was wrapped around her shoulder. "Come on," he said, "let's have a look at your uncle's house and see if it's all your gran cracks it up to be." They walked up the steps together but just as they were about to go in, the gate swung open and Dave's truck rumbled to a halt. He jumped out and bounded up the steps two at a time, hesitating only as he reached the door. There was a moment's uncertainty as the brothers faced one another and then Dan reached out his hand.

"How are you, Dave? Thanks for taking such good care of the kids." Dave visibly relaxed and shook his brother's hand warmly, whilst simultaneously returning Jane's reassuring smile.

"Don't anyone bother about me then," protested a voice from the bottom of the steps. Everyone span round.

"Gran!" shouted Jenny and David together as they ran down to greet her.

"Reet then, Jen lass," said Dave, "let's 'ave 'kettle on; might finally get a decent brew now 'cavalry's 'ere."

They sat together in the living room; Dan and Jane squeezed in on the settee and Jenny nestled at their feet, arms draped across her father's knees, whilst David turned The Chair round and set it to massage and their parents told them all about New York. Dave puffed out his cheeks and shook his head in disbelief when he heard about the mugging, whilst David simply stared at his father in lime pickle-eating, open-mouthed awe. Dan's gentle teasing of how Jane had won round The Client but lost the race to the foyer earned him a surprisingly vigorous punch on the arm before Jane described their trip to Harlem and the exciting news about Strivers' Row. But when she began to explain about needing to spend more time in New York, her voice faltered and she finally slowed to an embarrassed silence.

Jenny felt a slight pressure coming from her father's foot. "Mum, it'll be fine, honest," she said reassuringly, and behind her she recognised her mother's hand tightening around her father's.

"Er Dave …" said Dan uncomfortably, "… we were wondering … if I have to go out to New York at all …". He took a deep breath, "…would it be possible for Jenny and David to come and stay again?" Jenny caught her grandmother's eye but Audrey quickly turned away. There was a long pause.

"I don't know what t' say fo' 'best, our kid; I mean life's a lot tougher up 'ere than city folk realise; this is big country up 'ere, tha knows!" But they couldn't keep up the pretence any longer and the two brothers each broke into a mischievous grin. "Course they can; whenever they feel like it. That's if they're up to it, o' course - what's tha reckon *tha pair*?"

Jenny smiled at David. "Oh we'll be fine with *an experienced 'illsman* like Uncle Dave to look after us, won't we David?"

"If this bad boy's here, it'll be alreet not it, Uncle?" replied David patting The Chair.

There was another pause, as relaxed as the last one was tense, in which Jenny caught Audrey out of the corner of her eye for a second time; she was radiating happiness, she'd never seen her grandmother look so lovely.

"I'm afraid I didn't get anything ready for lunch," she said finally.

"Staff!" exclaimed Dave shaking his head. Dan laughed.

"Leave her alone, you two!" said Audrey. "I think she's done wonderful putting up with your daft goings on, and David. … Did you know I tried to call on Saturday night and he didn't even answer. And that answer phone thing's a complete waste of time; you really need to sort it, our David. Anyway, Jenny, you've done more than enough; if someone will run me down to the post office, we can all have pork sandwiches for lunch - my treat."

"Put thee money away, Mam; Danny 'n' me'll sort it. Any roads, I need t' talk t'im abaht summat." Everyone turned to look at the two brothers. "Tha can all stop nebbin' 'n all. Keep 'beaks out on it; bit o' business, that's all - nowt t' do wi' anyone else. … Come on Danny, tha can see what 'truck can do … eh, if tha's owt left, tha might make me an offer. If 'pencil's' sharp enough I might even …" he paused and looked round the room, "… throw in a Big Apple Pie. … BIG APPLE PIE!! What abaht that 'un, Davey lad, THROW IN A BIG APPLE PIE!"

After they'd gone, Jane and Jenny went into the kitchen to find some plates. "Mum," asked Jenny, "would we have time go to Hathersage this afternoon?"

"If it doesn't take too long and someone can take us. Why?"

"Oh nothing, *bit o' business*, that's all. Can you bring your credit card?"

Dave and Dan returned with an Exped Expedition (£504.95) sized box of pork sandwiches and enough parkin to fill even David. After lunch, Audrey insisted on washing up and whilst she was making tea, Jenny sidled up to Jane and asked again about Hathersage. “Okay,” she said, furrowing her brow, “as soon as we’ve had our tea we’ll go. Does David want to come?”

“Oh, er, I don’t think so.”

“Well, don’t you think you should ask him?”

“Please, Mum, can’t it be just you and me?”

Jane smiled tenderly at her daughter. “Okay, you’ve obviously got something in mind.”

“Thanks, Mum, I’ll fetch our coats.”

Jenny wasn’t sure how Dave would react to her and Jane slipping away on their own, but to her surprise he seemed almost relieved. “Special treat; tha can take truck, allus turns a few ‘eads. Tha can use ‘disabled sticker ‘n’ all.” Neither Jane nor Jenny had given any thought as to how they would get there and Dave’s suggestion took Jane by surprise. “Oh, er, if you’re sure. I’ve never driven anything that, er, *impressive* before.”

Dave beamed. “Piece o’ cake, old lass. Come on, I’ll show thee ‘controls. Any roads, tha’ll be used t’ a left ‘ooker after New York. … Eh, what abaht that then; we met a kid from there when we was ‘eadin’ ov’r ‘tops. All ov’r place ‘e were – didn’t know ‘odds between ‘Pennines ‘n’ ‘Peak District, ‘n’ ‘im a geography student! Eh, wonder if ‘e’s still out there, Jen lass!” Jenny braced herself for Dave’s onslaught, but for the second time in two days she’d misjudged him and, letting the moment pass, he grabbed his El Alamo and headed for the door. He paused to pick up the keys and turned momentarily to grin at his niece before firing off a conspiratorial wink in her direction. She smiled and sent one back.

After a seemingly endless explanation of its unique driving requirements, Dave, who may well have been regretting his impetuosity, insisted on reversing out of the drive himself. With one last review of his instructions and a final, final check to see if there were any questions, he reluctantly stepped back from his beloved truck, rapped it twice on the roof and watched with concern as Jane pulled slowly away.

At that moment, sitting on her own in the front seat beside her mother, Jenny couldn't think of anywhere she'd rather be. They drove slowly down the hill and before they'd reached the top pub she was already telling Jane all about the walk and Tom and James and Cathy, and Sam and Jess and The Lumps. She talked without drawing breath, only pausing to give her mother directions, not knowing if she were responding to the excitement of their adventures or her nervousness about the upcoming conversation.

She finally ran out of things to say just as they arrived in Hathersage. They drew up in the exact same parking spot that Dave had used on Saturday. Jane was just about to step down when Jenny grasped her arm. "Mum, is everything *really* okay?" she asked, her eyes filling with tears once more.

Jane closed the door and sighed deeply. "Honestly? We'll have to see, but Dad and I are in a better place than we've been for years, and to be honest, I've had my eyes open to a few things as well."

"Like what?"

"Like I can't make everybody be what I want them to be and," she paused, "... that I get too focussed on the business and forget what effect it has on everyone else."

"Then why are you going back to New York?"

It was Jane's turn to fight back the tears. "Jenny, if I thought for one moment that you didn't want me to go then I wouldn't."

Jenny sat quietly, mulling over her response. "Of course I don't want you to go, but I want you to be *happy* and you do come home in a much better mood."

"Do I?" asked Jane taken aback.

"Absolutely and we don't mind staying with Uncle Dave. In fact ..." she slowed almost to a halt as the full effect of what she was saying dawned on her, "... it could be quite cool."

"Honestly?"

"Honestly. David told me he liked it here and I think I've got

Uncle Dave sussed by now, and …" she slowed again, "I do like the people here."

Jane sunk back into her seat and pulled her thumb and forefinger along the bottom of her eyes, pinching her nose at the bridge. "You're not just saying that are you, Jenny? You would say wouldn't you?"

"No," said Jenny smiling, "I really mean it."

"Well that's that then," said Jane with an enormous sigh. "We'll just have to give it a go and see what happens. We've been stuck in traffic for far too long; Dad and I have been so worried, but maybe we're *finally* back on the move." She sighed again; it helped. Then she smiled at her daughter, who replied in kind. "I believe you mentioned credit cards."

24

Shopping completed, Jane and Jenny headed back to Highfield as quickly as Jane's caution would allow, but as they turned up past the post office they were met head on by a speeding four-wheel drive truck and its racketing horsebox. Jane stamped on the brakes and swerved to the edge of the road. The two vehicles somehow squeezed passed one another, clipping wing mirrors as they did so. Jane pulled up sharply, hands glued to the steering wheel.

"Everyone okay?" asked the other driver breezily, as she wandered over in a surprisingly nonchalant fashion. "No damage, I think," she added, casually clicking the truck's wing mirror back into place. "Oh … hello Jenny … thought you'd gone to Hathersage."

Jenny looked up, surprised to be addressed by name. It was the Female Doctor, whose earlier equanimity seemed to be quickly ebbing away. "We … er … didn't think you'd be back just yet." Jenny looked at her in confusion. "Oh, er, we were just calling in at your uncle's," The Female Doctor went on nervously, "to drop off some silage. Oh dear … er … wait a minute … let me think; er … I think we'd just better have a really good look round - just to check there's no more damage." And with that she bobbed down and disappeared from sight. Jane turned to Jenny, who could only shrug her shoulders and raise her upturned hands in bewilderment. After what seemed like an age, The Female Doctor still showed no signs of resurfacing, so Jane rather nervously craned her neck out of the window to see what had become of her.

"Are you okay?" she asked. The confusion in Jane's voice was evident; it's source was the sight of The Female Doctor lying on her back, half hidden under the truck, examining its tyres and wheel arches and anything else she could think of in the most minute detail. Eventually catching Jane's eye, The Female Doctor smiled sheepishly and slowly rose to her feet, "Can't *actually* see anything," she reported breathlessly through the window, "do you have a torch? I think we should probably drive down to the garage, just to be on the safe side, don't you? It's only on the corner, by the cricket pitch. … Do you know it? Oh, of course not, you're not from round here are you? London isn't it? … And aren't you working on a big case in New York or something? Oh, mind you, he doesn't open on Mondays. … Oh dear, I *am* sorry; must pay more attention in future. …. Look, at least we can swap insurance details - just in case."

"I'm sure everything's fine," replied Jane, at a complete loss to explain The Female Doctor's behaviour.

"Well, I'll just get you one of my cards out of the car, just in case."

The Doctor walked slowly back over to her own vehicle, and then apparently having second thoughts, she began to examine the horsebox with almost as much attention as she had given to Dave's truck.

Finally satisfied, she disappeared into the four wheel drive and after another excruciatingly long wait, returned with her name, address and 'phone number scrawled on the torn off corner of a cardboard box. "So you're Jenny's mum," said The Female Doctor casually, "Dave's told us all about you. We're up the hill, by the pylon." Jane furrowed her brow. "Oh, yes, of course … the Robinsons … Alice."

"Pleased to meet you," replied Jane, politely twisting her hand out through the window.

The Female Doctor stood there in silence, seemingly unaware of Jane's outstretched hand. She stared straight at Jenny as if trying to think of the right way of saying what she had to say, but when the words wouldn't come she eventually fell back on a somewhat confusing, "Goodbye then, Jenny, hope it all works out," and hurried back to her car. As Jane drew cautiously away,

Jenny thought she caught a glimpse of The Female Doctor opening her mobile ‘phone.

“Better not tell Dave,” her mother said conspiratorially. “… Strange woman.”

“Yeah,” replied Jenny thoughtfully.

Not knowing how to operate the remote control for the gate, Jane drew the truck up by the side of the road. To her surprise, Dan ran out of the house, dragging David after him. “Come on,” he shouted enthusiastically, “we’re going for a walk.”

“But it’s starting to rain.”

“So it is. Stay there and I’ll fetch an umbrella and see if Dave’s got any waterproofs.”

“Dan?!”

Dan ran back into the house and was back at the truck before Jane and Jenny had had time to gather their shopping and get out. “Come on then, let’s go!”

“But I don’t want to go for a walk,” moaned Jane.

“Come on!” ordered Dan with a raise of his eyebrows. Jane stared at him intently and then finally catching on, feigned another feeble attempt at resistance before climbing down and pulling on someone’s raincoat. “He’s been like this since that business at the Centurion – thinks he’s Superman. … We’re not going far are we? We’re already late.”

“No just, ten minutes or so, we could all do with some fresh air before the journey.” Jenny was just about to protest when she saw her father’s arm gently rise up and fasten around Jane’s waist. Her opposition melted. “Come on Davey lad, let’s show city folks ‘ow ‘illsmens carry on ov’r them tops. Last one there’s a Wednesdayite.” She ran off up the hill with no idea where she was going. David galloped after her with even less. As they watched their children run up the hill, Dan pulled Jane towards him.

"It's going alright, isn't it?" she asked somewhat anxiously.

"It's about to go a whole lot better," replied Dan cryptically.

Five minutes into their walk, Dan's 'phone rang, and after the most cursory conversation he announced that he had had enough and they were going back. The others shrugged and turned back down the hill. When they arrived back at the house, Dave was standing by the gate, examining the wing mirror of his truck in great detail. Jane looked at Jenny and winced. Jenny smiled back and walked over to Dave, and then to everyone's surprise, she leaned over and kissed him on the cheek. "These are for you," she said, pulling a small bag out her pocket.

Dave was speechless. He reached into the bag and pulled out a smaller bag made of fine black cloth. A sly grin began to spread across his face. Jenny smiled, "They're from David and me, to say 'thank-you' … for everything."

Dave opened the bag and carefully pulled out a pair of Oakley Carbon Blade Black Iridium Polarised sunglasses. He was completely overwhelmed and turned quickly away to try them on. "Top gear, these," he said with a slight cough. "Thanks *tha pair,* I don't know what t' say."

"Absolute bargain, then!" laughed Jenny.

"Top gear for a top uncle!" shouted David, "and I've got something for you as well." He reached inside his coat and pulled out Dave's abandoned Viking Peregrine 10 x 42 EDs. "Tha might need these to see us in front of thee if we go on another walk."

Dave laughed and pretended to cuff David over the gate. "Now, tha can see I'm made up, I really am, but I don't want *tha pair* thinkin' tha's got 'better o' t'old Uncle Dave just yet. So, *I've* got summat tha might be interested in. … Come on, Davey first!" He marched off towards the stables, beckoning the others to follow. "What's tha make o' that then, sunshine?" beamed Dave as he flung open the door with a flourish.

"Is it mine?" asked David incredulously.

"Sure is, Davey lad; Cannondale Trail 7. Top gear, 'from 'States - just like 'truck." David walked up to the silver bike and just stared, not daring to touch it.

"Are you sure it's mine?" he asked. Everyone laughed.

"Pretty sure, lad, although if tha sees an American bloke runnin' after thee, tha'd better pedal like mad."

David opened his eyes wide. "Why, is it his?"

"Maybe, tha can't be too sure. Tha'd better get a bit o' trainin' in, sharpish like," said Dave, nodding towards the road. David turned to look at his father, who grinned and produced a matching cycle helmet from behind his back.

"Cool, thanks," was all David could say. He grabbed the helmet, put it on backwards and wheeled the bike out onto the road. "Thanks Mum, thanks Dad, thanks Gran, thanks Jenny, thanks John, thanks Meg and *thanks Uncle Dave; a right Unitedite."*

"Turn th''elmet round," shouted Dave. David struggled with the catch for a few seconds and then, having refastened his helmet the right way, he looked up triumphantly and shouted, "To Hathersage and beyond." As he pedalled away up the hill, Jenny turned and smiled warmly at her uncle.

"'n' what abaht thee, young lady? What's in t'other stable?" Jenny followed him across the yard, trembling with excitement. Dave opened the stable door and ushered her in. She stopped stock still in the doorway, unable to move. Chewing contently on bale of hay was the white pony.

"What…?" she began, but now it was her turn to be lost for words. "What …?" She stalled again. "Is…?"

"Now don't wet theesen; I've not bought 'im, but 'Doctors reckon 'e needs a bit more lookin' after, 'n' they've not 'time. … What 'e *really* needs is a bit o' fresh air. So, we've come t' an agreement that 'e'll stay 'ere as long as someone can take him out - not all 'time … just now 'n' again, like. … Does tha know anyone?"

Jenny squealed with delight and threw her arms in the air, jumping up and down in excitement. "But what about during the week?" she asked, suddenly filled with anxiety for her pony.

"Young Tommy said 'e'd muck 'im out, 'n' John'll chip in wi' owt that needs doin'. So it's just up t' thee really. Fancy comin' up fo' odd week-end?"

Jenny turned and beamed at her parents, "Mum, Dad?" she asked, eyes wide to popping.

"Well …" began Dan slowly, "it wouldn't hurt to nip back to New York now and then."

"Oh yes! Yes! Yes! Yes!" yelled Jenny. She forced herself to calm down and then walked solemnly over to the pony. "Hello boy," she whispered, stroking him gently. "What's your name?"

"Jasper," said Dan, "he's four and very friendly. Think you and him could get on?"

Jenny ran over to her parents and hugged them both. "We'll be fine, we'll all be fine," she said, muzzling into her father's shoulder. After a few minutes, the adults left the two new friends together, already caught up in the long and happy process of getting to know another, whilst Dave, John and Meg went off to look for David..

"You are clever," whispered Jane as she and Dan climbed the steps to the house side by side. "Thank you."

"Don't thank me, thank the Strivers – it was their idea."

Time was pressing on and before long the bags were packed and lined up at the door. As Dan dragged David out of The Chair, Jenny briefly disappeared into the kitchen before racing her brother to the stables. She stroked and hugged Jasper one last time and David patted his bike and told it to be good until the week-end. Dave, secretly delighted to show how easily the truck's cabin could accommodate six people *and* their luggage, drove them to the station and he and Audrey insisted on walking them to the platform. Jenny smiled as they pulled up into the same parking lot. This time there were more than enough willing hands to help with the luggage. The train arrived more or less on time and they made their farewells.

"Thanks for everything," said Dan, shaking his brother's hand firmly.

"We'll need t' 'ave a chat 'fore long, thee 'n' me," said Dave seriously.

"I know. … We will."

"Thanks Dave," said Jane warmly, holding out her hand and swallowing hard, "we're in your debt."

"Don't worry abaht it, lass, just 'ave a word wi' that lad o' yours, 'n' see if tha can talk some sense into 'im." Jane looked at him quizzically. "Football - 'e needs t' start followin' a decent team."

"I'll see what I can do," she smiled.

"Bye, Uncle Dave," shouted David from the train. "I'll beat thee on t' Wild West Rodeo next time."

"No chance lad, I'll be able t' get some practice in, now *tha pair's* out o' road."

"Bye, Uncle Dave, thanks again. … See you at the week-end."

"Bye, lass - lookin' forward to it."

Dave and Audrey watched until the train disappeared and then Dave drove her home. He didn't stay long; for some reason he wanted to be back at his own house. He followed the road out of town, singing along with Willy as he left the city lights behind. He'd taken the long way round, over the dam and allowed himself a gentle smile as he passed the Highfield sign, before slowing almost to a stop over the bridge beside the bowling green. He accelerated gently around the cricket pitch – 'just enough'- and then up and out into the night, smiling again and waving to Tom and Cathy as he left the top village. A minute later he was pulling onto the drive.

He unlocked the door, turned on the lights and walked in, leaving the door ajar. Somehow the house didn't seem as empty as before and for the first time since the renovation he didn't go over to The Chair and turn on the television. He wandered into the kitchen and was surprised to see a note on the side next to a small cardboard box. He lifted the note and read,

Dear Uncle Dave, Dad says you need something called a 'frequency converter' for your microwave. He knows someone who can get one for you (proper gear – no cheap tack 'ere, tha knows) and we can bring it up next time we come.

P.S. In the meantime, this will let you enjoy the lights!

Dave stood speechless, staring from the note to the Menumaster and back again to the note. Then from nowhere, a wave of emotion surged up from the depths of his being, so powerful that he was forced to reach out for the work surface to stop himself falling. To his amazement, he recognised it as pure, childlike joy. But this sprang not from the anticipation of showing his visitors what the Menumaster could do, appetising as that might be. Neither was it in response to his niece and nephew's gratitude for everything he'd done for them or the thoughtfulness of their gift. And whilst he was both thrilled and delighted to be the beneficiary once again of Dan's knowledge and attention to detail, not even this was the source of the exhilaration he felt coursing through every vein. No, the thread that tied the childlike smile to the happiness that threatened to burst open his chest was one simple, hitherto unimaginable truth, the importance of which it had taken until this moment to realise – he had his brother back.

Holding the note by its corner as though fearing it might somehow disintegrate if he gripped it too firmly, he read it again. A single tear formed in the corner of his eye and skiddled down his cheek. As he wiped it away, he read on, this time taking note of the P.S. He opened the box, and the smile, if possible, grew even wider as he ripped open the La Guardia Airport bag and pulled out an adaptor for an American plug. He went straight over to the sink, plugged the adaptor into the nearest wall socket, pushed its plug into the adaptor and stood back to watch the MFS18 flicker into life. He reached out to press the buttons on the control panel but suddenly halted and let out a contented sigh. "Just enough; just enough to let 'em know." And he reached out again and turned off the socket at the wall. But there was one more surprise; without exactly knowing why, he picked up the note once more and turned it over. This time the grin threatened to tear his face in two:

Thanks again Uncle Dave. Tha did alreet. Love from your fellow 'illsmens, Jenny and David.

"*Tha did alreet,*" he chuckled to himself: "Tha did 'n' all, t'old Uncle Dave!" Shivering at the draught, he went back to close the front door and stood quietly for a moment taking in the hills and the gathering night. He was just in time to see John walking up the road with Meg. His old friend smiled and waved. Dave replied in kind, and, still smiling, took one last look at the place where he finally belonged, and then quietly closed the door. He was home.